PAUL M. COOK, D.Phil. (2010), University of Oxford, is an Affiliate Professor at Asbury Theological Seminary. He also teaches at Florida State University.

A Sign and a Wonder

Supplements

to

Vetus Testamentum

VOLUME 147

A Sign and a Wonder

The Redactional Formation of Isaiah 18–20

By

Paul M. Cook

BRILL

LEIDEN • BOSTON
2011

This book is printed on acid-free paper.

Library of Congress Cataloging-in-Publication Data

Cook, Paul M. (Paul Michael), 1976–
  A sign and a wonder : the redactional formation of Isaiah 18–20 / by Paul M. Cook.
    p. cm. — (Supplements to Vetus Testamentum, ISSN 0083-5889 ; v. 147)
  "This book is a revised version of my doctoral thesis that was accepted
by the Faculty of Oriental Studies at the University of Oxford in 2009"—
Acknowledgements.
  Includes bibliographical references and index.
  ISBN 978-90-04-20591-8 (hardback : alk. paper)
  1. Egypt in the Bible. 2. Ethiopia in the Bible. 3. Bible. O.T. Isaiah I, 18–20—
Criticism, Redaction. 4. Bible. O.T. Isaiah I, 13–23—Criticism, interpretation, etc. I. Title.

  BS1199.E59C66 2011
  224'.10663—dc22

                                                            2011011257

ISSN 0083-5889
ISBN 978 90 04 20591 8

PRINTED BY DRUKKERIJ WILCO B.V. - AMERSFOORT, THE NETHERLANDS

For Jennifer

CONTENTS

ACKNOWLEDGEMENTS

This book is a revised version of my doctoral thesis that was accepted by the Faculty of Oriental Studies at the University of Oxford in 2009. As such, many individuals have contributed in some way to the thesis or its revision. My doctoral supervisor, Professor Hugh Williamson, has been an enthusiastic and encouraging guide. I have especially appreciated his accessibility, attention to detail, and vast knowledge of both primary and secondary material.

Many others at the University of Oxford have read or heard portions of the work as it was in progress. Professor John Barton and Dr. Philip Johnston (now Senior Tutor at Hughes Hall, Cambridge) served as assessors of the thesis at various stages. I am especially grateful to Professor John Day and Dr. Eryl Davies (of Bangor University) for providing helpful comments as examiners.

My thanks go to Professor Hans Barstad and members of the editorial board of *Vetus Testamentum* who accepted the thesis for publication and offered helpful suggestions for improvement.

I completed the revised version while at The Florida State University, where the Department of Religion has been most helpful. I am especially thankful for comments of support from the chair of the department, Dr. John Corrigan, from Dr. David Levenson, and from many others. Dr. Matthew Goff has been particularly attentive, since he has read early versions of the manuscript and provided many helpful comments.

Members of my family and my wife's family have always been supportive, and have offered numerous prayers on our behalf. Also, Dr. Bill Arnold, of Asbury Theological Seminary, has continued to provide encouragement and assistance, as well as the initial nudge to study at Oxford. I am also grateful for support from Drs. James and Barbara Holsinger.

Finally, my wife, Jennifer, has contributed more than anyone else to this project. It is to her that I owe the greatest debt of gratitude and it is to her that this book is dedicated with much love.

ABBREVIATIONS

ÄAT	Ägypten und Altes Testament
AB	Anchor Bible
ABD	*Anchor Bible Dictionary*. Edited by David Noel Freedman. 6 vols. New York: Doubleday, 1992.
ABR	*Australian Biblical Review*
AcOr	*Acta orientalia*
AegT	Aegyptiaca Treverensia
AEL	*Ancient Egyptian Literature*. Edited by Miriam Lichtheim. 3 vols. Berkeley and Los Angeles: University of California Press, 2006.
AfO	*Archiv für Orientforschung*
AJET	*Africa Journal of Evangelical Theology*
AJSL	*American Journal of Semitic Languages and Literature*
ALUOS	*Annual of Leeds University Oriental Society*
ANEP	*The Ancient Near East in Pictures Relating to the Old Testament*. Edited by James B. Pritchard. 2d ed. Princeton: Princeton University Press, 1969.
ANET	*Ancient Near Eastern Texts Relating to the Old Testament*. Edited by James B. Pritchard. 3d ed. Princeton: Princeton University Press, 1969.
AOAT	Alter Orient und Altes Testament
ARAB	*Ancient Records of Assyria and Babylonia*. Edited by Daniel David Luckenbill. 2 vols. Chicago: University of Chicago Press, 1926–27.
ArBib	The Aramaic Bible
ArOr	*Archiv Orientální*
ASTI	*Annual of the Swedish Theological Institute*
ATANT	Abhandlungen zur Theologie des Alten und Neuen Testaments
ATDan	Acta theologica danica
AUSS	*Andrews University Seminary Studies*
BA	*Biblical Archaeologist*
BAR	*Biblical Archaeology Review*
BASOR	*Bulletin of the American Schools of Oriental Research*
BAT	Die Botschaft des Alten Testaments

BBB	Bonner biblische Beiträge
BBR	*Bulletin for Biblical Research*
BDB	*A Hebrew and English Lexicon of the Old Testament.* F. Brown, S. R. Driver, and C. A. Briggs. Oxford: Clarendon, 1907.
BE	Bibliothèque d'Étude
BETL	Bibliotheca ephemeridum theologicarum lovaniensium
BHS	*Biblia Hebraica Stuttgartensia.* Edited by K. Elliger and W. Rudolph. Stuttgart: Deutsche Bibelgesellschaft, 1997.
Bib	*Biblica*
BibOr	Biblica et orientalia
BibTS	Biblisch-Theologische Studien
BIOSCS	*Bulletin of the International Organization for Septuagint and Cognate Studies*
BIS	Biblical Interpretation Series
BSac	*Bibliotheca sacra*
BTA	Bible and Theology in Africa
BurH	*Buried History*
BWANT	Beiträge zur Wissenschaft vom Alten und Neuen Testament
BZ	*Biblische Zeitschrift*
BZAW	Beihefte zur Zeitschrift für die alttestamentliche Wissenschaft
CBC	Cambridge Bible Commentary
CBQ	*Catholic Biblical Quarterly*
CHANE	Culture and History of the Ancient Near East
CHJ	*Cambridge History of Judaism.* Edited by W. D. Davies and Louis Finkelstein. 4 vols. Cambridge: Cambridge University Press, 1984–2006.
ConBOT	Coniectanea biblica: Old Testament Series
COP	Cambridge Oriental Publications
COS	*The Context of Scripture.* Edited by William W. Hallo. 3 vols. Leiden: Brill, 1997–2002.
DDD	*Dictionary of Deities and Demons in the Bible.* Edited by Karel van der Toorn, Bob Becking, and Pieter W. van der Horst. 2d ed. Leiden: Brill, 1999.
DS	Demotische Studien
EBib	*Etudes bibliques*
EF	Erlanger Forschungen
ErIsr	*Eretz-Israel*

FAT	Forschungen zum Alten Testament
FO	*Folia orientalia*
FOTL	Forms of the Old Testament Literature
FRLANT	Forschungen zur Religion und Literatur des Alten und Neuen Testaments
GM	*Göttinger Miszellen*
GN	Geographical Name
HALOT	*The Hebrew and Aramaic Lexicon of the Old Testament.* L. Koehler, W. Baumgartner, and J. J. Stamm. Translated and edited under the supervision of M. E. J. Richardson. 5 vols. Leiden: Brill, 1994–2000.
HAT	Handbuch zum Alten Testament
HBS	Herders biblische Studien
HCS	Hellenistic Culture and Society
HKAT	Handkommentar zum Alten Testament
HO	Handbuch der Orientalistik
HSM	Harvard Semitic Monographs
HTKAT	Herders theologischer Kommentar zum Alten Testament
HTR	*Harvard Theological Review*
HUCA	*Hebrew Union College Annual*
IBC	Interpretation: A Bible Commentary for Teaching and Preaching
ICC	International Critical Commentary
IEJ	*Israel Exploration Journal*
Int	*Interpretation*
JAOS	*Journal of the American Oriental Society*
JARCE	*Journal of the American Research Center in Egypt*
JBL	*Journal of Biblical Literature*
JCS	*Journal of Cuneiform Studies*
JEA	*Journal of Egyptian Archaeology*
JHS	*Journal of Hebrew Scriptures*
JJS	*Journal of Jewish Studies*
JNES	*Journal of Near Eastern Studies*
JPS	Jewish Publication Society
JQR	*Jewish Quarterly Review*
JSJ	*Journal for the Study of Judaism in the Persian, Hellenistic, and Roman Periods*
JSOT	*Journal for the Study of the Old Testament*
JSOTSup	Journal for the Study of the Old Testament: Supplement Series

JSS	*Journal of Semitic Studies*
JSSEA	*Journal of the Society for the Study of Egyptian Antiquities*
JTS	*Journal of Theological Studies*
KAT	Kommentar zum Alten Testament
KHC	Kurzer Hand-Commentar zum Alten Testament
LHBOTS	Library of Hebrew Bible/Old Testament Studies
LSTS	Library of Second Temple Studies
LXX	Septuagint
MdB	*Le Monde de la Bible*
MT	Masoretic Text
NASB	New American Standard Bible
NCB	New Century Bible
NHE	Natural History of Egypt
NIBCOT	New International Biblical Commentary on the Old Testament
NICOT	New International Commentary on the Old Testament
NIV	New International Version
NRSV	New Revised Standard Version
Numen	*Numen: International Review for the History of Religions*
OBO	Orbis biblicus et orientalis
OBT	Overtures to Biblical Theology
OIS	Oriental Institute Seminars
OLA	Orientalia lovaniensia analecta
OLZ	*Orientalistische Literaturzeitung*
Or	*Orientalia*
OTL	Old Testament Library
OtSt	*Oudtestamentische Studiën*
OTWSA	*Ou-Testamentiese Werkgemeenskap in Suid-Afrika*
PIBA	Proceedings of the Irish Biblical Association
PRSt	*Perspectives in Religious Studies*
RB	*Revue biblique*
RBén	*Revue bénédictine*
RevExp	*Review and Expositor*
RSR	*Recherches de science religieuse*
SAAS	State Archives of Assyria Studies
SBLDS	Society of Biblical Literature Dissertation Series
SBLSCS	Society of Biblical Literature Septuagint and Cognate Studies
SBLSymS	Society of Biblical Literature Symposium Series
SBS	Stuttgarter Bibelstudien

SBT	Studies in Biblical Theology
ScrCI	*Scripta Classica Israelica*
SEÅ	*Svensk exegetisk årsbok*
SHCANE	Studies in the History and Culture of the Ancient Near East
SJOT	*Scandinavian Journal of the Old Testament*
SOTSMS	Society for Old Testament Studies Monograph Series
ST	*Studia theologica*
StBL	Studies in Biblical Literature
SWBA	Social World of Biblical Antiquity
TA	*Tel Aviv*
TAD	*Textbook of Aramaic Documents from Ancient Egypt.* Edited by Bezalel Porten and Ada Yardeni. 4 vols. Jerusalem: Hebrew University Department of the History of the Jewish People, 1986–99.
TBS	The Biblical Seminar
TDOT	*Theological Dictionary of the Old Testament.* Edited by G. Johannes Botterweck, Helmer Ringgren, and Heinz-Josef Fabry. Translated by Geoffrey W. Bromiley, John T. Willis, David E. Green, and Douglas W. Stott. 15 vols. Grand Rapids: Eerdmans, 1974–.
Transeu	*Transeuphratène*
TZ	*Theologische Zeitschrift*
UF	*Ugarit-Forschungen*
UTR	Utrechtse Theologische Reeks
VAB	Vorderasiatische Bibliothek
VT	*Vetus Testamentum*
VTSup	Vetus Testamentum Supplements
WBC	Word Biblical Commentary
WMANT	Wissenschaftliche Monographien zum Alten und Neuen Testament
WO	*Die Welt des Orients*
WUNT	Wissenschaftliche Untersuchungen zum Neuen Testament
ZAW	*Zeitschrift für die alttestamentliche Wissenschaft*
ZBK	Zürcher Bibelkommentare
ZDMG	*Zeitschrift der deutschen morgenländischen Gesellschaft*

CHAPTER ONE

INTRODUCTION AND SURVEY OF RESEARCH

1. Introduction

Like many other prophetic books of the Hebrew Bible, the book of Isaiah contains a section of material devoted primarily to prophetic oracles concerning foreign nations, located in Isaiah 13–23. Although the central focus on foreign nations seems define these chapters as a distinct literary unit within the book, the formation of that unit is not immediately obvious. The disagreement among scholars about how this material came to be brought together is due primarily to the diversity of the material. For one thing, these chapters do not exclusively relate to foreign nations. The oracle addressed to the 'Valley of Vision' (22:1–14), for example, is usually understood as a judgment against Jerusalem and Judah. From the perspective of the formation of Isa 13–23, however, a more significant element is the variation in the types of literature represented in these chapters. Many of the literary units in Isa 13–23 are introduced by a מַשָּׂא ('oracle') formula, but there are other formulaic headings represented as well. Moreover, these chapters also contain narrative material in addition to the more common prophetic oracles. Questions regarding how these texts relate to each other and how they came to be brought together present considerable challenges to trace the processes that have led to the current shape of Isa 13–23.

This book does not aim to identify every step in the development of all of the texts in Isa 13–23, although it will propose a new approach to the general formation of the collection. In particular, the present goal is to give careful attention to the formation of Isa 18–20, which is a smaller group of material united by its thematic interest in the nations of Cush and Egypt, despite its literary diversity. This is an important group of chapters to study for the formation of the larger collection, because many of the challenges that apply to the formation of 18–20 are also applicable to the shaping of the larger collection in 13–23.

The majority of the oracles in Isa 13–23 are introduced by a מַשָּׂא ('oracle') superscription (13:1; 15:1; 17:1; 19:1; 21:1, 11, 13; 22:1; 23:1).

However, two other oracles begin with הוֹי ('woe'; 17:12; 18:1), another has a מַשָּׂא heading that does not conform to the others (14:28), and a few passages contain no title (14:24–27; 20:1–6; 22:15–25). Upon initial examination, it might appear that the מַשָּׂא oracles have played a central role in the assembly of the collection, but the addition of the non-conforming material would also need to be explained. In addition, the diachronic study of Isa 13–23 is hindered further by recognition that מַשָּׂא and non-מַשָּׂא passages alike could contain material that stems from the eighth century B.C.E. as well as later periods.

This is also the case for Isa 18–20, which is similarly diverse. The Egypt oracle in Isa 19 begins with מַשָּׂא, but the Cush oracle that precedes it is one of only two הוֹי oracles within Isa 13–23. These are followed in Isa 20 by the only narrative about the prophet Isaiah to appear within Isa 13–23. Despite such literary variation, the common concern in these three chapters for the nations of Cush and Egypt holds this small unit together within the larger collection of nations oracles. Moreover, the fact that they have been compiled without particular regard for their literary form suggests that the thematic interest in these nations is the prevailing element in the formation of the group.

2. Survey of Research

Critical approaches to the formation of Isa 13–23 have typically assumed the incorporation of the מַשָּׂא oracles into the book as a single collection, with the main point of dispute being whether this preceded or followed the non-מַשָּׂא texts. Thus, the following discussion surveys contributions to the study of these chapters along these two lines. However, there is no basis for the assumption shared by both, regarding the addition of a comprehensive collection of מַשָּׂא oracles. Moreover, the variety of literary material in these chapters poses additional challenges to the usual approaches. These difficulties will be addressed by a fresh proposal for the formation of Isa 13–23. Since our primary concern is with Isa 18–20, we will also bring attention toward the implications for the formation of these chapters within the literary context of Isa 13–23.

1. *The Secondary Addition of a* מַשָּׂא *Collection*

One major group of scholars proposes that the present shape of Isa 13–23 has been produced by the addition of a collection of מַשָּׂא

oracles to pre-existing material in the book of Isaiah. Karl Marti's work is representative of the tendency to emphasize the distinction between מַשָּׂא and non-מַשָּׂא texts in the growth of the collection. According to Marti, the earliest group of oracles consisted of a small amount of Isaianic material, primarily within what is now Isa 17; 18; 20; 22.[1] Perhaps during the third or second century B.C.E. a complete collection of מַשָּׂא oracles was broken up and distributed among these early texts, along with the addition of Isa 24–27.[2]

In Marti's reconstruction, the מַשָּׂא oracle about Egypt in Isa 19 would have been deliberately positioned between the Cush oracle (Isa 18) and the narrative about Cush and Egypt (Isa 20) on account of its thematic affiliation.[3] In his view, the earliest portion of the Egypt oracle (19:1–4) cannot be authentic, primarily because the high concentration of references to Egypt is deemed inferior to the supposed polished style of the eighth-century prophet Isaiah.[4] Instead, he supposes that the description in these verses of harsh treatment of Egypt and internal calamity among its citizens best describes the conquest of the final Egyptian dynasty by the Persian king Artaxerxes III Ochus (359–338).[5]

Marti detects additional elements of expansion in Isa 13–23 subsequent to the addition of the מַשָּׂא collection. For example, the portrayal of Yhwh worship in Egypt in 19:16–25 is viewed against the historical background of the construction of a Jewish temple at Leontopolis by Onias in the mid-second century B.C.E.[6] Assuming that 19:16–25 contains some of the latest material in Isa 13–23, this purported reference to the Leontopolis temple fixes the late-second century as a *terminus a quo* for the completion of Isa 13–23.[7] Of course, Marti's dating is no longer tenable, since the large Isaiah scroll from Qumran (1QIsaᵃ) can be reasonably dated as early as 150–125 B.C.E.[8] Thus, however the

---

[1] Karl Marti, *Das Buch Jesaja* (KHC 10; Tübingen: Mohr [Siebeck], 1900), xvi. Similarly, cf. R. B. Y. Scott, "The Book of Isaiah Chaps. 1–39," in *The Interpreter's Bible* (ed. George A. Buttrick; 12 vols.; New York: Abingdon, 1951–1957), 5:159–60.

[2] Marti, *Jesaja*, xix.

[3] Marti, *Jesaja*, xvi.

[4] Marti, *Jesaja*, 152.

[5] Marti, *Jesaja*, 155; following Bernhard Duhm, *Das Buch Jesaia* (4th ed.; HKAT; Göttingen: Vandenhoeck & Ruprecht, 1922 [1892¹]), 140–1.

[6] Josephus, *Ant.* 13.3.1–2; *J.W.* 7.10.3.

[7] Marti, *Jesaja*, 158–9; cf. Duhm, *Jesaia*, 145.

[8] Emanuel Tov, "The Text of Isaiah at Qumran," in *Writing and Reading the Scroll of Isaiah* (ed. Craig C. Broyles and Craig A. Evans; 2 vols.; VTSup 70; Leiden: Brill, 1997), 2:494; following Frank Moore Cross, *The Ancient Library of Qumran* (3d ed.;

formation of Isa 13–23 is conceived, it must have been completed before this period.

George Buchanan Gray similarly views the so-called 'untitled' oracles (14:24–27, 28–32; 17:12–14; 18; 20; 22:15–25) as generally older material that may have been preserved within the book itself before the addition of the מַשָּׂא collection.[9] Because some of the מַשָּׂא oracles reflect late- or post-exilic circumstances, such as the fall of Babylon (e.g., 13:1–14:4; 21:1–10), Gray assumes that the comprehensive collection of מַשָּׂא oracles, which he perceives as a distinct 'Book of Oracles,' would not have been formed before that period. He proposes that these oracles were assembled independently into a separate corpus before being added to the 'untitled' material.

As for the מַשָּׂא oracle about Egypt in Isa 19, Gray agrees with earlier critical opinions that the 'inelegant' style of verses 1–4 rules out Isaianic authorship, but he is hesitant to follow Marti and Bernhard Duhm in assigning this oracle to the reign of Artaxerxes Ochus.[10] The references to a pharaoh in verses 1–4, 11–15 suggest an earlier period in Egypt's history, perhaps shortly after the Babylonian exile. He views the five 'in that day' passages in 19:16–25 as a single unit, and like many of his critical predecessors, he associates these verses with the temple at Leontopolis in the second century B.C.E.

Because the מַשָּׂא superscription is a common feature of most of the oracles in Isa 13–23, both Marti and Duhm assume that this recurring element identifies a corpus of מַשָּׂא oracles that was added to supplement earlier oracular texts in Isaiah. This view also holds that the supposed מַשָּׂא collection circulated independently before its incorporation into the book of Isaiah. As we have already observed, Marti and Gray assume that the מַשָּׂא collection could not have been added prior to the post-exilic period on the basis of those oracles that refer to the fall of Babylon, but this does not imply that all of the מַשָּׂא were composed at that time. On the contrary, Gray asserts that the earliest portion of the Damascus oracle beginning at 17:1 could derive from

---

Sheffield: Sheffield Academic Press, 1995), 176; See also Solomon A. Birnbaum, "The Dates of the Cave Scrolls," *BASOR* 115 (1949): 20–22; Frank Moore Cross, "The Development of the Jewish Scripts," in *The Bible and the Ancient Near East: Essays in Honor of William Foxwell Albright* (ed. G. Ernest Wright; London: Routledge & Kegan Paul, 1961), 135–6.

[9] George Buchanan Gray, *The Book of Isaiah: I–XXVII* (ICC; Edinburgh: T. & T. Clark, 1912), li.

[10] Gray, *Isaiah*, 320–3.

the time of Isaiah.[11] However, this notion implies that such Isaianic material circulated independently of other authentic oracles before being reunited during the post-exilic period. While this may be technically possible, it is more likely either that all genuine material would be preserved together, or that any distinctively Isaianic characteristics would be lost in the process of transmission outside of the book, in which case it would no longer be identifiable as such.

Although later decades saw greater interest in the redactional formation of the book of Isaiah, proposals continued to maintain that a complete corpus of מַשָּׂא oracles was added to an earlier core of non-מַשָּׂא material. Georg Fohrer, for example, identifies seven broad stages in the formation of Isa 1–39.[12] He supposes that non-מַשָּׂא texts, such as Isa 18; 20, comprised an early collection of nations oracles, some of which are probably Isaianic and would have been included at an early stage in the formation of the book. Sometime after the exile the independent collection of מַשָּׂא oracles was broken up and redistributed among the pre-existing מַשָּׂא texts.

Hermann Barth is probably best known for positing a large-scale reworking of Isa 1–39 during the seventh century B.C.E.[13] Assuming that Isaiah ben Amoz pronounced only judgment on Judah to be carried out by Assyria (e.g., 10:5–6), Barth points to anti-Assyrian texts (e.g., 14:24–25; 30:27–33) as evidence for an Assyrian Redaction (*Assur Redaktion*) of the book in connection with the fall of Assyria during the reign of King Josiah of Judah (640–609 B.C.E.). This *Assur Redaktion* is thought to emphasize Yhwh's plan to rebuild the Davidic empire under Josiah and accounts for much of the current shape of Isa 2–32.

Barth detects some affinities in Isa 18; 20 with 14:4b+6–20a; 17:4–6, and so concludes that these passages must have been included as part of the *Assur Redaktion*.[14] Although he identifies older material in

---

[11] Gray, *Isaiah*, 297–8.

[12] Georg Fohrer, "The Origin, Tradition and Composition of Isaiah I–XXXIX," *ALUOS* 3 (1961–62): 3–38; = "Entstehung, Komposition und Überlieferung von Jesaja 1–39," in *Studien zur alttestamentlichen Prophetie (1949–1965)* (ed. Georg Fohrer; BZAW 99; Berlin: Töpelmann, 1967), 113–47; idem, *Das Buch Jesaja* (3 vols.; ZBK; Zürich: Zwingli, 1960–1964), 1:2–17.

[13] Hermann Barth, *Die Jesaja-Worte in der Josiazeit: Israel und Assur als Thema einer produktiven Neuinterpretation der Jesajaüberlieferung* (WMANT 48; Neukirchen-Vluyn: Neukirchener Verlag, 1977).

[14] Barth, *Jesaja-Worte*, 216–17.

the collection of מַשָּׂא oracles (or מַשָּׂא-*Sammlung*), this unit circulated independently of the book before being added shortly after
the exile as a foundation for subsequent promises of salvation and
redemption of Israel. As previous scholars have done, Barth accepts
the anti-Babylonian מַשָּׂא oracles (13:1–14:23; 21:1–10) as the basis for
dating the formation of the מַשָּׂא-*Sammlung*.[15] Still later, perhaps at
the beginning of the fourth century B.C.E., other material that speaks
favorably of foreign nations, such as 19:18–25, was added to counter-
act prior judgment against them.

Hans Wildberger's proposal for the formation of Isa 13–23 is mainly
dependent on the suggestions made by Fohrer and earlier scholars.[16]
While Barth attributes much of the non-מַשָּׂא material to the *Assur
Redaktion*, Wildberger supposes that the early collection was formed
primarily of authentic passages. At a later point, the collection of מַשָּׂא
oracles was incorporated into the group, during the course of which
מַשָּׂא superscriptions were also added to a few pre-existing oracles. He
suggests that the main impetus for the addition of the מַשָּׂא collection
was the occurrence of the מַשָּׂא heading at 14:28, which possibly traces
back to Isaiah ben Amoz, in his view. Thus, the later editor who added
the מַשָּׂא collection may have sought to align it with the work of the
eighth-century prophet.

A key point in Wildberger's view is the notion that the מַשָּׂא superscription was applied secondarily to certain pre-existing oracles (*viz.*,
17:1–7: 22:1–15). This proposal is distinguished from earlier approaches
that assume that all of the 'מַשָּׂא oracles' (i.e., those that now have the
superscription) were incorporated into the book as a single collection.
An important advantage of this notion is that it releases some of the
מַשָּׂא oracles from the constraint of being dated on the basis of others
that plausibly relate to a later period. However, this raises additional
challenges. By what criteria, then, would it be possible to determine
which oracles have מַשָּׂא headings that were secondarily added? Also,
if it is supposed that *some* of the מַשָּׂא titles are secondary, could this
not theoretically be the case for *all* of them? If so, this would preclude
the basic presupposition of the incorporation of a מַשָּׂא collection into

---

[15] Barth, *Jesaja-Worte*, 216–17, 290–92.
[16] Hans Wildberger, *Isaiah 13–27* (trans. Thomas H. Trapp; Minneapolis: Fortress,
1997), 1–2.

Isa 13–23. Although Wildberger is not directly concerned with these matters, we will return to them in due course.

Although Wildberger's perspective reflects a helpful sensitivity to the dating of individual oracles rather than the whole collection, his suggestion creates additional difficulties. For one thing, the notion that the מַשָּׂא superscription has been applied to some of the pre-existing texts only begs the question why it has not been added to others (e.g., 14:24–27; 18; 20). Also, Wildberger views an early version of the מַשָּׂא oracle about Egypt in 19 as Isaianic,[17] but includes this particular oracle within the collection that was subsequently added to the book. On one hand, he fails to establish criteria for determining that 17:1–7 and 22:1–15 (which currently have מַשָּׂא titles) pre-existed without the title as part of the core collection of early material. On the other hand, he provides no basis for the assumption that 19:1–4, 11–15 was a component of the added מַשָּׂא collection. Wildberger argues for the authenticity of all of these texts, but seems to determine arbitrarily which ones were part of an early collection and which were added subsequently. In the case of Isa 19, Wildberger asserts that it has been strategically placed between 18 and 20 on the basis of common interest in Egypt and Cush,[18] but this does not preclude the possibility of its insertion prior to the addition of the מַשָּׂא collection. In other words, Wildberger has not clearly demonstrated that the Egypt oracle must be taken as a component of the מַשָּׂא collection. Finally, Wildberger's claim that on one hand the earliest form of the Egypt oracle originated from the eighth century prophet, while on the other hand it was added along with a collection of מַשָּׂא oracles implies that Isaianic material circulated independently before being reintegrated with other Isaianic writings.

Similarly, Ronald Clements includes the מַשָּׂא oracle about Damascus at Isa 17:1–6 among the initial core of texts (along with 14:28–32; 18:1–7; 20:1–6) to which a מַשָּׂא collection was supposedly added, but because of the diversity of these texts, Clements is reluctant to view them as a cohesive literary unit.[19] Because 17:1–6 focuses on Aram and Israel, Clements includes this among the early oracles, and like

---

[17] Wildberger, *Isaiah 13–27*, 233–6.
[18] Wildberger, *Isaiah 13–27*, 233.
[19] Ronald E. Clements, *Isaiah 1–39* (NCB; Grand Rapids: Eerdmans; London: Marshall, Morgan & Scott, 1980), 129–30; see also Knud Jeppesen, "The *Maśśā᾽ Bābel* in Isaiah 13–14," PIBA 9 (1985): 63–80.

Wildberger, supposes that the מַשָּׂא title was added so that it would conform to the מַשָּׂא collection.[20] However, Clements offers no explanation regarding why the מַשָּׂא title was never added to the other oracles of the early group.

With some variation in certain points of detail, all of the scholars in this group subscribe to the general view that the current shape of Isa 13–23 was largely brought about by the addition of a collection of מַשָּׂא oracles to a group of pre-existing texts. Also, the approximate date for the addition of the collection is determined by components of the מַשָּׂא collection. In most cases, the incorporation of the מַשָּׂא collection is assigned to the early post-exilic period on the basis of the oracles describing the fall of Babylon in 13:1–14:23 and 21:1–10. Since Marti dates the earliest part of the מַשָּׂא oracle about Egypt in Isa 19 to the fourth century B.C.E., he conceives of the addition of the collection at a later point, possibly along with Isa 24–27, sometime during the third century.[21] Others, such as Wildberger and Clements, find earlier material among the מַשָּׂא texts and so propose that the superscription was applied to pre-existing oracles in some cases.

Several difficulties arise with the idea that the group of nations oracles in Isa 13–23 has been shaped largely by the contribution of a collection of מַשָּׂא oracles to a handful of earlier texts. The greatest challenge relates to the underlying assumption that there was such a collection in the first place. As the next chapter will consider more thoroughly, the Hebrew Bible contains no other collections of מַשָּׂא oracles, such as is thought to have been added to Isaiah. As a matter of fact, there are no individual מַשָּׂא oracles to speak of in the Hebrew Bible, such as those in the book of Isaiah.[22] Moreover, מַשָּׂא appears only as a superficial introductory element in the oracles of Isa 13–23, rather than as an integral part of the body of each oracle. Simply put, if Wildberger and Clements suppose that the title was secondarily added to some of the so-called מַשָּׂא oracles (e.g., 17:1), it is not implausible to suppose that such could be the case with all of them.

Another problem associated with the incorporation of a comprehensive מַשָּׂא collection is that it often leads its adherents to date the

---

[20] Clements, *Isaiah 1–39*, 157–8.
[21] Marti, *Jesaja*, xix.
[22] Chapter 2, below, will show that the introductory use of מַשָּׂא in Nah 1:1; Hab 1:1; Zech 9:1; 12:1; Mal 1:1 involves textual units larger than a single oracle, in which case these occurrences do not identify individual so-called מַשָּׂא oracles.

incorporation, if not also the composition, of individual oracles on the basis of some in the group. As we have seen however, some of the מַשָּׂא texts may have been composed in the eighth century B.C.E., while others are almost certainly more recent. Moreover, Wildberger's proposal for the secondary addition of certain מַשָּׂא superscriptions weakens the basic premise of the addition of a מַשָּׂא collection.

Finally, this view presumes the notion of an organized collection of oracles in an early recension of the book, to which the מַשָּׂא collection was added. Wildberger, for example, follows Fohrer's suggestion that the possibly Isaianic מַשָּׂא heading at 14:28 provided the primary impetus for the addition of the מַשָּׂא collection.[23] However, the assertion of an early collection of non-מַשָּׂא texts is challenged by the nonuniformity of these passages. Although opinions vary on which texts should be included, this group may have consisted of an untitled declaration of Assyria's destruction (14:24–27), an oracle against Philistia with an unusual מַשָּׂא heading at 14:28, an unspecified הוֹי oracle beginning at 17:12, followed by another הוֹי oracle against Cush beginning at 18:1, and the narrative about Egypt and Cush in 20:1. However, most of these texts have something to do with foreign nations, 20:1–6 contains a narrative rather than an oracle, and 17:12–14 refers to nations only generally, without specifying any one in particular. Therefore, it is difficult to conceive of this early assemblage as anything like an organized collection of nations oracles, much less one that could serve as the platform for the supposed addition of a much larger מַשָּׂא collection.

2. *The Priority of a* מַשָּׂא *Collection*

Some of these difficulties are addressed by a different group of scholars who advance the opposite proposition that all of the non-מַשָּׂא texts are later additions to a collection of מַשָּׂא oracles. An early proponent of this view is T. K. Cheyne, who posits that the מַשָּׂא collection was supplemented with authentic material (14:24–27; 17:12–14; 18; 20) in order to lend authenticity to the entire collection.[24] In the

---

[23] Wildberger, *Isaiah 13–27*, 1–2.

[24] T. K. Cheyne, *Introduction to the Book of Isaiah* (London: Adam and Charles Black, 1895), xxiv–xxv; see also Heinrich Friedrich Hackmann, *Die Zukunftserwartung des Jesaia* (Göttingen: Vandenhoeck & Ruprecht, 1893), 13. Cheyne's proposals for the development of Isa 13–23 are echoed substantially by G. H. Box, *The Book of Isaiah* (London: Pitman, 1908), 72, 89–95. Matthijs J. de Jong (*Isaiah among the Ancient*

present arrangement of the מַשָּׂא oracles, only the first superscription (13:1) makes any explicit claim to Isaianic authorship: "the מַשָּׂא about Babylon, which Isaiah ben Amoz saw." No other מַשָּׂא oracle directly asserts authenticity, and the title at 13:1 is very likely a secondary element, which leads Cheyne to conclude that the מַשָּׂא oracles initially give no indication of Isaianic authorship. Thus, he asserts that only later, with the introduction of genuine material (14:24–27; 17:12–14; 18; 20), is any movement made toward deliberately ascribing authenticity to the collection.

However, it is possible to draw precisely the opposite conclusion from Cheyne's observations. The appearance of the מַשָּׂא superscriptions produces the outcome of linking each of the components with the first in the series. Since the oracle that begins at Isa 13:1 claims to be a מַשָּׂא that Isaiah saw, a reader could infer that this characteristic applies to each מַשָּׂא oracle that follows.[25] Regardless of whether they were actually composed by the eighth-century prophet, it cannot be said that the מַשָּׂא oracles are unconcerned with claims of Isaianic authorship, as Cheyne asserts.

Furthermore, among those passages cited in Cheyne's list of later Isaianic insertions (14:24–27; 17:12–14; 18; 20), we may point out that only Isa 20 explicitly names Isaiah, and not one of these claims to be written by him.[26] Therefore, there is no basis for the assertion that the insertion of these texts could effectively claim Isaianic authorship for the entire collection. If this were the primary impetus for the incorporation of these verses into the collection, one would rather expect them to contain explicit references to Isaiah ben Amoz, possibly in the form of a heading similar to 13:1. Thus, even if these non-מַשָּׂא passages are genuine, their insertion contributes very little toward rendering authenticity to the entire collection.

Near Eastern Prophets: A Comparative Study of the Earliest Stages of the Isaiah Tradition and the Neo-Assyrian Prophecies [VTSup 117; Leiden: Brill, 2007], 139–40, 150–1) holds a similar view, although he includes 19:1–4 among the inserted passages. Thus, he asserts that מַשָּׂא was secondarily added at 19:1, but offers no explanation for why the heading was not applied to other insertions.

[25] Otto Kaiser (*Isaiah 13–39* [trans. R. A. Wilson; OTL; Philadelphia: Westminster; London: SCM, 1974], 1) makes the point that by designating the first מַשָּׂא oracle as Isaianic (13:1), the editor claims that those that follow also derive from the prophet.

[26] Isaiah 14:24–25 contains first-person speech, which could be interpreted as implicitly Isaianic, but this factor alone does not demonstrate authenticity, much less transfer that quality to other passages.

Since Isa 18 and 20 are cited among Cheyne's authentic insertions into the מַשָּׂא collection, more can be said about his understanding of the relationship between these chapters and the intervening מַשָּׂא oracle about Egypt. Despite the focus on Cush and Egypt in the following chapters, Cheyne is inclined to link the insertion of the הוֹי oracle at 18:1–6 with the preceding הוֹי oracle at 17:12–14.[27] He cites a common 'artistic structure' and historical background relating to the Assyrian campaign against Jerusalem in 701 B.C.E. concerning both הוֹי oracles as the basis for the insertion of the Cush oracle at 18. Against this assertion, however, neither passage contains any explicit association with the 701 siege of Jerusalem, and Cheyne does not elaborate on his interpretation of their structure beyond the common introductory particle.

In light of Cheyne's view that the non-מַשָּׂא passages have been distributed among the מַשָּׂא oracles, a more plausible suggestion would be that the Cush oracle of 18 has been added with an eye toward the מַשָּׂא oracle about Egypt in 19 or the narrative about both nations in 20. It would appear that the thematic links with these chapters provide a stronger basis of influence for the insertion of 18 than the הוֹי oracle at 17:12–14. Moreover, the הוֹי oracle at 17:12–14 exhibits no explicit thematic ties with the surrounding material, which may suggest that rather than prompting the insertion of the הוֹי oracle about Cush at 18, the latter oracle has played the influential role.

Cheyne briefly entertains the possibility that the additions of Isa 18 and 20 to the מַשָּׂא collection are interrelated, but he ultimately remains unconvinced on account of their disparate perspectives on Assyria's future.[28] Thus, 18:4–6 speaks of Yhwh's quiet observance before pruning immature vines, which Cheyne understands to refer to the ultimate destruction of Assyria and the deliverance of Jerusalem in light of Sennacherib's siege in 701 B.C.E. This interpretation of Isa 18 would conflict with the portrayal of Assyria's subjugation of Egypt and Cush in Isa 20, which is explicitly identified with the Ashdod revolt of 711. Against Cheyne's interpretation, however, the Cush oracle of Isa 18 makes no specific mention of Assyria, nor is there any indication that 18:4–6 refers to its judgment and the implied deliverance of Jerusalem. Although this matter will be taken up more thoroughly at a later

---

[27] Cheyne, *Isaiah*, 95.
[28] Cheyne, *Isaiah*, 97–8.

point (see Chapter 3, below), we may note that if 18 is not interpreted
to proclaim judgment against Assyria, the insertion of 18 and 20 as a
coordinated effort is more plausible.

In summary, Cheyne argues for the formation of Isa 13–23 in two
main stages: the addition of a מַשָּׂא collection, followed by the incorporation of other material. In his view, the latter stage is responsible
not only for 14:24–27; 17:12–14; 18; 20, but also for a number of editorial expansions to the מַשָּׂא oracles. However, this presents a number of challenges concerning the juxtaposition of diverse material in
a single editorial movement. It is rather unlikely, for example, that
19:23–25, which Cheyne interprets as the hope for peaceful international relations between Egypt and Assyria, would be added along with
the narrative in Isa 20, which depicts the humiliating tyranny of Egypt
and Cush by Assyria. Therefore, it is reasonable to expect that the formation of Isa 13–23 involved additional stages of development over an
extended period of time.

Otto Kaiser also adopts the view that various passages were added
to a core collection of מַשָּׂא oracles.[29] Since the Babylon oracles can
be dated no earlier than the late exilic period, Kaiser assumes that the
entire מַשָּׂא collection would not have been added to the book before
that time. Those passages that lack the superscription would have been
incorporated even later. In the case of the variant use of מַשָּׂא in the
heading at 14:28, Kaiser suggests that this was added to a later oracle
in imitation of the pre-existing מַשָּׂא material.[30]

The basic notion that non-מַשָּׂא texts have been added subsequently
to the מַשָּׂא oracles is not implausible. However, Kaiser accepts the
prevailing view that the addition of all the מַשָּׂא oracles must be dated
no earlier than the late exilic period on the basis of the Babylon oracles.
As with those who argue for the priority of the non-מַשָּׂא texts, this
position depends on the underlying assumption that the מַשָּׂא oracles
constitute a comprehensive collection that was added to the book *en
bloc*. It is rather surprising that Kaiser advances this view, considering
his suggestion that the מַשָּׂא heading at 14:28 has been fashioned in

---

[29] Kaiser, *Isaiah 13–39*, 1–5. For similar proposals, see Walther Eichrodt, *Der Herr
der Geschichte: Jesaja 13–23, 28–39* (BAT 17/2; Stuttgart: Calwer Verlag, 1967), 9–10;
Uwe Becker, *Jesaja: Von der Botschaft zum Buch* (FRLANT 178; Göttingen: Vandenhoeck & Ruprecht, 1997), 271–2.

[30] Kaiser, *Isaiah 13–39*, 2; also Friedrich Huber, *Jahwe, Juda und die anderen Völker
beim Propheten Jesaja* (BZAW 137; Berlin: de Gruyter, 1976), 102 n. 72.

the likeness of the others. As it happens, the heading at 14:28 would be a very poor imitation of the other superscriptions because it fails to name the addressee as the others do. If anything, the formation of 14:28 seems to be influenced primarily by 6:1 (see the discussion in Chapter 2, below). More significantly for our purposes, however, Kaiser's suggestion can be taken to advance the possibility that some of the מַשָּׂא headings in Isa 13–23 very well could be imitations of earlier superscriptions. This notion will be addressed more fully in the next chapter.

We may also include in this group those scholars who emphasize the role of the מַשָּׂא superscriptions in the structural arrangement of Isa 13–23.[31] For example, Marvin Sweeney's concern is not so much to demonstrate that the מַשָּׂא texts chronologically preceded others, but rather, to analyze these texts in the final structural form of 13–23. Sweeney posits that the מַשָּׂא superscription identifies a specific genre of literature and thereby delineates the structural divisions for these chapters.[32] Under the assumption that the final form of 13–23 consists entirely of מַשָּׂא texts or 'prophetic pronouncements,' Sweeney regards anything that lacks this superscription as 'extraneous material,' which is "subordinated structurally to the pronouncement forms."[33]

By way of example, the present arrangement of Isa 13–23 includes a מַשָּׂא superscription at 17:1 to introduce the Damascus oracle, and the next מַשָּׂא heading does not appear until the beginning of the Egypt oracle at 19:1, so Sweeney views 17:1–18:7 as a single מַשָּׂא unit (a 'prophetic pronouncement'). This structural arrangement subsumes the Cush oracle (18:1–7) as part of the מַשָּׂא about Damascus (17:1–18:7). In addition to the reference to a different nation in Isa 18, the boundaries of this oracle are established by the introductory הוֹי ('woe') particle at 18:1 and the start of the oracle about Egypt at 19:1.

Despite these factors, Sweeney supports his view in part by observing common agricultural themes in 17:4–6, 10–11, 13 and also 18:5–6. More substantially, Sweeney includes 18:1–7 as part of the preceding מַשָּׂא unit on the basis of certain essential elements of a מַשָּׂא genre as

---

[31] Marvin A. Sweeney, *Isaiah 1–39* (FOTL 16; Grand Rapids: Eerdmans, 1996), 212–17; idem, *King Josiah of Judah: The Lost Messiah of Israel* (Oxford: Oxford University Press, 2001), 244–7.

[32] Sweeney, *Isaiah 1–39*, 534–5.

[33] Sweeney, *Isaiah 1–39*, 212. This position is adopted by Brevard S. Childs, *Isaiah* (OTL; Louisville; Westminster John Knox, 2001), 114.

identified by Richard Weis.[34] According to Weis's analysis of the genre, a מַשָּׂא oracle should include, among other things, an explanation of Yhwh's direct involvement in human affairs. Sweeney finds no reference to Yhwh's activity anywhere in Isa 17, so he concludes that the portrayal of Yhwh pruning young shoots and branches in 18:3–6 supplies the essential component for the מַשָּׂא oracle that begins at 17:1.[35] However, it should be noted that 17:13 supplies a description of Yhwh rebuking the roaring nations, so that 18:3–6 need not be included with 17:1–14 as part of the same literary unit on this basis. Of course, this verse appears as part of a הוֹי oracle beginning at 17:12, in which case this part of chapter 17 also may arguably be distinguished from the מַשָּׂא unit beginning at 17:1. Nonetheless, the appearance of Yhwh's activity in 17:13 suffices to exclude 18:3–6 on the basis of Weis's criteria for the מַשָּׂא genre as accepted by Sweeney.

In a similar fashion, Sweeney groups Isa 19–20 as a single מַשָּׂא oracle, because the מַשָּׂא superscription at 19:1 does not recur until 21:1. While many commentators would date the origins of 19:18–25 sometime after the exilic period, Sweeney views these verses against the historical background of Manasseh's support for Assurbanipal's Egyptian campaigns during the mid-seventh century B.C.E.[36] The narrative of Isa 20 ostensibly refers to the Ashdod revolt in 711, but Sweeney relates this passage to Josiah's opposition of Egypt in the late seventh century.[37] There is no need to take issue with Sweeney's historical analysis of these texts here (see Chapters 4–5, below), but the inclusion of the narrative of 20:1–6 as part of the מַשָּׂא oracle about Egypt in 19 demonstrates his inclination to subordinate every literary unit in 13–23 as a component of a מַשָּׂא oracle.

By establishing the מַשָּׂא superscriptions as the defining structural elements of Isa 13–23, Sweeney does not identify any non-מַשָּׂא mate-

---

[34] Richard D. Weis, "A Definition of the Genre Maśśāʾ in the Hebrew Bible" (Ph.D. diss., Claremont Graduate School, 1986); idem, "Oracle, Old Testament," *ABD* 5:28–9. For discussion and evaluation of Weis's claims regarding a מַשָּׂא genre, see Chapter 2, below, and also Brian C. Jones, *Howling over Moab: Irony and Rhetoric in Isaiah 15–16* (SBLDS 157; Atlanta: Scholars Press, 1996), 65–74.

[35] Sweeney, *Isaiah 1–39*, 254; Childs, *Isaiah*, 135–8.

[36] See "Campaigns against Egypt, Syria, and Palestine," translated by A. Leo Oppenheim (*ANET*, 294–7); Sweeney, *Isaiah 1–39*, 272; also Willem A. M. Beuken, *Jesaja 13–27* (HTKAT; Freiburg: Herder, 2007), 179–80.

[37] Sweeney, *Isaiah 1–39*, 273. For further discussion of Sweeney's proposed seventh-century 'Josianic' redaction of the nations oracles, see his *King Josiah of Judah*, 244–8.

rial within these chapters. However, this structural function of the מַשָּׂא superscriptions and their role in the identification of a supposed מַשָּׂא genre are matters that remain to be demonstrated, rather than simply assumed, since several factors speak against them. To begin, the presence of Isa 18:1–7 as an oracle against a foreign nation that lacks the מַשָּׂא superscription suggests that the primary function of this superscription is not to identify any particular literary genre. The evidence for including 18:1–7 with the preceding material is not compelling, and there is no reason to subordinate this oracle about Cush as a component of the Damascus oracle simply because it lacks a מַשָּׂא superscription.

Also, the variant מַשָּׂא heading at Isa 14:28 weakens the assumption that the superscriptions serve as a formal element of a particular oracular genre. Except for 14:28, all of the מַשָּׂא superscriptions are immediately followed by the name of the addressee, such as מַשָּׂא בָּבֶל ('oracle about Babylon') at 13:1. Rather than this 'מַשָּׂא GN' formula, 14:28 has הָיָה הַמַּשָּׂא הַזֶּה ('this oracle came') following the temporal phrase בִּשְׁנַת־מוֹת הַמֶּלֶךְ אָחָז ('in the year of the death of King Ahaz'; cf. 6:1). Although proponents of a מַשָּׂא genre as a literary form would agree that at the very least מַשָּׂא is an essential element of the genre, the occurrence at 14:28 witnesses against uniformity even among the titles. If the מַשָּׂא titles were intended either as a genre identifier or a structural indicator, one would expect the heading at 14:28 to have been modified to conform to the others.

Furthermore, the grouping of chapters 18–20 according to their thematic interest in Cush and Egypt seems to preclude the structural organization of 13–23 according to the מַשָּׂא headings. The fact that these chapters contain a combination of מַשָּׂא and non-מַשָּׂא passages about these nations seems hardly accidental. More to the point, the current arrangement of non-מַשָּׂא texts surrounding the מַשָּׂא oracle about Egypt indicates thematic ties that cross the structural boundaries that Sweeney seeks to establish.

A similar emphasis on the structural role of the מַשָּׂא superscriptions lies at the heart of work by Leon J. Liebreich, who proposes a scheme for the formation of the entire book of Isaiah.[38] Liebreich

---

[38] Leon J. Liebreich, "The Compilation of the Book of Isaiah," *JQR* 46 (1955–56): 259–77; 47 (1956–57): 114–38. Others who organize Isa 13–23 around the מַשָּׂא titles include Ulrich Berges, *Das Buch Jesaja: Komposition und Endgestalt* (HBS 16; Freiburg: Herder, 1998), 139–45; Beuken, *Jesaja 13–27*, 23–6.

begins his study by observing that the verb חזה ('to see') appears at the
beginning of major divisions in the first part of the book, namely, 1:1;
2:1; 13:1. From these three superscriptions, Liebreich posits three corresponding types of prophetic utterances: a חָזוֹן (cf. 1:1) is primarily
denunciatory in character, a דְּבַר (cf. 2:1) is thought to be more positive, while a מַשָּׂא (cf. 13:1) addresses foreign nations.[39] He identifies
four main divisions within Isa 1–39, with the nations oracles located
in Division II, which spans 13–27. Individual prophecies in this section are distinguished solely by the occurrence of the מַשָּׂא superscriptions, so that oracles without the title (e.g., 18) are evidently taken
as components of מַשָּׂא material. Also, Liebreich associates the מַשָּׂא
superscription at 14:28 with the others, despite the points of variation
that we have already noted.

Liebreich proposes that Isa 13–27 consists of two groups of five
מַשָּׂא oracles, called Divisions IIA and IIB (beginning at 13:1; 14:28;
15:1; 17:1; 19:1 and 21:1, 11, 13; 22:1; 23:1), which are joined together
by a transitional passage at chapter 20.[40] He supports this outline by
identifying a number of parallel elements between the two bodies of
material, such as a six-fold recurrence of the בַּיּוֹם הַהוּא ('in that day')
formula concluding each set of מַשָּׂא prophecies (19:16, 18, 19, 21, 23,
24 and 25:9; 26:1; 27:1, 2, 12, 13).

While Sweeney assigns the entire contents of Isa 13–23 to some part
of a מַשָּׂא oracle, Liebreich distinguishes 20:1–6 as a non-מַשָּׂא unit
and designates it as a bridge between the two bodies of מַשָּׂא texts. The
function of this narrative as a transitional passage is established on the
basis of two links with the surrounding chapters. The description of
the king of Assyria in 20:1, 4, 6 corresponds with mention of Assyria
in 19:23–25, while reference to Yhwh speaking (דִּבֶּר יְהוָה) in 20:2 is
understood as a link with the same expression at 21:17; 22:25; 24:3;
25:8. Despite these common elements, Liebreich fails to discuss how
the narrative provides a transition from one מַשָּׂא group to another
and how these textual links are supposed to contribute toward that
end. Rather, it appears that these common elements are more coincidental than intentional. A more plausible basis for 20:1–6 functioning

[39] Liebreich, "Compilation," *JQR* 46 (1955–56): 260–1.
[40] Liebreich, "Compilation," *JQR* 46 (1955–56): 265–6.

as a transitional passage would be a word or theme held in common with both the preceding and following material.[41]

Liebreich's evidence for dividing Isa 13–27 into two groups of מַשָּׂא oracles is similarly arbitrary. For example, Liebreich has does not show why Isa 24–27, which is not introduced by מַשָּׂא, should be included along with the second group of oracles. The inclusion of these chapters implies that they are to be understood as part of the מַשָּׂא oracle beginning at 23:1. He attempts to explain that 24:1–25:8 are 'intervening chapters' preceding the second series of six בַּיּוֹם הַהוּא phrases, which is supported by superficial parallels between 24:1–25:8 and the supposed transitional passage at 20.[42] However, according to his own arrangement, Isa 20 cannot be viewed as a structural parallel with 24:1–25:8, since the six בַּיּוֹם הַהוּא phrases *precede* the transitional passage (19:16, 18, 19, 21, 23, 24) at 20, while these formulae *follow* the intervening chapters (25:9; 26:1; 27:1, 2, 12, 13) of 24:1–25:8.

In Liebreich's studies, a structural arrangement that could be merely coincidental (two 'groups' of five מַשָּׂא superscriptions) is unduly forced to bear the weight of his proposal for the deliberate formation of the collection. Furthermore, his effort to demonstrate structural symmetry ultimately disregards other units of material, such as those oracles that lack the מַשָּׂא superscription, or the distinction of Isa 24–27 as a separate literary unit. This treatment of the text results in a circular analysis, since the support for his claims is based on the validity of the thesis.

Some mention should also be made of the study by Allan Jenkins, which admittedly demonstrates greater interest in the structural arrangement of Isa 13–23 than in the redactional development of these chapters.[43] Thus, Jenkins generally declines to speculate on the processes leading to the assembly of the collection, but he does consider the frequent occurrence of the מַשָּׂא superscription to be evidence of "an ordered and deliberate arrangement."[44]

---

[41] For example, in order to posit Isa 20 as a transition between 13–19 and 21–27, Liebreich might have pointed out the recurring mention of Assyria in 20, as well as at the conclusion of both sections (19:23–25; 27:13). In any event, this also seems to be mere coincidence rather than evidence of literary shaping.

[42] Liebreich, "Compilation," *JQR* 46 (1955–56): 266.

[43] Allan K. Jenkins, "The Development of the Isaiah Tradition in Is 13–23," in *The Book of Isaiah—Le Livre de Isaïe: Les oracles et leurs relecture. Unité et complexité de l'ouvrage* (ed. Jacques Vermeylen; BETL 81; Leuven: Peeters, 1989), 237–51.

[44] Jenkins, "Development," 238.

Jenkins argues for a division of two major sections of oracles that are thematically arranged according to neighboring states (14:28–17:14; Philistia, Moab, Damascus) and great political powers (18–21; Ethiopia, Egypt, Babylon). It is interesting to note that despite Jenkins' assertions about the structural role of the מַשָּׂא title, he associates the beginning of the second cluster of oracles with the הוֹי oracle about Cush at 18:1. In addition, he gives little attention to specifying how the remaining material enclosing the two groups (13:1–14:27; 22–23) fits into this rubric. There are also difficulties with the criteria that he has established for the identification of the two major groups of oracles. While 'neighboring nations' purportedly defines the first group (14:28–17:14), this characteristic could be plausibly attributed to the material about Egypt (19) as well. Similarly, no suggestion is offered for how 'Dumah' (21:11–12), for example, might be considered a major world power, even though this is supposedly the defining characteristic of the second group.[45] In the end, this structural arrangement provides little insight into the formation of Isa 13–23.

3. *Alternative Approaches*

Most commentators have adopted one of the foregoing positions, namely, that Isa 13–23 was formed by the addition of a מַשָּׂא collection, either before or after the incorporation of the non-מַשָּׂא texts. Both opinions depend on the underlying premise that most or all of these מַשָּׂא oracles were added to the book as a collection. However, the evidence speaks against this assumption, despite its prevalence. For one thing, the מַשָּׂא oracles seem to exhibit considerable variety in their date of composition. As we have seen, some may stem from the eighth century B.C.E., while others cannot be plausibly dated much earlier than end of the exile. They are also inconsistent with regard to such characteristics as literary form, length, and content. The example at 14:28 shows that even the מַשָּׂא titles are not entirely uniform, and the presumed reference to Jerusalem in the 'Valley of Vision' oracle (22:1–14) indicates that these cannot even be categorized exclusively as oracles against foreign nations.

---

[45] The designation 'Dumah' is uncertain, but 21:11 mentions Seir (Edom), which arguably could more plausibly be considered a neighboring nation than a significant power.

Another challenge is presented by the observation that at least some of the מַשָּׂא superscriptions are secondary additions to the oracles. Unless it can be shown that the title has direct bearing on either the composition or incorporation of oracles, it provides an unreliable basis for dating the oracle that it introduces. Moreover, it is worth pointing out that there are no other collections of מַשָּׂא oracles in the Hebrew Bible, such as is thought to have been incorporated into the book of Isaiah. For that matter, the Hebrew Bible contains no individual מַשָּׂא oracles like those of Isa 13–23, except at Isa 30:6.[46]

Finally, any proposal for the formation of Isa 13–23 must address the fact that both titled and untitled literary units are brought together within the collection. As we have observed, the מַשָּׂא titles have been frequently employed as the basis for distinguishing between stages in the formation of 13–23. Despite such attempts, other characteristics of the textual material are not so easily divided along the same lines. For example, both the מַשָּׂא and non-מַשָּׂא texts contain material that can be arguably dated to the eighth century B.C.E. as well as later periods. In addition, the grouping of Cush and Egypt material in Isa 18–20 witnesses to thematic ties that transcend attempts at division according to oracular titles. Furthermore, the scholarly divide concerning the priority of either מַשָּׂא or non-מַשָּׂא texts suggests that this criterion cannot sustain arguments in either direction.

In light of the foregoing comments, we should mention a few scholars whose proposals for the formation of Isa 13–23 are more or less indifferent to the distinction of the מַשָּׂא superscription. Despite Bernhard Duhm's substantial influence on the critical study of the formation of Isaiah, his suggestions for Isa 13–23 did not attract as many followers as his delineation of Trito-Isaiah (Isa 56–66). Duhm views Isa 13–23 (plus 30:6–7, which also begins with מַשָּׂא) as one of several independent 'booklets' (*Büchlein*) that were assembled together to produce the book of Isaiah, because 13:1 introduces Isaiah as if he were an unknown figure.[47] According to Duhm, this booklet initially consisted of a small collection of five oracles that are now found in 14:28–20:6,

---

[46] The occurrences at Nah 1:1; Hab 1:1; Zech 9:1; 12:1; Mal 1:1 all introduce larger textual units.

[47] Duhm, *Jesaia*, 12–13. See also Sigmund Mowinckel, "Die Komposition des Jesajabuches Kap. 1–39," *AcOr* 11 (1932): 276–8; Joachim Becker, *Isaias: Der Prophet und sein Buch* (SBS 30; Stuttgart: Katholisches Bibelwerk, 1968), 63–6.

excluding the הוֹי oracles at 17:12–18:7, which were later insertions.[48] Despite the appearance of both מַשָּׂא and non-מַשָּׂא material in this group, Duhm detects thematic homogeneity among them, and asserts that concern for the land of Philistia in the first and last units (14:28–32; 20:1–6) provides an appropriate enclosure for the collection. This initial group of oracles (Isa 14:28–20:6) was later supplemented with a separate collection of five shorter מַשָּׂא oracles. Four of these are contained within Isa 21–22, while the fifth has since been displaced to its current position at 30:6–7. The redactor who added this second group also enclosed the new collection with the מַשָּׂא oracles about Babylon (13:1–14:23) and Tyre (23).[49]

Duhm's early proposal is attractive for advocating the growth of Isa 13–23 by increments that are not strictly defined by the מַשָּׂא superscription, but his view of these chapters as an independent booklet is less plausible. Although he offers no basis besides thematic coherence within the units, his position is clearly distinguished from subsequent views that involve the incorporation of a self-contained collection of מַשָּׂא oracles. As the following chapter will show, the general view of the integration of מַשָּׂא texts in multiple stages is similar in some respects to that which is advanced by the present study.

Jacques Vermeylen approaches the subject of the formation of Isa 13–23 with the assumption that the earliest stages of the formation of these chapters contain the oldest material, as his proposed reconstruction of the formation of Isa 18–20 illustrates.[50] In his view, a portion of the Cush oracle (18:1–2, 4) and the narrative of 20:1–6 would have been gathered with other Isaianic material during the initial phase. Vermeylen suggests that sometime later, perhaps during the exilic period, 19:1–4, 11–15 was supposedly added as a Deuteronomistic commentary on the preceding Cush oracle. He draws this conclusion on the basis of the concern in 19:1–4, 11–15 for matters of piety and worship, as well as the renunciation of Egypt's purported

---

[48] For the subsequent insertion of 17:12–18:7 Duhm follows earlier commentators, including Georg Heinrich August von Ewald, *Commentary on the Prophets of the Old Testament* (trans. J. Frederick Smith; London: Williams and Norgate, 1876), 243–4; and August Dillmann, *Der Prophet Jesaia* (Leipzig: Hirzel, 1890), 164–70.

[49] Duhm, *Jesaia*, 12–13.

[50] Jacques Vermeylen, *Du prophète Isaïe à l'apocalyptique: Isaïe, I–XXXV* (2 vols.; *EBib*; Paris: Gabalda, 1977–78), 1:286. A similar approach, involving two stages of development for Isa 21, is taken by A. A. Macintosh, *Isaiah XXI: A Palimpsest* (Cambridge: Cambridge University Press, 1980).

wisdom.[51] It was not until the first half of the fifth century B.C.E. that these chapters were first deliberately formulated into a collection of foreign nations oracles, when the מַשָּׂא superscriptions were supposedly applied. Vermeylen claims that this period was marked by a diminished interest in particular nationalities, so the reworking tends to compare non-Jews with other nations by means of general descriptions, as demonstrated in such additions as 18:3, 5–6; 19:5–10. In his view, a subsequent stage emphasizes a conflict between pious and impious Jews, producing texts like 19:16–17, in which wayward Jews are supposedly compared with foreigners. Finally, greater interest in the conversion of foreigners is shown during the Hellenistic period, during which 18:7; 19:18–25 were added to the group.[52]

Vermeylen's emphasis on the gradual development of Isa 13–23 within the book of Isaiah offers a helpful perspective on the formation of these chapters. However, his dating of particular texts is occasionally arbitrary, and seems to be based more on their alignment with his comprehensive seven-stage scheme for the formation of Isa 1–35 than on a careful consideration of specific texts. His characterization of 19:1–4, 11–15 as Deuteronomistic, for example, is unconvincing.[53] In addition, Vermeylen criticizes other proposals that fail to account for the fact that the מַשָּׂא superscription has not been applied to every oracle in Isa 13–23, but he offers little explanation for the absence of the superscription in the Cush oracle of Isa 18.[54] In the end, although Vermeylen has offered a broad paradigm on to which he projects his conception of the formation of Isa 13–23, his proposal fails to address thoroughly some of the deficiencies that he has identified in other perspectives.

Another helpful way forward has been offered by Joseph Blenkinsopp, who proposes that the formation of Isa 13–23 came about in a series of increments, beginning from a collection of early sayings that initially lacked the מַשָּׂא superscription (14:24–27, 28–31; 15:1–16:11; 17:1–3, 4–6; 18:1–6; 19:1–15).[55] Picking up Barth's notion of an *Assur Redaktion*, Blenkinsopp suggests that this group of oracles served as an extension of the material relating to Assyria in the first part of

[51] Vermeylen, *Du prophète Isaïe*, 1:320–1.
[52] Vermeylen, *Du prophète Isaïe*, 1:347–8.
[53] For discussion of Isa 19, see Chapter 4, below.
[54] Vermeylen, *Du prophète Isaïe*, 1:318.
[55] Joseph Blenkinsopp, *Isaiah 1–39* (AB 19; New York: Doubleday, 2000), 272.

the book and that it might have been formulated during the seventh century B.C.E., when the fall of the Assyrian empire was on the near horizon.

In Blenkinsopp's view, the collection was enclosed with the oracles against Babylon in Isa 13–14 and 21:1–10 no earlier than the sixth century B.C.E. At a later point, מַשָּׂא superscriptions were added to some of the existing oracles and new מַשָּׂא oracles were added, namely those addressing Dumah (21:11–12), the Wilderness (21:13–15), the Valley of Vision (22:1–8), and Tyre (23:1–16).[56]

Blenkinsopp's suggestion that the מַשָּׂא titles were added to certain oracles seems to give due consideration to the secondary nature of the superscriptions. However, he explains that the pre-existing oracles against Assyria (14:24–27), Philistia (14:28–31), and Israel (17:4–6) never received a title because they were "of less contemporaneous relevance."[57] Since the secondary application of the titles serves to provide an element of uniformity, it would seem that the contemporaneous relevance is an unlikely criterion. Moreover, the occurrence of the superscription at the beginning of the Damascus oracle at 17:1 also argues against this possibility. In addition, we may note that מַשָּׂא does indeed occur at 14:28, even though it is different from the others in the collection.

3. Summary

As we have observed, most commentators propose that the greater part of Isa 13–23 was formed by the addition of a collection of מַשָּׂא oracles, either before or after the incorporation of the remaining material. Both views depend on the assumption that these מַשָּׂא texts constitute a comprehensive literary corpus that was worked into the book of Isaiah, despite significant challenges that have been mentioned. These difficulties demonstrate a need for a re-evaluation of common assumptions about the formation of Isa 13–23. Therefore, Chapter 2, below, advances a new proposal for the broad stages in the development of this broad collection, which serves as a basis for the formation of the Cush-Egypt group in Isa 18–20 as well. Chapters 3–5 deal with

---

[56] Blenkinsopp, *Isaiah 1–39*, 272–3.
[57] Blenkinsopp, *Isaiah 1–39*, 272.

the internal development of each of the chapters of Isa 18–20. From that point, Chapter 6 specifically addresses the formation of Isa 18–20 into a group of literary material concerning Cush and Egypt, followed by a concluding chapter that discusses a few broader implications of the study. The English translations of biblical texts are primarily my own, although they are frequently based on the New Revised Standard Version. Verse references follow the numbering of the Masoretic Text, with English references given in parentheses, where they differ.

CHAPTER TWO

THE NATIONS ORACLES IN ISAIAH 13–23

1. INTRODUCTION

The previous chapter surveyed the two main approaches to the formation of Isa 13–23 that have characterized most critical interpretations of Isaiah. Some argue that a collection of מַשָּׂא oracles was added to those texts that lack the superscription, while others posit that the collection of מַשָּׂא oracles came first, with the non-מַשָּׂא texts being subsequently interspersed among them. Proponents of both positions usually assume that the מַשָּׂא texts constitute a complete corpus of literary material that was added to the book at some point.

However, several factors challenge the underlying notion of an independent collection of מַשָּׂא oracles. First, while other prophetic books feature collections of foreign nations oracles (Jer 46–51; Ezek 25–32; Amos 1–2; Zeph 2:4–15), there are no other מַשָּׂא collections in the Hebrew Bible, such as is supposed to have been added to the book of Isaiah. מַשָּׂא is used elsewhere as a prophetic superscription at Isa 30:6; Nah 1:1; Hab 1:1; Zech 9:1; 12:1; Mal 1:1, but these superscriptions occur individually, they often introduce larger textual units,[1] and they are not uniform.

Another argument against the insertion of a complete collection of מַשָּׂא oracles can be raised from the diversity of the מַשָּׂא oracles in Isa 13–23. As the following discussion will show, scholars have been unable to identify any common formal elements among those texts that are introduced by מַשָּׂא. Also, even considering the likelihood that many of the oracles have received additional expansion, the present forms range considerably in length from the two verses of the Dumah oracle (21:11–12) to the two chapters of the Moab oracle (15–16). In addition, some oracles appear to address the fall of Babylon, presumably at the end of the exilic period (13:1–14:23; 21:1–10), while others

---

[1] Michael H. Floyd, "The מַשָּׂא (maśśāʾ) as a Type of Prophetic Book," *JBL* 121 (2002): 401–22.

may plausibly relate to the eighth century B.C.E. (e.g., 17:1–6; 22:1–8). As the previous chapter noted, this has caused difficulty for tracing the development of such an independent collection and for dating its subsequent incorporation into the book of Isaiah.

Finally, even the מַשָּׂא superscriptions themselves in Isa 13–23 are diverse, as will be discussed in greater detail shortly. For the moment, we may observe that most of the oracles have a 'מַשָּׂא GN' title, but the heading at 14:28 uses מַשָּׂא in a unique way. In addition, the title at 13:1 is of the 'מַשָּׂא GN' variety, but it has been modified to parallel the introduction at 2:1. Thus, while the מַשָּׂא title is presumably the key unifying component for the purported collection, there is some variance in how it appears in Isa 13–23, and to a greater degree, elsewhere in the Hebrew Bible.

Because מַשָּׂא is a common feature of much of the material in Isa 13–23, it presumably plays a key role in the development of these chapters. In light of the difficulties with the notion of an independent מַשָּׂא collection, however, a different approach must be taken toward the formation of Isa 13–23. The following discussion advances the proposal that מַשָּׂא titles were applied to oracles from the earliest stage in the development of a collection of nations oracles within the literary context of the book of Isaiah. In addition, this chapter will distinguish two main movements in the development of the מַשָּׂא material. This approach is a more plausible alternative to the usual assumption of the incorporation of a comprehensive collection of מַשָּׂא oracles. The incremental application of the מַשָּׂא superscriptions seeks to resolve apparent conflicts concerning מַשָּׂא material that can be plausibly dated either to the eighth century B.C.E. or to later periods, while maintaining that the collection has developed within the literary context of the book of Isaiah. Following a survey of current discussion concerning מַשָּׂא oracles, we will offer a fresh proposal for the formation of Isa 13–23.

2. The מַשָּׂא Oracles in Isaiah 13–23

The word מַשָּׂא appears ten times as an introductory element in Isa 13–23,[2] and a similar occurrence can also be found at Isa 30:6. Nearly

---

[2] Isaiah 13:1; 14:28; 15:1; 17:1; 19:1; 21:1, 11, 13; 22:1; 23:1.

all of these use the term to formulate a 'מַשָּׂא GN' superscription, such
as מַשָּׂא בָּבֶל ('oracle concerning Babylon'), found at 13:1. A variation
appears at 14:28, in which the term is included as part of a longer introduction to the oracle about Philistia: בִּשְׁנַת־מוֹת הַמֶּלֶךְ אָחָז הָיָה הַמַּשָּׂא
הַזֶּה ('In the year of the death of King Ahaz, this oracle came').

In addition to these occurrences in Isaiah, the book of Nahum is
introduced by a 'מַשָּׂא GN' superscription similar to those in Isaiah,
while a different sort of מַשָּׂא title appears at Hab 1:1 (cf. Isa 13:1), and
yet another מַשָּׂא variation begins each of the final three sections of the
book of the Twelve (Zech 9:1; 12:1; Mal 1:1). The term also appears
in reference to prophecy at 2 Kgs 9:25; Jer 23:33–39; Lam 2:14; Ezek
12:10; 2 Chr 24:27; Prov 30:1; 31:1.[3] Otherwise, most occurrences of
the word in the Hebrew Bible describe a burden that is carried or
lifted up without any prophetic connotation.[4] Finally, the term appears
within a musical context (1 Chr 15:22, 27) and is also the name of a
place (Gen 25:14; 1 Chr 1:30).

Wherever מַשָּׂא is understood without dispute to mean 'burden,' it is
usually thought to be linked etymologically with the verb נשׂא ('to lift
up, carry'). Some scholars interpret the prophetic occurrences of the
term on the same basis, and thus propose that מַשָּׂא in such instances
refers to some kind of prophetic 'burden.'[5] Henry Gehman, for example, supports this view by citing several biblical instances in which a
prophetic figure 'lifts up' (נשׂא) the message.[6] Balaam, for example, is
said to lift up his saying (מָשָׁל; Num 23:7, 18; 24:3, 15, 20, 21, 23; cf.
Isa 14:4; Mic 2:4; Hab 2:6), and prophets occasionally lift up a lament
(קִינָה; Jer 7:29; 9:9; Ezek 19:1; 26:17; 27:2, 32; 28:12; 32:2; Amos 5:1).

---

[3] It is unclear whether the occurrences at Prov 30:1; 31:1 should be understood to
describe prophetic speech.

[4] Exodus 23:5; Num 4:15, 19, 24, 27, 31, 32, 47, 49; 11:11, 17; Deut 1:12; 2 Sam
15:33; 19:36; 2 Kgs 5:17; 8:9; 2 Chr 17:11; 19:7; 20:25; 35:3; Neh 13:15, 19; Job 7:20;
Ps 38:5 (4); Isa 22:25; 46:1, 2; Jer 17:21, 22, 24, 27; Ezek 24:25; Hos 8:10.

[5] Henry S. Gehman, "The 'Burden' of the Prophets," *JQR* 31 (1940–41): 107–21; see
also P. A. H. de Boer, "An Inquiry into the Meaning of the Term מַשָּׂא," *OtSt* 5 (1948):
197–214; Barry B. Margulis, "Studies in the Oracles against the Nations" (Ph.D. diss.,
Brandeis University, 1967), 202; J. A. Naudé, "*Maśśā'* in the OT with Special Reference
to the Prophets," *OTWSA* 12 (1969): 91–100; Magne Sæbø, *Sacharja 9–14: Untersuchungen von Text und Form* (WMANT 34; Neukirchen-Vluyn: Neukirchener Verlag,
1969), 137–40; Robert R. Wilson, *Prophecy and Society in Ancient Israel* (Philadelphia:
Fortress, 1980), 249, cf. 257–9; John D. W. Watts, *Isaiah 1–33* (rev. ed.; WBC 24;
Nashville: Thomas Nelson, 2005), 236–7. Similarly, the Vulgate consistently translates
all occurrences of מַשָּׂא in prophetic superscriptions as *onus*.

[6] Gehman, "'Burden,'" 110–14.

In Gehman's view, a 'burden' from God comes to the prophet, who then takes up the מַשָּׂא and conveys it to the nation or individual being addressed. Thus, the prophetic burden is to be understood as a message of judgment or calamity against the recipients.

Against this view, the messages associated with מַשָּׂא are not always burdensome or ominous in nature (e.g., Lam 2:14; Prov 30:1; 31:1). For this reason, others argue for a sense along the lines of 'utterance' or 'pronouncement' (= מַשָּׂא II) within the context of prophecy. This homonym of מַשָּׂא I ('burden') is often thought to derive separately from the verb נשׂא, perhaps by means of the expression נשׂא קוֹל, 'to lift one's voice.'[7] Other attempts to relate the term etymologically to the verb נשׂא include 'taking up' lots for divination,[8] and 'lifting the hand,' either as a solemn oath or as a prophetic curse.[9] Alternatively, Richard Weis associates מַשָּׂא with the noun מַשְׂאֵת ('smoke signal'; Judg 20:38, 40; Jer 6:1; also Lachish Ostracon 4.10), in which case מַשָּׂא is interpreted to denote a signal of Yhwh's intentions as communicated by the prophetic lookout.[10]

Despite a solid basis for the distinction of a sense for מַשָּׂא aside from 'burden', the derivation from נשׂא קוֹל is difficult to sustain, since in no case in the Hebrew Bible is a prophetic figure ever said to lift up his or her voice to speak a מַשָּׂא. Rather, the idea of lifting the voice most commonly involves an expression of grief or crying out for some other purpose, and is often collocated with such verbs as בכה ('to weep'; Gen 21:16; 27:38; 29:11; Num 14:1; Judg 2:4; 21:2; Ruth 1:9, 14; 1 Sam 11:4; 24:17; 30:4; 2 Sam 3:32; 13:36; Job 2:12; Jer 9:9), צעק

---

[7] H.-P. Müller, "מַשָּׂא," *TDOT* 9:20–24; also Johannis D. Michaelis, *Observationes philologicae et criticae in Jeremiae Vaticinia et Threnos* (ed. Johannes Friedericus Schleusner; Göttingen: Vandenhoeck & Ruprecht, 1793), 199–201; Karl Heinrich Graf, *Der Prophet Jeremia* (Leipzig: Weigel, 1862), 315; Karl Marti, *Das Buch Jesaja* (KHC 10; Tübingen: Mohr [Siebeck], 1900), 117; Ronald E. Clements, *Isaiah 1–39* (NCB; Grand Rapids: Eerdmans, 1980), 132; "מַשָּׂא II," *HALOT* 2:639–40. According to Otto Procksch (*Jesaja I* [KAT 9/1; Leipzig: Deichert, 1930], 184), Campegius Vitringa (1659–1722) was the first to link this sense of מַשָּׂא with lifting the voice.

[8] Thus, Procksch (*Jesaia I*, 184) translates מַשָּׂא as 'Schicksalspruch.'

[9] R. B. Y. Scott, "The Meaning of *massāʾ* as an Oracle Title," *JBL* 67 (1948): v–vi; idem, "The Literary Structure of Isaiah's Oracles," in *Studies in Old Testament Prophecy Presented to Theodore H. Robinson* (ed. H. H. Rowley; Edinburgh: T. & T. Clark, 1950), 178.

[10] Richard D. Weis, "A Definition of the Genre Maśśāʾ in the Hebrew Bible" (Ph.D. diss., Claremont Graduate School, 1986), 353–7. Victor Sasson ("An Unrecognized 'Smoke Signal' in Isaiah xxx 27," *VT* 33 [1983]: 90–95) relates the unusual form מַשְׂאָה in MT Isa 30:27 to מַשְׂאֵת as well.

('to cry out'; Isa 42:2), and קרא ('to call'; Judg 9:7).[11] However, 2 Kgs 9:25 speaks of lifting up (נשא) a מַשָּׂא, with clear reference to a prophetic utterance rather than any kind of physical burden or load. This would seem to affirm an etymological connection between the noun מַשָּׂא and the verb נשא, even if its development cannot be traced.

The notion that מַשָּׂא I ('burden') and מַשָּׂא II ('utterance') are homonyms is given further support by a play on this word in Jer 23:33–39. In 23:33, the people ask for a מַשָּׂא from Yhwh, to which the prophet is instructed to respond by declaring that the people themselves are the מַשָּׂא.[12] The context clearly indicates that the first occurrence of the term refers to a prophetic message or 'word' (cf. 23:36), which may or may not have been expected to be burdensome. By contrast, the sense 'burden' must be applied within the same verse to the rejoinder that '*you* are the מַשָּׂא,'[13] since this is something that will be cast off (נטש). This is confirmed by the recurrence in 23:39 of נטש, again in reference to casting off the people/burden, along with the addition of the verb נשא ('to lift up') as a play on מַשָּׂא.[14]

When מַשָּׂא means 'utterance' or 'oracle' in the Hebrew Bible, the term is used primarily as an introduction to prophetic material. The most sustained treatment of the prophetic use of מַשָּׂא has been carried out by Richard Weis in his unpublished dissertation, which is summarized briefly in an article he produced for the *Anchor Bible Dictionary*.[15] Weis's main objective is to argue for מַשָּׂא as a specific literary genre. He defines a מַשָּׂא as a prophetic clarification of a previous message from Yhwh, brought about either by misunderstanding about the divine intention or by changes that have taken place in the unfolding of human events. In Ezek 12:10–16, for example, the prophet is

---

[11] Other instances include an expression of arrogance (2 Kgs 19:22/Isa 37:23) and lifting the voice in praise or joy (Ps 93:3; Isa 24:14; 52:8).

[12] William McKane, "משא in Jeremiah 23:33–40," in *Prophecy: Essays Presented to Georg Fohrer on His Sixty-fifth Birthday* (ed. J. A. Emerton; BZAW 150; Berlin: de Gruyter, 1980), 35–54; idem, *Jeremiah* (2 vols.; ICC; Edinburgh: T. & T. Clark, 1986–96), 1:597–604. The NRSV and JPS translate all occurrences of מַשָּׂא in Jer 23:33–39 as 'burden', while the NASB and NIV (for example) translate the first occurrence as 'oracle'.

[13] LXX ὑμεῖς ἐστε τὸ λῆμμα (= אַתֶּם הַמַּשָּׂא) is preferred over MT אֶת־מַה־מַשָּׂא.

[14] A few Hebrew manuscripts and several versions support reading וְנָשִׁיתִי (a variant of וְנָשָׁאתִי) and נָשָׁא rather than וְנָשִׁיתִי... נָשָׁא in MT Jer 23:39. See McKane, "משא in Jeremiah 23:33–40," 51; idem, *Jeremiah*, 1:602.

[15] Weis, "Definition of the Genre Maśśāʾ"; idem, "Oracle, Old Testament," *ABD* 5:28–9.

instructed to give a מַשָּׂא in order to explain the meaning of his actions (12:7) and to respond to the uncertainty of its significance (12:9).[16]

In Weis's view, the general absence of common features among מַשָּׂא texts requires that the definition of the genre must be established primarily by its function rather than its form. Nonetheless, he is able to ascertain a few characteristics that typify מַשָּׂא texts, such as their lack of prophetic messenger formulae, their association with either a דְּבַר יְהוָה ('word of Yhwh') or a general revelation from Yhwh, and their relation to specific historical situations.[17]

Although Weis has offered a comprehensive survey of the מַשָּׂא texts, his central methodological focus is on the מַשָּׂא texts in their final form, whereas the present study is primarily concerned with the diachronic development of Isa 13–23. Weis's identification of certain characteristics among texts that are labeled מַשָּׂא in their present form provides limited insight into the formation of Isa 13–23 if some of these characteristics are shown to be editorial additions to earlier material. Thus, it may be possible to argue for a מַשָּׂא genre in the final form of the texts, but this is entirely different from asserting that they were composed as such.

In fact, one would need to look no further than the likelihood that many of the מַשָּׂא headings themselves are secondary additions to the texts that they introduce, a matter that will be given fuller treatment in due course. Needless to say, a text without the מַשָּׂא heading can hardly be classified according to that genre. Weis is certainly aware of this difficulty, but in his view, the problem is eliminated if merely one example can be located in which the text and the term are integrally linked from the outset. He proceeds to provide two such examples (Isa 14:28–32; Zech 9:1–11:3),[18] but the difficulty is not so easily resolved. Even if Weis is correct that these texts have incorporated the term מַשָּׂא from the earliest point of composition, it does not follow that such is the case in all instances. To the contrary, if a text has been assigned a מַשָּׂא title secondarily, any association with this purported genre has been produced by a later editor, rather than by the original author.

---

[16] See Weis, "Definition of the Genre Maśśāʾ," 249–50.
[17] For additional characteristics, see Weis, "Definition of the Genre Maśśāʾ," 78.
[18] Weis, "Definition of the Genre Maśśāʾ," 259–62.

This difficulty has been observed by Brian Jones, who offers the following critique:

> Weis does not wish for us to agree only that he has produced an accept-
> able final form interpretation of the texts; he wants us to accept that
> his readings form a reliable basis for the delineation of genre as it was
> understood by the eighth and seventh century prophets. His method is
> synchronic/final-form as it pertains to the individual texts, but it leads
> him to diachronic/historical conclusions.[19]

In this way, Weis seems to assume that the final form of the מַשָּׂא texts
can provide a reliable basis for his conclusions about their initial composition. For example, he claims, "In terms of the genre's constitution,
at the level of the final form of the text of the Hebrew Bible a *maśśā*
is a prophetic speech or text unit, *composed by a prophet* in order to
show how YHWH's acting or intention will or does manifest itself in
human affairs."[20]

As we have already noted, Weis concedes the dearth of common
formal elements among the מַשָּׂא texts. As with the מַשָּׂא titles, however, Weis would need to demonstrate that any formal components
that can be identified were present in the earliest version of the מַשָּׂא if
they are to be viewed as compositional characteristics. Otherwise, any
common elements among the מַשָּׂא texts would indicate only that the
oracles were *shaped* in accordance with the supposed מַשָּׂא genre, not
necessarily that they were *composed* as such.

Moreover, the basic claim regarding the existence of a מַשָּׂא genre
is further weakened by the recognition that those texts that are introduced by מַשָּׂא have a variety of literary characteristics. Thus, as
John Goldingay has noted, a מַשָּׂא "can be (among other things) an
imaginative picture, a lament, or a poem—in other words, any kind
of prophetic composition."[21] Mark Boda observes that Weis's appeal
to the 'intention' as the single unifying characteristic of a מַשָּׂא genre
underscores the difficulty of finding any common elements by which

---

[19] Brian C. Jones, *Howling over Moab: Irony and Rhetoric in Isaiah 15–16* (SBLDS
157; Atlanta: Scholars Press, 1996), 71.

[20] Weis, "Definition of the Genre Maśśāʾ," 271 (emphasis added). By contrast, Floyd
("מַשָּׂא [*Maśśāʾ*]," 401–22) is careful to distinguish מַשָּׂא as a supposed genre of prophetic *literature* (in its final form) from its use in prophetic *speech* (as originally given;
see p. 407).

[21] John Goldingay, *Isaiah* (NIBCOT; Peabody, Mass.: Hendrickson, 2001), 91;
quoted in Mark J. Boda, "Freeing the Burden of Prophecy: *Maśśāʾ* and the Legitimacy
of Prophecy in Zech 9–14," *Bib* 87 (2006): 350.

to establish a definition of the genre. Moreover, many other prophetic speech forms have the same intention, even though some of the מַשָּׂא texts themselves do not easily share this characteristic.

> In the end, not only must he try to fit the many 'deviations' into his hypothesis, but must generalize the intention to the point that it could describe many prophetic texts which are not *maśśā'*.... This feature [of 'intention'] cannot be limited to *maśśā'*.[22]

Despite these difficulties, Marvin Sweeney depends substantially on Weis's definition of a מַשָּׂא genre for his own analysis of Isa 13–23. However, Sweeney goes beyond Weis by advancing the claim that the מַשָּׂא texts, or 'pronouncement forms,' as he calls them, provide the organizational structure for the contents of this section of Isaiah. In Sweeney's view, those textual units that are not introduced by מַשָּׂא constitute 'extraneous material' that is "subordinated structurally to the pronouncement forms."[23] For example, a מַשָּׂא superscription begins an oracle concerning Damascus at 17:1 and does not recur until 19:1, at the start of the Egypt oracle. However, intervening verses (17:1–18:7) incorporate a הוֹי ('woe') oracle at 17:12–14, followed by another at 18:1–7, which addresses Cush. Sweeney proposes that these passages should be nonetheless subordinated structurally with 17:1–11 as part of the pronouncement form that spans 17:1–18:7. Accordingly, 17:12–14 is understood to relate to the preceding Damascus pronouncement (17:1–11) by rebuking nations that threaten Zion, and 18:1–7 (especially verses 3, 7) demonstrates the nations' recognition of Yhwh in response.[24]

Also, Sweeney upholds Weis's claim that a text belonging to the מַשָּׂא genre should include mention of Yhwh's activity in human affairs. Since he is unable to locate a description of Yhwh's involvement within 17:1–18:7 until 18:3–6, he concludes that the latter verses must be taken as an essential element of the מַשָּׂא concerning Damascus. He finds additional support for the inclusion of 18:1–7 with the Damascus oracle on the basis of his observation that agricultural imagery unifies the various subunits of the oracle.

Concerning Sweeney's claim that the subunits of Isa 17:1–18:7 are unified by agricultural imagery, we may observe that the הוֹי oracle at

[22] Boda, "Freeing the Burden of Prophecy," 349.
[23] Marvin A. Sweeney, *Isaiah 1–39* (FOTL 16; Grand Rapids: Eerdmans, 1996), 212.
[24] Sweeney, *Isaiah 1–39*, 213, 258.

17:12–14 has little, if anything, to do with agriculture, but instead compares the thundering of would-be plunderers to the roar of the mighty sea. Only a brief reference to wind-blown chaff in these verses can be remotely considered agricultural, especially by comparison to 17:4–6, 10–11. Moreover, this attempt to link 18:1–7 with the preceding material on the basis of its thematic content ignores the more obvious connection that this Cush oracle has with the Egypt oracle (19:1–25) and the narrative concerning Cush and Egypt (20:1–6) that follow.

With regard to the assumption that the מַשָּׂא genre requires a description of Yhwh's activity, we may observe that although Yhwh is not explicitly mentioned in Isa 17, the rebuke of the nations in 17:13 certainly implies Yhwh's involvement, and Sweeney himself attributes this rebuke to Yhwh. Thus, the inclusion of 17:12–14 could satisfy the criteria of Yhwh's involvement in the מַשָּׂא, without necessitating the incorporation of 18:1–7.[25] In any event, Weis himself prefers to limit the boundaries of the מַשָּׂא concerning Damascus to 17:1–11. In contrast to Sweeney, he concedes that this particular מַשָּׂא omits explicit reference to Yhwh's activity.[26]

More significantly, however, Sweeney's insistence that 18:1–7 provides an essential element of the מַשָּׂא that begins at 17:1 creates an inherent conflict with his additional view that 18:1–7 is extraneous material to be subordinated by the מַשָּׂא structure. Simply put, if 18:1–7 is to be understood as part of the מַשָּׂא itself, it cannot also be extraneous to the מַשָּׂא. In addition to arguing that the Cush oracle should not be taken as part of the מַשָּׂא concerning Damascus, we would propose that this הוֹי oracle concerning Cush can stand on its own as a distinct literary unit within Isa 13–23, without being subordinated in any way to the preceding material. Moreover, the present study will seek to demonstrate a redactional link with the material that follows, rather than a literary link with the preceding chapter.

Before moving on, some mention should be made of John Geyer's form-critical approach to the collections of foreign nations oracles in the books of Isaiah (13–23), Jeremiah (46–51), and Ezekiel (26–32), which he designates as ON-IJE.[27] Rather than showing concern only

---

[25] However, the introductory הוֹי particle at 17:12 suggests that 17:12–14 is a distinct textual unit from the preceding material.

[26] Weis, "Definition of the Genre Maśśāʾ," 128–9.

[27] Geyer outlines the form and structure of the ON-IJE in the first chapter of his monograph, *Mythology and Lament: Studies in the Oracles about the Nations*

for מַשָּׂא oracles, or even the material in Isaiah, Geyer looks more broadly for a common structural form among the nations oracles in the collections of these three books. In support of his main thesis concerning the influence of 'mythical' texts on the oracles, Geyer identifies a common form among the ON-IJE that includes (1) a superscription, followed by elements of (2) destruction,[28] (3) lamentation, (4) flight, and (5) reference to Yhwh.[29]

However, two main difficulties weaken Geyer's formal analysis of these oracles. First, Geyer never specifies whether he is identifying elements of the final form of the oracles or an earlier stage of development, but an introductory comment implies interest in their original composition:

> If each oracle is composed within a set form common to them all then we are dealing with a specific kind of literature that can be analysed and it will be possible to ask where this form of literature originated and what its purpose was.[30]

Despite this statement, however, his treatment of the oracles appears to be inconsistent. On one hand, he takes Isa 19:1–25, for example, as a single oracle concerning Egypt and identifies all five formal elements within the span of those verses. Such a view presumes the compositional unity of the entire chapter, a notion that has been rejected almost unanimously by critical scholars (see Chapter 4, below). On the other hand, Geyer's consideration of Isa 13:1–8 + 14:1–3 as a single textual unit demonstrates clear indifference to the final form of the text. In either case, Geyer's application of his proposed formal elements to justify his delimitation of the boundaries of each oracle results in a circular approach to his search for a common structure.

More significantly, Geyer has failed to establish substantial criteria for his identification of each of the structural elements. He offers some discussion of Jer 47:1–7 as an example, but even here, little explanation

---

(Aldershot: Ashgate, 2004), which is largely reprinted from "Mythology and Culture in the Oracles Against the Nations," *VT* 36 (1986): 129–45. Ezekiel 25 is omitted from Geyer's analysis of the ON-IJE because he finds the form to be more akin to the nations oracles in Amos.

[28] The 'destruction' passages are examined more closely in John B. Geyer, "Desolation and Cosmos," *VT* 49 (1999): 49–64.

[29] Geyer, *Mythology and Lament*, 10–12. See also idem, "Blood and the Nations in Ritual and Myth," *VT* 57 (2007): 1–20; idem, "Another Look at the Oracles about the Nations in the Hebrew Bible: A Response to A. C. Hagedorn," *VT* 59 (2009): 80–87.

[30] Geyer, *Mythology and Lament*, 9.

of each element is given besides a statement about how this passage illustrates the form. Although this particular example fits the pattern, no evidence is provided to substantiate his identification of each element in the other oracles. As a result, his application of the formal elements to other oracles is occasionally forced. For example, it is not at all clear how Isa 14:31 ("Wail, O gate; cry, O city; melt, O Philistia, all of you! For from the north smoke comes, and there is no straggler in its ranks") is supposed to function as both a flight passage and a lamentation text. Moreover, oracles that lack certain formal elements are left without discussion, such as the Cush oracle of Isa 18, which is missing both the lament and flight elements.[31]

In sum, Geyer seeks to identify a formal structure for the composition of the ON-IJE in the hopes of tracing the origins of a specific type of literature, but the challenges to his analysis suggest that the identification of a common literary structure for these oracles remains elusive. A convincing case for the ON-IJE as a distinct literary form would require far more attention to the identification of any formal elements, as well as much more rigorous discussion of the numerous departures from the supposed formal structure. Against Geyer's proposal, it is entirely plausible that the oracles within these collections may share some recognizable broad similarities without a common form.

With regard to the formation of Isa 13–23, various attempts to establish a מַשָּׂא genre have been less than satisfactory. It may be possible to identify common features of biblical texts that are introduced by מַשָּׂא in their final form, but the results of such an inquiry cannot support the assertion of מַשָּׂא as a compositional genre. In any case, the question of genre does little to advance a solution to the growth of Isa 13–23.

The following discussion finds its basis in the recognition that for at least some of the מַשָּׂא texts the superscriptions have been applied secondarily. In fact, nearly every occurrence of the 'מַשָּׂא GN' superscription in these chapters has been formulated by extracting the name of the entity or a key phrase from the body of the oracle. Because of this, there is no basis for the assumption that the מַשָּׂא oracles have been added *en bloc* to the book of Isaiah. Rather, it is entirely plausible that the superscription could have been added either simultaneously

---

[31] Geyer, *Mythology and Lament*, 16–17.

with or after the incorporation of the oracles. It is equally plausible to suppose that other additions to the collection were never assigned a superscription.

3. The מַשָּׂא Titles in Isaiah 13–23

Among those studies that focus on the מַשָּׂא texts, few have given considerable attention to the variety of מַשָּׂא introductions, but Weis articulates some distinctions, as follows.[32] A 'simple title' usually consists of the term מַשָּׂא followed by the addressee, such as מַשָּׂא מוֹאָב ('oracle concerning Moab') at Isa 15:1. Most of the headings in Isa 13–23 (also 30:6) are of this variety. Another form of heading, which Weis calls an 'expanded title' or 'superscription,' involves an extension of the simple מַשָּׂא title. At Isa 13:1, for example, the simple title מַשָּׂא בָּבֶל ('oracle concerning Babylon') has been expanded with the phrase אֲשֶׁר חָזָה יְשַׁעְיָהוּ בֶּן־אָמוֹץ ("which Isaiah son of Amoz saw"). Finally, an 'introductory sentence' uses מַשָּׂא to refer to the prophecy in a prosaic manner that is not as detached from the oracle as the simple titles and expanded titles. Thus, Isa 14:28 introduces the Philistia oracle with the sentence בִּשְׁנַת־מוֹת הַמֶּלֶךְ אָחָז הָיָה הַמַּשָּׂא הַזֶּה ("in the year of the death of King Ahaz, this oracle came").

As these examples demonstrate, all three types of מַשָּׂא headings can be found within Isa 13–23. Outside of Isaiah, מַשָּׂא appears as an introductory element at Nah 1:1; Hab 1:1; Zech 9:1; 12:1; Mal 1:1 (Weis also includes 2 Kgs 9:25; Ezek 12:10 as introductory sentences). Among these, מַשָּׂא נִינְוֵה ('oracle concerning Nineveh') at the beginning of the book of Nahum is like the simple 'מַשָּׂא GN' titles in Isa 13–23,[33] while Hab 1:1 (הַמַּשָּׂא אֲשֶׁר חָזָה חֲבַקּוּק הַנָּבִיא; 'the oracle that Habakkuk the prophet saw') is syntactically identical to the expanded title at Isa 13:1. The headings at Zech 9:1; 12:1; Mal 1:1 share the common expanded title מַשָּׂא דְבַר־יְהוָה ('the oracle [of] the word of Yhwh'),

---

[32] Weis, "Definition of the Genre Maśśāʾ," 67.

[33] By contrast, Weis views Nah 1:1 as an 'expanded title,' presumably because it is followed by another title, סֵפֶר חֲזוֹן נַחוּם הָאֶלְקֹשִׁי ('the book of the vision of Nahum the Elkoshite'). However, it appears that the latter heading may have been an earlier title of the book of Nahum (cf. Isa 1:1; Obad 1:1), in which case מַשָּׂא נִינְוֵה would actually be the expansion.

which is different from anything in Isaiah.[34] In this regard, it should be noted that whenever מַשָּׂא is used as a prophetic superscription outside of the book of Isaiah, it introduces textual units larger than a single oracle, including entire books.[35] In addition, all of these headings probably postdate the earliest of the מַשָּׂא titles in the book of Isaiah, in which case it is conceivable that at least some of the introductory uses of מַשָּׂא elsewhere in the Hebrew Bible have been influenced by the occurrences in Isaiah. Thus, some of the nations oracles in Isaiah very likely represent the earliest instances of the application of מַשָּׂא as a title.

Concerning the simple 'מַשָּׂא GN' titles in Isa 13–23, it is important to note that because they are titles, the superscriptions are detached from the main body of the oracle. This can be seen clearly in Isa 15:1, for example, where the superscription is external to parallel expressions:

Isa 15:1	Oracle concerning Moab.	מַשָּׂא מוֹאָב
	Because Ar is laid waste in a night, Moab is destroyed;	כִּי בְּלֵיל שֻׁדַּד עָר מוֹאָב נִדְמָה
	Because Kir is laid waste in a night, Moab is destroyed.	כִּי בְּלֵיל שֻׁדַּד קִיר־מוֹאָב נִדְמָה

Since each title is not an integral part of the oracle that follows it, it would be difficult to maintain that the addition of the title is contemporaneous with the composition of the oracle. To the contrary, a closer examination of this oracle and others indicates that the title is very likely a secondary element.

We may also observe that the identification of Moab in the superscription at 15:1 is redundant, since the nation is already named in the initial line of the body of the oracle. This particular feature can be detected in the oracles about Damascus (17:1) and Egypt (19:1) as well as Moab (15:1), but in none of the others. Moreover, the Damascus and Egypt oracles already have sufficient introductions of their

---

[34] Although the three titles at Zech 9:1; 12:1; Mal 1:1 are identical, Weis designates Zech 9:1 as a simple title, while those at Zech 12:1; Mal 1:1 are considered expanded titles.

[35] See Floyd, "מַשָּׂא (maśśā')," 401–22.

own, consisting of the particle הִנֵּה followed by a participial phrase.[36] We may infer that in these cases, the secondary addition of the 'מַשָּׂא GN' formula does not serve principally to identify the addressee of the oracle, but rather, to provide a common element that links these oracles together as a group.

Despite the frequency of the 'מַשָּׂא GN' title in Isa 13–23, none of the remaining oracles shares the characteristic of naming the addressee within the first verse of the oracle in addition to the title.[37] In the case of the Babylon oracle beginning at 13:1, Babylon is not mentioned after the superscription until 13:19 (also 14:4, 22). The Valley of Vision (22:1, 5) and Tyre (23:1, 5, 8, 15, 17) oracles also name the addressee only at some later point. The Wilderness of the Sea (מִדְבַּר־יָם) oracle refers to wilderness (מִדְבָּר) within the first verse (21:1), but the exact title from the superscription is never again used,[38] and the Desert oracle mentions the desert in the initial verse (21:13), but the contents of the oracle actually seem to address the 'caravans of Dedanites.'

Thus, despite the common 'מַשָּׂא GN' title, two basic patterns emerge in the way it is applied to oracles in Isa 13–23, a distinction that has gone almost entirely unnoticed.[39] As already noted, in those instances where the addressee is not immediately named, the superscription has been formulated using an element taken from the contents of the body

---

[36] For the introductory use of הִנֵּה + participle, see Isa 3:1; 10:33; 24:1; 30:27 (cf. 8:7; 13:9, 17; 21:9; 22:17; 26:21; 37:7; 38:8; 39:6).

[37] This is also true of מַשָּׂא בַּהֲמוֹת נֶגֶב ('oracle concerning the beasts of the Negeb') at Isa 30:6. Similarly, the book of Nahum begins with מַשָּׂא נִינְוֵה ('oracle concerning Nineveh'), but Nineveh is not mentioned again until Nah 2:9 (also 3:7).

[38] The meaning of MT מַשָּׂא מִדְבַּר־יָם ('oracle concerning the wilderness of the sea') is unclear. Moreover, 'sea' is missing from LXX while 1QIsaᵃ has משא דבר ים ('oracle concerning the matter of the sea'), resulting in a number of alternative suggestions. See, for example, William Henry Cobb, "Isaiah xxi. 1–10 Reëxamined," *JBL* 17 (1898): 40–61; Edouard-Paul Dhorme, "Le désert de la mer (Isaïe, XXI)," *RB* 31 (1922): 403–6; Julian Obermann, "Yahweh's Victory over the Babylonian Pantheon: The Archetype of Is. 21:1–10," *JBL* 48 (1929): 307–28; René Dussaud, "Sur le chemin de Suse et de Babylone," *Annuaire de l'institut de philologie et de l'histoire orientales et slaves* 4 (1936): 143–50; R. B. Y. Scott, "Isaiah XXI 1–10: The Inside of a Prophet's Mind," *VT* 2 (1952): 279–80; G. R. Driver, "Isaiah I–XXXIX: Textual and Linguistic Problems," *JSS* 13 (1968): 46–7; A. A. Macintosh, *Isaiah XXI: A Palimpsest* (Cambridge: Cambridge University Press, 1980), 4–7; Binyamin Uffenheimer, "The Desert of the Sea Pronouncement (Isaiah 21:1–10)," in *Pomegranates and Golden Bells: Studies in Biblical, Jewish, and Near Eastern Ritual, Law, and Literature in Honor of Jacob Milgrom* (ed. David P. Wright, David Noel Freedman, and Avi Hurvitz; Winona Lake, Ind.: Eisenbrauns, 1995), 677–88.

[39] Kaiser (*Isaiah 13–39*, 1–2) notes this characteristic, but fails to draw from it any conclusions regarding the formation of Isa 13–23.

of the oracle.[40] This would suggest that the title was fashioned for the purpose of bringing each oracle into conformity with a pre-existing pattern.

Against the frequent assumption that a complete collection of מַשָּׂא oracles was added to the book of Isaiah, the two patterns in the application of the 'מַשָּׂא GN' superscriptions point to two movements in the development of the מַשָּׂא material within the book of Isaiah. The resumptive mention of the addressee in 15:1; 17:1; 19:1 indicates an effort to unify an initial group, while the remaining occurrences of the superscription have been supplied in extension of that paradigm.

As we previously observed, the reiteration of the addressee in 15:1; 17:1; 19:1 suggests that the oracles were not composed as מַשָּׂא texts, but rather, the title was added to the oracles when they were compiled to form the initial collection of foreign nations oracles. This raises questions concerning when this group was assembled and what led to the application of מַשָּׂא as a unifying element. Both inquiries can be addressed by means of a closer examination of the Philistia oracle at Isa 14:28–32.

To borrow Weis's terminology, מַשָּׂא appears in 14:28 as part of an 'introductory sentence' rather than a 'simple title,' the only such occurrence in Isaiah:

Isa 14:28	In the year of the death of King Ahaz, this oracle came.	בִּשְׁנַת־מוֹת הַמֶּלֶךְ אָחָז הָיָה הַמַּשָּׂא הַזֶּה

This particular מַשָּׂא introduction begins with a temporal phrase that associates the oracle with the death of King Ahaz. In contrast to the 'מַשָּׂא GN' superscriptions, the מַשָּׂא heading at 14:28 does not name the addressee, although Philistia appears in the first verse of the body of the oracle (14:29). In this respect, the Philistia oracle is like the 'מַשָּׂא GN' oracles concerning Moab (15:1), Damascus (17:1), and Egypt (19:1), which also name the addressee in the initial verse of the body of the oracle. In view of the proposal that these particular oracles may have formed an early collection held together by the common מַשָּׂא titles, it would appear that the oracle about Philistia once stood

---

[40] In the brief oracles about Dumah (Isa 21:11) and the beasts of the Negeb (30:6), the addressees are never again mentioned.

as the first in the series. In that case, the singularity of the מַשָּׂא introduction at 14:28 can be explained by its position at the head of the
group. Rather than being a variation of the more common 'מַשָּׂא GN'
form,[41] the heading at 14:28 functioned as a precursor for the subsequent development of the מַשָּׂא titles. Clearly, the 'מַשָּׂא GN' titles were
not formulated to imitate the heading at 14:28 precisely, but rather, to
provide a formal element for the cohesion of the group. Thus, while
the Philistia oracle is introduced in conjunction with the death of King
Ahaz, the other three members of the initial group (beginning at 15:1;
17:1; 19:1) are associated with it by virtue of their מַשָּׂא titles.

The preceding discussion has concluded that the earliest collection
of nations oracles consisted of the four relating to Philistia, Moab,
Damascus, and Egypt. The strategic position of Isa 14:28 at the head
of this early group can be supported by a comparison with the introduction at 6:1:

Isa 6:1	In the year of the death of King Uzziah, I saw the Lord.	בִּשְׁנַת־מוֹת הַמֶּלֶךְ עֻזִּיָּהוּ וָאֶרְאֶה אֶת־אֲדֹנָי
Isa 14:28	In the year of the death of King Ahaz, this oracle came.	בִּשְׁנַת־מוֹת הַמֶּלֶךְ אָחָז הָיָה הַמַּשָּׂא הַזֶּה

Some commentators suggest reading וָאֶחֱזֶה ('I saw') instead of MT
אָחָז הָיָה in 14:28, which would create a close syntactical and semantic
correspondence with וָאֶרְאֶה ('I saw') in 6:1.[42] This would also eliminate specific mention of Ahaz, whose implied role as an oppressor of

[41] Kaiser (*Isaiah 13–39*, 2) proposed that מַשָּׂא in Isa 14:28 was composed in imitation of the more common 'מַשָּׂא GN' headings; see also Friedrich Huber, *Jahwe, Juda
und die anderen Völker beim Propheten Jesaja* (BZAW 137; Berlin: de Gruyter, 1976),
102 n. 72.

[42] See *BHS* and Julius A. Bewer, "Critical Notes on Old Testament Passages," in *Old
Testament and Semitic Studies in Memory of William Rainey Harper* (ed. Robert Francis Harper, Francis Brown, and George Foot Moore; 2 vols.; Chicago, 1908), 2:224–6;
idem, "The Date in Isa. 14:28," *AJSL* 54 (1937): 62; idem, "Textkritische Bemerkungen
zum alten Testament," in *Festschrift Alfred Bertholet zum 80. Geburtstag* (ed. Walter
Baumgartner, Otto Eissfeldt, Karl Elliger, and Leonhard Rost; Tübingen: Mohr [Sie-
beck], 1950), 65–6; Charles C. Torrey, "Some Important Editorial Operations in the
Book of Isaiah," *JBL* 57 (1938): 109–22; see also Jacques Vermeylen, *Du prophète Isaïe
à l'apocalyptique: Isaïe, I–XXXV* (2 vols.; EBib; Paris: Gabalda, 1977–78), 1:299–300.

Philistia seems to be historically problematic (cf. 2 Chr 28:16–18).[43] However, not only does this proposal lack textual support, the removal of the reference to King Ahaz only disrupts the parallel reference to the death of King Uzziah in 6:1. Furthermore, the similar phrases in Jer 26:1; 27:1; 36:1 (see below) support reading the verb הָיָה in 14:28 with MT.

Either way, each reading seeks to preserve a syntactical parallel between Isa 6:1 and 14:28. Since 6:1 is widely recognized as an introduction to one of the earliest textual units of the book, the use of the same heading at 14:28 suggests that the latter verse once marked the beginning of a corresponding section of foreign nations oracles in an earlier recension of the book.[44] In addition to the parallel headings, these two passages are further linked together by the common thematic elements of flying seraphs (6:2, 6; 14:29; cf. 30:6) accompanied by smoke (6:4; 14:31). Except for the single reference to a flying seraph at Isa 30:6, these two themes are not found individually, let alone jointly, elsewhere in the book of Isaiah. It seems likely, therefore, that this initial group of nations oracles was compiled at an early point in the formation of the book, in conjunction with the unit beginning at 6:1.

Although we have designated Isa 14:28 as the beginning of the earliest collection of nations oracles, the current form of the collection begins with an oracle about Babylon at 13:1. The addition of this oracle at the start of the collection would have prompted the attachment of its title, which extends the 'מַשָּׂא GN' superscription:[45]

---

[43] The date of 14:28–32 is often disputed in large part because the breaking of the rod, which is the cause of the Philistine rejoicing, is a more suitable description for the death of Sargon II in 705 B.C.E. than the death of Ahaz (cf. 9:3 [4]; 10:5, 15, 24). From a literary perspective, however, the reference to the death of Ahaz in 14:28 does not function as much to establish the historical background of the oracle as to form a structural parallel with 6:1. For discussion of 14:28–32 in addition to the commentaries, see Kemper Fullerton, "Isaiah 14:28–32," *AJSL* 42 (1926): 86–109; W. A. Irwin, "The Exposition of Isaiah 14:28–32," *AJSL* 44 (1928): 73–87; Joachim Begrich, "Jesaja 14,28–32: Ein Beitrag zur Chronologie der israelitisch-judäischen Königszeit," *ZDMG* 86 (1932): 66–79; Hayim Tadmor, "Philistia under Assyrian Rule," *BA* 29 (1966): 86–102; Bernard Gosse, "Isaïe 14,28–32 et les traditions sur Isaïe d'Isaïe 36–39 et Isaïe 20,1–6," *BZ* 35 (1991): 97–98; idem, "Isaïe VI et la tradition isaïenne," *VT* 42 (1992): 340–9.

[44] H. G. M. Williamson, *The Book Called Isaiah: Deutero-Isaiah's Role in Composition and Redaction* (Oxford: Oxford University Press, 1994), 162–4.

[45] Seth Erlandsson (*The Burden of Babylon: A Study of Isaiah 13:2–14:23* [ConBOT 4; Lund: Gleerup, 1970]) attempts to situate the מַשָּׂא בָּבֶל against the historical background of 701 B.C.E. Because of its relation to the fall of Babylon and the structural link between 2:1 and 13:1, however, his case is not ultimately convincing.

Isa 13:1	Oracle concerning Babylon that Isaiah ben Amoz saw.	מַשָּׂא בָּבֶל אֲשֶׁר חָזָה יְשַׁעְיָהוּ בֶּן־אָמוֹץ

This heading, which now introduces the entire section in Isa 13–23, is syntactically identical to the introduction at 2:1:

Isa 2:1	The word that Isaiah ben Amoz saw.	הַדָּבָר אֲשֶׁר חָזָה יְשַׁעְיָהוּ בֶּן־אָמוֹץ

Introductory formulae involving a word (דָּבָר) that the prophet saw (אֲשֶׁר חָזָה), such as that which appears at Isa 2:1, can also be found at the beginning of the books of Amos and Micah.[46] This suggests not only that a previous form of the book of Isaiah may have begun at what is now Isa 2:1, but also that 13:1 has been modeled after this introduction.[47] At the same time, the substitution of מַשָּׂא בָּבֶל at 13:1 for הַדָּבָר indicates that the heading has also been adapted to coordinate with the early collection of 'מַשָּׂא GN' titles. These sets of parallel headings at 6:1; 14:28 and 2:1; 13:1 suggest that the two stages in the current proposal for the formation of Isa 13–23 correspond with the broader development of the book of Isaiah.[48]

The preceding discussion has proposed that in the course of the placement of the Babylon oracle at the beginning of the pre-existing collection, the introduction at 13:1 was formulated to correspond with the 'מַשָּׂא GN' titles of the early group (14:28; 15:1; 17:1; 19:1), as well

---

[46] David Noel Freedman, "Headings in the Books of the Eighth-Century Prophets," *AUSS* 25 (1987): 9–26.

[47] Some commentators interpret Isa 2:1 as a concluding section to the first chapter of Isaiah, following the influence of Georg Fohrer ("Jesaja 1 als Zusammenfassung der Verkündigung Jesajas," *ZAW* 74 [1962]: 251–68), along with the suggestion of Peter R. Ackroyd ("Note on Isaiah 2:1," *ZAW* 75 [1963]: 320–1) that 2:1 has been inserted to lend authenticity to 2:2–4; see Anthony J. Tomasino, "Isaiah 1.1–2.4 and 63–66, and the Composition of the Isaianic Corpus," *JSOT* 57 (1993): 81–98; John Goldingay, "Isaiah I 1 and II 1," *VT* 48 (1998): 326–32. However, Marvin A. Sweeney (*Isaiah 1–4 and the Post-Exilic Understanding of the Isaianic Tradition* [BZAW 171; Berlin: de Gruyter, 1988], 134 n. 87) points out that 2:1 ("the word...concerning Judah and Jerusalem") makes little sense in reference only to 2:2–4 because the latter verses have nothing to do with Judah.

[48] See Williamson, *The Book Called Isaiah*, 153–4; idem, "Synchronic and Diachronic in Isaian Perspectives," in *Synchronic or Diachronic?: A Debate on Method in Old Testament Exegesis* (ed. Johannes C. de Moor; OtSt 34; Leiden: Brill, 1995), 221–3.

as the introduction at 2:1. Thus, the introductions at 2:1 and 13:1 are identical, with the exception that 13:1 has מַשָּׂא בָּבֶל instead of הַדָּבָר. Along the same lines, it is notable that Hab 1:1 (הַמַּשָּׂא אֲשֶׁר חָזָה חֲבַקּוּק הַנָּבִיא) also closely imitates Isa 13:1, while the superscriptions at Zech 9:1; 12:1; Mal 1:1 combine מַשָּׂא and דְּבַר together: מַשָּׂא דְבַר־יְהוָה ('an oracle [of] the word of Yhwh').[49] With regard to the intersection of מַשָּׂא and דָּבָר in introductory formulae, we may compare Isa 14:28 with the headings at Jer 26:1; 27:1; 36:1, all of which are syntactically identical:

Isa 14:28	In the year of the death of King Ahaz, this oracle came.	בִּשְׁנַת־מוֹת הַמֶּלֶךְ אָחָז הָיָה הַמַּשָּׂא הַזֶּה
Jer 26:1	In the beginning of the reign of Jehoiakim son of Josiah, king of Judah, this word came from Yhwh.	בְּרֵאשִׁית מַמְלְכוּת יְהוֹיָקִים בֶּן־יֹאשִׁיָּהוּ מֶלֶךְ יְהוּדָה הָיָה הַדָּבָר הַזֶּה מֵאֵת יְהוָה
Jer 27:1[50]	In the beginning of the reign of Jehoiakim son of Josiah, king of Judah, this word came to Jeremiah from Yhwh.	בְּרֵאשִׁית מַמְלֶכֶת יְהוֹיָקִם בֶּן־יֹאשִׁיָּהוּ מֶלֶךְ יְהוּדָה הָיָה הַדָּבָר הַזֶּה אֶל־יִרְמְיָה מֵאֵת יְהוָה
Jer 36:1	In the fourth year of Jehoiakim son of Josiah, king of Judah, this word came to Jeremiah.	וַיְהִי בַּשָּׁנָה הָרְבִיעִת לִיהוֹיָקִים בֶּן־יֹאשִׁיָּהוּ מֶלֶךְ יְהוּדָה הָיָה הַדָּבָר הַזֶּה אֶל־יִרְמְיָהוּ מֵאֵת יְהוָה

Each of these verses begins with a similar temporal phrase concerning the king followed by a statement that either 'this word' (Jer 26:1; 27:1; 36:1) or 'this oracle' (Isa 14:28) came. Gene M. Tucker posits that מַשָּׂא eventually came to be used as a general introduction of prophetic speech, in a way that is 'roughly synonymous' with introductory uses

---

[49] While it was previously noted that Jer 23:33–39 involves a play on the meaning of מַשָּׂא (see McKane, "מַשָּׂא in Jeremiah 23:33–40," 35–54; idem, *Jeremiah*, 1:597–604), these verses may provide an additional example of the confluence of מַשָּׂא and דָּבָר (cf. Jer 23:36).

[50] Although MT Jer 27:1 names Jehoiakim, the rest of the chapter refers to Zedekiah (27:3, 12). The entire verse is omitted from the LXX, which may indicate that MT 27:1 reflects a later insertion in imitation of 26:1. For discussion, see McKane, *Jeremiah*, 2:685–6.

of דָּבָר ('word').[51] At least these particular examples would seem to support some level of semantic correspondence between the use of דָּבָר and מַשָּׂא as prophetic superscriptions.

According to Weis's analysis, the מַשָּׂא genre is analogous to the דְּבַר יְהוָה ('word of Yhwh') as a type of prophetic literature. In his view, the primary difference is that the source of the דְּבַר יְהוָה is Yhwh, while a מַשָּׂא is produced by the prophet, although it may relate to and even clarify the דְּבַר יְהוָה.[52] Accordingly, Weis interprets Jer 23:35–40 as a prohibition specifically against a מַשָּׂא יְהוָה, since a human composition should not be characterized as deriving from Yhwh. He also asserts that this understanding of a מַשָּׂא as a human composition is probably a subsequent development from a דְּבַר יְהוָה.[53]

If there is any direct relationship between the introductory formulae at Isa 14:28 and Jer 26:1; 27:1; 36:1, it would appear that the latter verses were influenced by Isa 14:28, since each of these Jeremiah texts includes the additional element מֵאֵת יְהוָה ('from Yhwh'), which is absent from Isaiah. This expression of a word coming from Yhwh resonates strongly with other literary material in the book of Jeremiah (7:1; 11:1; 18:1; 21:1; 26:1; 27:1; 30:1; 32:1; 34:1, 8, 12; 35:1; 36:1; 40:1; cf. 37:17), but only occurs elsewhere in the Hebrew Bible at Ezek 33:30.[54] By contrast, if the formula at Isa 14:28 were borrowed from these, one would expect to find מֵאֵת יְהוָה as an integral element of the formulaic expression. With regard to the interchange between דָּבָר and מַשָּׂא, the headings at Jer 26:1; 27:1; 36:1 may provide an instance in which דָּבָר is applied in a manner that is derived from the use of מַשָּׂא. In addition, the possibility that these verses in Jeremiah have been borrowed

---

[51] Gene M. Tucker, "Prophetic Superscriptions and the Growth of the Canon," in *Canon and Authority: Essays in Old Testament Religion and Theology* (ed. George W. Coats and Burke O. Long; Philadelphia: Fortress, 1977), 64–5; see also Erlandsson, *The Burden of Babylon*, 64–5; John N. Oswalt, *The Book of Isaiah, Chapters 1–39* (NICOT; Grand Rapids: Eerdmans, 1986), 296.

[52] Weis, "Definition of the Genre Maśśāʾ," 99–103.

[53] Müller (*TDOT* 9:23) cites the use of משא as a parallel to הדבר לבוא ("the word concerning the future") in 1Q27 fragment 1, 1:8, which seems to speak against the sharp distinction that Weis proposes.

[54] For discussion of this and other formulae characteristic of Jeremiah, see Peter K. D. Neumann, "Das Wort, das geschehen ist…: Zum Problem der Wortempfangsterminologie in Jer. I–XXV," *VT* 23 (1973): 171–217; Theodor Seidl, "Datierung und Wortereignis: Beobachtungen zum Horizont von Jer 27, 1," *BZ* 21 (1977): 23–44, 184–99; idem, "Die Wortereignisformel in Jeremia: Beobachtungen zu den Formen der Redeeröffnung in Jeremia, im Anschluß an Jer 27, 1. 2," *BZ* 23 (1979): 20–47.

from Isa 14:28 supports our earlier determination that the occurrence of מַשָּׂא in that verse comprises the earliest application of the term in the book of Isaiah, from which the 'מַשָּׂא GN' titles were developed.

4. Conclusion

It is quite likely that many of the oracles have received some measure of internal reworking and enhancement, but the complex task of tracing all the redactional strata of Isa 13–23 exceeds the present aim. Rather, the preceding discussion can be summarized by identifying three main types of contributions to the development of the collection.

We have proposed that only four oracles constituted the earliest collection of nations oracles. This initial group began with the oracle about Philistia (14:28–32), and the remaining oracles included those concerning Moab (15–16), Damascus (17), and Egypt (19). In the case of the latter three oracles, the resumptive naming of the addressee in both the superscription and the initial verse of the oracle suggests that they were collected sometime after their composition. Nonetheless, the corresponding headings at 6:1 and 14:28 suggest that this brief collection was assembled at an early stage in the development of the book. Moreover, since these may represent the earliest occurrences of the 'מַשָּׂא GN' title in the Hebrew Bible, and since the repetition of the addressee in both the superscription and the initial verse of the oracle never occurs elsewhere, it is likely that this title was not an inherited literary form. Rather, we have proposed that the title was contrived as a means of extending the initial occurrence of מַשָּׂא at 14:28 to each of the oracles of the group. Moreover, we should note that the oracles concerning these particular political entities form a comprehensive group of pronouncements concerning Judah's neighbors to the west, east, north, and south, respectively.

Over the course of possibly several stages, מַשָּׂא titles were added to most of the subsequent additions as a means of assimilating them into the collection. In nearly every case, the title has borrowed a term or phrase from the oracle itself. Despite the common 'מַשָּׂא GN' titles, these additions can be distinguished from the initial group because they lack the repetition of the addressee within the initial verse of the oracle. On one hand, it is possible that these oracles could have included pre-existing material, as in the case of the Valley of Vision

oracle in Isa 22, much of which is generally thought to be Isaianic. On
the other hand, there is nothing in principle to preclude the possibility
that some of the oracles have been composed specifically for integration into the collection. Either way, the perpetuation of the 'מַשָּׂא GN'
superscriptions suggests redactional interest in assimilating these oracles into the existing collection. Among the oracles of this group, the
most conspicuous may be the Babylon oracle beginning at 13:1. This
oracle has been deliberately added as the new head of the collection
of nations oracles, which is indicated not only by its placement at the
front, but also by its modification of the introduction to correspond
with Isa 2:1.

Finally, some of the material in Isa 13–23 lacks any form of מַשָּׂא
superscription (e.g., Isa 14:24–27; 17:12–14; 18; 20; 22:15–25). Without a unifying element (such as the מַשָּׂא title), it would appear that
these texts have been incorporated into the collection under a variety
of influences, rather than by a single redactional effort. For this reason,
individual explanations would have to be sought for the incorporation of each text on a case-by-case basis. Isaiah 14:24–27, for example,
has several close linguistic and thematic ties with Isa 10, which may
indicate that its current location is primarily due to the insertion of
intervening material.[55] By contrast, the prose material in 22:15–25
seems to be an expansion of the Valley of Vision oracle that precedes
it. Whatever impulses have brought these texts to their current literary position, we may observe that in every case, the application of a
uniform מַשָּׂא title is no longer a prevailing concern.

It would be beyond the present focus to offer detailed discussion
of the processes leading to the incorporation of all of these non-מַשָּׂא
texts. However, two of the texts in this category are of central importance for the present study because of their ties to each other and to
the מַשָּׂא oracle concerning Egypt. Specifically, the הוֹי oracle concerning Cush (18) and the biographical narrative involving Cush and Egypt
(20) are linked together by their interest in the same nations, a feature
that is shared with the intervening oracle about Egypt (19). Since the
preceding discussion has identified the Egypt oracle as a component
of the initial group of nations oracles, it follows that this oracle has
served as the thematic focal point for the addition of the Cush oracle

---

[55] Vermeylen, *Du prophète Isaïe*, 296–7; Williamson, *The Book Called Isaiah*,
162–3.

and the Cush/Egypt narrative that now surrounds it. Thus, a central issue for the ensuing discussion will be the influences that have produced this small group of diverse literary material concerning Cush and Egypt within the larger collection of nations oracles. This matter will be taken up in Chapter 6 below, following a discussion of the internal development within each of the chapters of Isa 18–20.

CHAPTER THREE

THE REDACTIONAL FORMATION OF ISAIAH 18

1. Introduction

Critical scholars have usually attributed the earliest form of the oracle about Cush in Isa 18 to Isaiah ben Amoz, frequently on the basis
of the relationship between this הוֹי oracle and the מַשָּׂא oracles that
predominate in Isa 13–23.[1] As the discussion in the chapters above
has shown, many scholars tend to date the incorporation of the מַשָּׂא
oracles to the late exilic period at the earliest, on the assumption
that they were added to the book as a single comprehensive collection. Accordingly, the Cush oracle in 18 is viewed along with other

---

[1] The biblical designation 'Cush' has been interpreted variously. 'Ethiopia' was
used by the Greeks and Romans to refer to an ambiguous area inhabited by dark-
skinned people, and therefore may be both inaccurate and anachronistic for most
occurrences of 'Cush' in the Hebrew Bible; D. M. Dixon, "The Origin of the Kingdom
of Kush (Napata-Meroë)," *JEA* 50 (1964): 123. Within the context of eighth-century
B.C.E. international affairs relating to Judah, references to Cush describe the Nubian
kingdom, which established the 25th Dynasty of rule over Egypt; J. Daniel Hays, "The
Cushites: A Black Nation in Ancient History," *BSac* 153 (1996): 270–80; idem, "The
Cushites: A Black Nation in the Bible," *BSac* 153 (1996): 396–409. Additional propos-
als for interpreting the biblical Cush include Sudan (Piers T. Crocker, "Cush and the
Bible," *BurH* 22 [1986]: 27–38; Robert W. Anderson Jr., "Zephaniah ben Cushi and
Cush of Benjamin: Traces of Cushite Presence in Syria-Palestine," in *The Pitcher Is
Broken: Memorial Essays for Gösta W. Ahlström* [ed. Steven W. Holloway and Lowell
K. Handy; JSOTSup 190; Sheffield: Sheffield Academic Press, 1995], 45–70), Africa
and Africans in general (David Tuesday Adamo, "The Images of Cush in the Old Tes-
tament: Reflections on African Hermeneutics," in *Interpreting the Old Testament in
Africa: Papers from the International Symposium on Africa and the Old Testament in
Nairobi, October 1999* [ed. Mary Getui, Knut Holter, and Victor Zinkuratire; BTA 2;
New York: Lang, 2001], 68; cf. "land *beyond* the rivers of Cush" in Isa 18:1), or a
small tribal group on Judah's southwestern border (Robert D. Haak, "'Cush' in Zephaniah," in *The Pitcher Is Broken: Memorial Essays for Gösta W. Ahlström* [ed. Steven
W. Holloway and Lowell K. Handy; JSOTSup 190; Sheffield: Sheffield Academic Press,
1995], 247–9). As Peter Unseth ("Hebrew Kush: Sudan, Ethiopia, or Where?," *AJET*
18 [1999]: 143–59) observes, the value of retaining the biblical term Cush (or Kush)
is that it avoids reference to modern geopolitical designations. For additional discussion, see Rodney Steven Sadler Jr., *Can a Cushite Change His Skin? An Examination of
Race, Ethnicity, and Othering in the Hebrew Bible* (LHBOTS 425; New York: T. & T.
Clark, 2005).

non-מַשָּׂא texts as one of the earliest elements of 13–23, to which the מַשָּׂא collection was subsequently added.[2] Others include the Cush oracle among several 'untitled' additions to the מַשָּׂא collection.[3] This view does not necessarily render the Cush oracle inauthentic, since T. K. Cheyne suggests that the הוֹי oracle about Cush was added to the מַשָּׂא collection along with other 'doubtlessly Isaianic' passages in order to make the entire collection of nations oracles appear more authentic.[4] These examples are indicative of a broad consensus concerning the date of the earliest elements of the Cush oracle, despite disagreement with regard to the formation of Isa 13–23.

The following discussion adheres to the position that the earliest form of the Cush oracle in Isa 18 reflects the circumstances of the eighth century B.C.E. At the same time, however, some elements of Isa 18 seem to be later contributions to the chapter. Verse 7, for example, is probably an expansion of the original oracle. Much of the content is repeated from verse 2 ("tall and smooth,... a people feared near and far," etc.) and the verse begins with the phrase בָּעֵת הַהִיא ("at that time"), which often introduces secondary material (cf. Jer 3:17, 18; 4:11; 33:15).[5] In addition, some of the themes, such as bringing tribute to Zion and "the place of the name," suggest that a later perspective has been added to the original oracle. Verse 3 is also probably a subsequent insertion. Here, the focus is broadened from the singular description of the Cushites to include "all the inhabitants of the world" (כָּל־יֹשְׁבֵי תֵבֵל), and the word תֵבֵל ('world') only appears in passages that are thought to be later contributions to the book (13:11; 14:17, 21;

---

[2] Karl Marti, *Das Buch Jesaja* (KHC 10; Tübingen: Mohr [Siebeck], 1900), xvi; George Buchanan Gray, *The Book of Isaiah: I–XXVII* (ICC; Edinburgh: T. & T. Clark, 1912), li; Georg Fohrer, "The Origin, Tradition and Composition of Isaiah I–XXXIX," *ALUOS* 3 (1961–62): 16–18; Jacques Vermeylen, *Du prophète Isaïe à l'apocalyptique: Isaïe, I–XXXV* (2 vols.; *EBib*; Paris: Gabalda, 1977–78), 1:285–6; Hans Wildberger, *Isaiah 13–27* (trans. Thomas H. Trapp; Minneapolis: Fortress, 1997), 1–2; Ronald E. Clements, *Isaiah 1–39* (NCB; Grand Rapids: Eerdmans; London: Marshall, Morgan & Scott, 1980), 130.

[3] T. K. Cheyne, *Introduction to the Book of Isaiah* (London: Adam and Charles Black, 1895), xxiv–xxv; G. H. Box, *The Book of Isaiah* (London: Pitman and Sons, 1908), 72; Walther Eichrodt, *Der Herr der Geschichte: Jesaja 13–23 und 28–39* (BAT 17/2; Stuttgart: Calwer Verlag, 1967), 9–10; Otto Kaiser, *Isaiah 13–39* (trans. R. A. Wilson; OTL; Philadelphia: Westminster; London: SCM, 1974), 1–2.

[4] Cheyne, *Isaiah*, xxiv–xxv.

[5] For בָּעֵת הַהִיא as a redactional introduction, see Simon J. De Vries, *From Old Revelation to New: A Tradition-Historical and Redaction-Critical Study of Temporal Transitions in Prophetic Prediction* (Grand Rapids: Eerdmans, 1995), 64–74.

24:4; 26:9, 18; 27:6; 34:1; 66:19). These redactional expansions will be given greater consideration after a discussion of the Cushite presence in the eighth century B.C.E. and the original unity of 18:1–2, 4–6.

2. Historical Considerations

The earliest form of the Cush oracle corresponds very well to the rise of the 25th Dynasty in Egypt during the late eighth century B.C.E., when the Cushite ruler Piankhy sought to assert control over the entire region of Nubia and Egypt.[6] Little is known about Piankhy's early years, but his victory stele found at the Nubian capital of Napata and dated around 727 B.C.E. describes a campaign in Upper and Middle Egypt during the twenty-first year of his reign.[7] Piankhy was unable to gain control over all of Lower Egypt, but he reportedly received

---

[6] For discussion of the rise of the Cushite (Nubian) empire, see Nicolas C. Grimal, *A History of Ancient Egypt* (trans. Ian Shaw; Oxford: Blackwell, 1992), 334–66; David O'Connor, *Ancient Nubia: Egypt's Rival in Africa* (Philadelphia: University Museum, University of Pennsylvania, 1993); Derek A. Welsby, *The Kingdom of Kush: The Napatan and Meroitic Empires* (London: British Museum Press, 1996); Meir Lubetski and Claire Gottlieb, "Isaiah 18: The Egyptian Nexus," in *Boundaries of the Ancient Near Eastern World: A Tribute to Cyrus H. Gordon* (ed. Meir Lubetski, Claire Gottlieb, and Sharon Keller; JSOTSup 273; Sheffield: Sheffield Academic Press, 1998), 364–84; Alviero Niccacci, "Isaiah XVIII–XX from an Egyptological Perspective," *VT* 48 (1998), 214–38; Kenneth A. Kitchen, "Regnal and Geneological Data of Ancient Egypt (Absolute Chronology I): The Historical Chronology of Ancient Egypt, A Current Assessment," in *The Synchronisation of Civilisations in the Eastern Mediterranean in the Second Millennium B.C.: Proceedings of an International Symposium at Schloß Haindorf, 15th–17th of November 1996 and at the Austrian Academy, Vienna, 11th–12th of May 1998* (ed. Manfred Bietak; Vienna: Österreichischen Akademie der Wissenschaften, 2000), 39–52, esp. 50–1; László Török, *The Kingdom of Kush: Handbook of the Napatan-Meroitic Civilization* (HO 31; Leiden: Brill, 1997), 131–88; Robert G. Morkot, *The Black Pharaohs: Egypt's Nubian Rulers* (London: Rubicon Press, 2000), 197–222; James K. Hoffmeier, "Egypt's Role in the Events of 701 B.C. in Jerusalem," in *Jerusalem in Bible and Archaeology: The First Temple Period* (ed. Andrew G. Vaughn and Ann E. Killebrew; SBLSymS 18; Atlanta: Society of Biblical Literature, 2003), 219–34.

[7] See "The Victory Stela of King Piye" (Miriam Lichtheim, *Ancient Egyptian Literature* [Berkeley and Los Angeles: University of California Press, 2006], 3:66–84); "The Victory Stela of King Piye (Piankhy)," translated by Miriam Lichtheim (*COS* 2.7:42–51); Tormod Eide et al., *Fontes Historiae Nubiorum: Textual Sources for the History of the Middle Nile Region between the Eighth Century BC and the Sixth Century AD* (4 vols.; Bergen: University of Bergen, 1994–2000), 1:62–118. Also, Nicolas C. Grimal, *La stèle triomphale de Pi(ʿankh)y au Musée du Caire* (Cairo: Institut Français d'Archéologie Orientale du Caire, 1981); Hans Goedicke, *Pi(ankh)y in Egypt: A Study of the Pi(ankh)y Stela* (Baltimore: Halgo, 1998).

tribute from Tefnakht, who ruled from the city of Sais in the western Delta.[8] Cush was the major controlling power over nearly all of Egypt during this period, with the possible exception of the eastern portion of the Delta.

Although the textual material relating to this period from Egypt is relatively scarce, the Assyrian inscriptions mention several encounters with Egypt and Cush.[9] For example, when Tiglath-pileser III advanced down the coast of Philistia in 734, Hanunu, the king of Gaza, fled to Egypt for refuge, but he later surrendered and was reinstalled in his former position. Tiglath-pileser then set up a stele at the Brook of Egypt to mark the southernmost limit of Assyrian influence, which describes an Egyptian king paying tribute to the Assyrians.[10] When Sargon II came to the Assyrian throne in 722, he opened a trading station with Egypt and sought to encourage commerce between the two empires.[11] Two years later, widespread revolt broke out against Assyria, with the cities of Arpad, Simira, Damascus, and Samaria participating. Hanunu of Gaza was also involved, and a certain Egyptian official named Reʾe provided military support, but Hanunu was captured by the Assyrians, and Reʾe fled back to Egypt. It was in connection with these events that Samaria was ultimately defeated.[12]

Some commentators view the composition of the Cush oracle of Isa 18 against the historical background of this part of the eighth century, usually on the assumption of a literary connection with the מַשָּׂא

---

[8] Donald B. Redford, "Sais and the Kushite Invasions of the Eighth Century B.C.," *JARCE* 22 (1985): 5–15; Hoffmeier, "Egypt's Role in the Events of 701 B.C.," 223–4.

[9] See Andreas Fuchs, *Die Annalen des Jahres 711 v. Chr. nach Prismenfragmenten aus Ninive und Assur* (SAAS 8; Helsinki: Neo-Assyrian Text Corpus Project, 1998), 81–96; J. J. M. Roberts, "Egypt, Assyria, Isaiah, and the Ashdod Affair: An Alternative Proposal," in *Jerusalem in Bible and Archaeology: The First Temple Period* (ed. Andrew G. Vaughn and Ann E. Killebrew; SBLSymS 18; Atlanta: Society of Biblical Literature, 2003), 268–9.

[10] Hayim Tadmor, *The Inscriptions of Tiglath-pileser III, King of Assyria* (Jerusalem: Israel Academy of Sciences and Humanities, 1994), 178–9, 190–1; Nadav Naʾaman, "The Brook of Egypt and Assyrian Policy on the Border of Egypt," *TA* 6 (1979): 68–90.

[11] Andreas Fuchs, *Die Inschriften Sargons II. aus Khorsabad* (Göttingen: Cuvillier, 1994), 88, 314; Hayim Tadmor, "The Campaigns of Sargon II of Assur: A Chronological-Historical Study," *JCS* 12 (1958): 35–6.

[12] K. Lawson Younger Jr., "Assyrian Involvement in the Southern Levant at the End of the Eighth Century B.C.E.," in *Jerusalem in Bible and Archaeology: The First Temple Period* (ed. Andrew G. Vaughn and Ann E. Killebrew; SBLSymS 18; Atlanta: Society of Biblical Literature, 2003), 237; idem, "The Fall of Samaria in Light of Recent Research," *CBQ* 61 (1999): 461–82.

unit that begins at 17:1.[13] Because the first part of Isa 17 describes the downfall of Damascus and Ephraim, it is supposed that 18 must also relate to the same period. In support of this, 2 Kgs 17:4 speaks of the Israelite king Hoshea withholding tribute from Assyria and sending messengers to a certain King So of Egypt,[14] presumably to solicit military aid in revolt against Assyria. Objections to the literary approach of including the Cush oracle with the מַשָּׂא oracle that begins at Isa 17:1 have already been raised in Chapter 2 above, and need not be repeated here. The greatest challenge to associating Isa 18 with this historical period stems from the confusion of Egypt and Cush in the biblical passages. This 'So' of 2 Kgs 17:4 is associated in the biblical text specifically with Egypt, whereas Isa 18:1–2 offers a distinctive description of people "beyond the rivers of Cush." In addition, Piankhy claims to have received tribute from Tefnakht in the western Delta, but he

---

[13] Marvin A. Sweeney, *Isaiah 1–39* (FOTL 16; Grand Rapids: Eerdmans, 1996), 258–62; also Eduard Meyer, *Geschichte des alten Ägyptens* (2 vols.; Berlin: Grote, 1887), 2:346–7; Marti, *Jesaja*, 150–1; Norman K. Gottwald, *All the Kingdoms of the Earth: Israelite Prophecy and International Relations in the Ancient Near East* (New York: Harper & Row, 1964), 162–3; Brevard S. Childs, *Isaiah and the Assyrian Crisis* (SBT 2/3. London: SCM, 1967), 46; Niccacci, "Isaiah XVIII–XX," 216; Willem A. M. Beuken, *Jesaja 13–27* (HTKAT; Freiburg: Herder, 2007), 151–2. John H. Hayes and Stuart A. Irvine (*Isaiah, the Eighth-Century Prophet: His Times and His Preaching* [Nashville: Abingdon, 1987], 252–4) link Isa 18 with this period, but not specifically with the Syro-Ephraimite conflict. In his commentary, Brevard S. Childs (*Isaiah* [OTL; Louisville: Westminster John Knox, 2001], 135–6, 138) groups Isa 18 as a literary unit with 17, but relates 18 historically to 701 B.C.E.

[14] The reference to So in 2 Kgs 17:4 has been most commonly understood as either Osorkon IV (Kenneth A. Kitchen, *The Third Intermediate Period in Egypt [1100–650 B.C.]* [2d ed. with supplement; Warminster: Aris & Phillips, 1986], 372–5; Hoffmeier, "Egypt's Role in the Events of 701 B.C.," 226) or Tefnakht (Ramadan Sayed, "Tefnakht ou Horus SI3-[ib]," *VT* 20 [1970]: 116–18; Henri Cazelles, "Problèmes de la guerre Syro-Ephraimite," *ErIsr* 14 [H. L. Ginsberg Volume, 1978]: 70*). However, Alberto R. W. Green ("The Identity of King So of Egypt—An Alternative Interpretation," *JNES* 52 [1993]: 99–108) defends an earlier proposal by Rudolf Kittel (*Geschichte des Volkes Israel* [2 vols.; 3d ed.; Gotha: Perthes, 1917], 2:536–7) that the biblical 'So" refers to Piankhy. Alternatively, it has been suggested that the Hebrew name *sô'* refers not to a person, but to the city of Sais (called *s3w* in Egyptian), which was Tefnakht's capital; cf. Hans Goedicke, "The End of 'So, King of Egypt,'" *BASOR* 171 (1963): 64–66; William F. Albright, "The Elimination of King 'So'," *BASOR* 171 (1963): 66; Donald B. Redford, "A Note on II Kings, 17, 4," *JSSEA* 11 (1981): 75–6; idem, "Sais and the Kushite Invasions," 15; Duane L. Christensen, "The Identity of 'King So' in Egypt (2 Kings XVII 4)," *VT* 39 (1989): 140–53; John Day, "The Problem of 'So, King of Egypt' in 2 Kings XVII 4," *VT* 42 (1992): 289–301; Pnina Galpaz-Feller, "Is That So? (2 Kings XVII 4)," *RB* 107 (2000): 338–47. For a recent survey in support of Kitchen's proposal, see Seung Il Kang, "A Philological Approach to the Problem of King So (2 Kgs 17:4)," *VT* 60 (2010): 241–8.

makes no mention of any control over the eastern Delta region.[15] To the contrary, Osorkon IV was still on his throne in the eastern Delta approximately ten years later, when he paid tribute to Sargon at the Brook of Egypt.[16] Thus, from the Judean perspective, it is unlikely that the Cushite military during these nascent years of influence in Egypt would have yet been considered 'feared near and far' and 'a nation mighty and powerful' (Isa 18:2).

The most likely period for potential Cushite involvement in Judean affairs would have been sometime after the death of Piankhy in 716 B.C.E., when the Cushite empire increased significantly in strength and influence under the reign of his brother Shabako, who succeeded him. Shabako relocated the capital of Cush further north to Memphis and executed Bakenrenef (Bocchoris), Tefnakht's son and successor in Sais. With this move, he seems to have established a much stronger grip over nearly the entire region of Egypt and Nubia.

In the years leading up to 711 B.C.E., King Azuri of Ashdod made plans to withhold tribute from Assyria and sent letters to neighboring kings to garner support for his revolt.[17] In response to this rebellion, Sargon removed Azuri and installed Ahimeti on the throne, who was promptly driven out by the people and replaced with a certain Yamani. Yamani reinvigorated the revolt, but fled to Egypt even before Sargon's army arrived, after which the Assyrians defeated Ashdod, deported its citizens, and appointed an Assyrian to govern the city.

Some have viewed this revolt of 711 B.C.E. as the historical background for Isaiah's Cush oracle, since Ashdod sought support from other cities in Philistia, as well as Judah, Edom, Moab, and Egypt.[18]

---

[15] See "The Victory Stela of King Piye" (*AEL* 3:66–84); "The Victory Stela of King Piye [Piankhy]" (*COS* 2.7:42–51); Grimal, *La stèle triomphale de Pi('ankh)y*; Naʾaman, "The Brook of Egypt," 68–90; idem, "The Historical Background of the Conquest of Samaria," *Bib* 71 (1990): 207–25.

[16] Ernst F. Weidner, "Šilkan(ḫe)ni, König von Muṣri, ein Zeitgenosse Sargons II. nach einem neuen Bruchstück der Prisma-Inschrift des assyrischen Königs," *AfO* 14 (1941–44): 40–53; Fuchs, *Die Annalen des Jahres 711*, 28–9, 57; Roberts, "Egypt, Assyria, Isaiah, and the Ashdod Affair," 269.

[17] See Roberts, "Egypt, Assyria, Isaiah, and the Ashdod Affair," 272–5; Anthony Spalinger, "The Year 712 B.C. and Its Implications for Egyptian History," *JARCE* 10 (1973): 95–101.

[18] Otto Procksch, *Jesaja I* (KAT 9/1; Leipzig: Deichert, 1930), 237–8; Georg Fohrer, *Das Buch Jesaja* (3 vols.; ZBK; Zürich: Zwingli, 1960–1964), 1:204–5; Edward J. Kissane, *The Book of Isaiah* (2 vols.; rev. ed.; Dublin: Browne and Nolan, 1960), 1:194; Vermeylen, *Du prophète Isaïe*, 1:317; John N. Oswalt, *The Book of Isaiah, Chapters 1–39* (NICOT; Grand Rapids: Eerdmans, 1986), 360; Clements, *Isaiah 1–39*, 163–4;

This event is also explicitly cited as the setting for Isa 20, in which the prophet enacts the capture of Egypt and Cush by Assyria. Against this proposal for Isa 18, however, there is no indication that Egypt, Cush, or Judah actually consented to participate in Ashdod's rebellion. Furthermore, the Cushites apparently delivered the rebellious leader Yamani over to Sargon, which would seem to indicate that they were uninterested in inciting conflict with Assyria at that point in time.[19]

Therefore, the most likely historical setting for the Cush oracle is probably Sennacherib's campaign against Judah in 701 B.C.E.[20] According to Sennacherib's *Annals*, the Philistine city of Ekron rebelled against Assyria and summoned the Egyptian and Cushite military for assistance.[21] The Egyptians supplied horses and chariots, but were defeated

---

J. J. M. Roberts, "Isaiah's Egyptian and Nubian Oracles," in *Israel's Prophets and Israel's Past: Essays on the Relationship of Prophetic Texts and Israelite History in Honor of John H. Hayes* (ed. Brad E. Kelle and Megan Bishop Moore; LHBOTS 446; London: T. & T. Clark, 2006), 205.

[19] According to the Assyrian account, the 'king of Melluḫḫa' (Nubia) returned Yamani; see "The Great 'Summary' Inscription," translated by K. Lawson Younger Jr. (*COS* 2.118E:296–7); "The Small 'Summary' Inscription," translated by K. Lawson Younger Jr. (*COS* 2.118F:297). Previously, Kitchen (*The Third Intermediate Period in Egypt*, 143–4) assumed that the 'king of Melluḫḫa' must be Shabako, but the recently discovered Assyrian inscription from Tang-i Var specifically names Shabataka as this king; see Grant Frame, "The Inscription of Sargon II at Tang-i Var," *Or* 68 (1999): 31–57, pls. i–xviii; "The Tang-i Var Inscription," translated by K. Lawson Younger Jr. (*COS* 2.118J:299–300); also Donald B. Redford, "A Note on the Chronology of Dynasty 25 and the Inscription of Sargon II at Tang-i Var," *Or* 68 (1999): 58–60; Dan'el Kahn, "The Inscription of Sargon II at Tang-i Var and the Chronology of Dynasty 25," *Or* 70 (2001): 1–18. This could place Shabataka on the throne at least four years earlier than was previously thought, but since Hoffmeier ("Egypt's Role in the Events of 701 B.C.," 227–9) remains convinced of Kitchen's earlier chronology that dates Shabako's death at 702, he proposes a co-regency between Shabako and Shabataka until that time; cf. Frank Yurco, "Sennacherib's Third Campaign and the Coregency of Shabaka and Shebitku," *Serapis* 6 (1980): 221–40; idem, "The Shabaka-Shebitku Coregency and the Supposed Second Campaign of Sennacherib against Judah: A Critical Assessment," *JBL* 110 (1991): 35–45; Kitchen, "Regnal and Geneological Data of Ancient Egypt," 39–52, esp. 50–1; idem, *The Third Intermediate Period in Egypt*, 154–61.

[20] See "Sennacherib's Siege of Jerusalem," translated by Mordechai Cogan (*COS* 2.119B:302–3). For discussion, see Childs, *Isaiah and the Assyrian Crisis*; Nadav Na'aman, "Sennacherib's 'Letter to God' on his Campaign to Judah," *BASOR* 214 (1974): 25–39; Francolino J. Gonçalves, *L'expédition de Sennachérib en Palestine dans la littérature hébraïque ancienne* (EBib 7; Paris: Gabalda; Leuven: Peeters, 1986); Antti Laato, "Hezekiah and the Assyrian Crisis in 701 B.C.," *SJOT* 2 (1987): 49–68; William R. Gallagher, *Sennacherib's Campaign to Judah: New Studies* (SHCANE 18; Leiden: Brill, 1999); William W. Hallo, "Jerusalem under Hezekiah: An Assyriological Perspective," in *Jerusalem: Its Sanctity and Centrality to Judaism, Christianity, and Islam* (ed. Lee I. Levine; New York: Continuum, 1999), 36–50.

[21] "Sennacherib's Siege of Jerusalem" (*COS* 2.119B:302–3).

at the battle of Eltekeh, and the leaders of Ekron were punished for their rebellion.[22] The biblical account implicates Hezekiah as a participant in the rebellion against Assyria, which resulted in Sennacherib's attack against Jerusalem (2 Kgs 19:9–10//Isa 37:9–10). Against this background, the condemnation of messengers in Isa 18 would raise a prophetic objection to Judah's complicity in the affair.[23]

Hezekiah's interest in seeking aid from Egypt seems to be a key element linking the Cush oracle of Isa 18 with the events of 701 B.C.E.[24] The dispatch of envoys in 18:1–2 could certainly refer to negotiations among Judah, Ekron, and Egypt/Cush to build support for resistance against Assyria. Hezekiah was apparently interested in obtaining Egyptian assistance (Isa 36:4–6), and other prophetic oracles in Isaiah

---

[22] There is some uncertainty about the precise chronology of the battle at Eltekeh in relation to Sennacherib's campaign in Judah. In addition, the reference to Taharqa in 2 Kgs 19:9 (//Isa 37:9) would be anachronistic if he did not ascend to the throne until a later period. Kenneth A. Kitchen ("Egypt, the Levant and Assyria in 701 B.C.," in *Fontes atque Pontes: Eine Festgabe für Hellmut Brunner* [ed. M. Görg; ÄAT 5; Wiesbaden: Harrassowitz, 1983], 243–53), for example, proposes two separate Egyptian armies (one at Eltekeh and the other led by Taharqa), while Hoffmeier ("Egypt's Role in the Events of 701 B.C.," 219–34) suggests a Shabataka/Taharqa coregency. However, Gallagher (*Sennacherib's Campaign to Judah*, 122–5, 221–3) questions the association of the battle of Eltekeh with the rumor of Taharqa in 2 Kgs 19:9, as well as Taharqa's involvement in the events of 701 B.C.E. For a survey and discussion of these issues, see Richard S. Hess, "Hezekiah and Sennacherib in 2 Kings 18–20," in *Zion, City of Our God* (ed. Richard S. Hess and Gordon J. Wenham; Grand Rapids: Eerdmans, 1999), 23–41.

[23] Hoffmeier ("Egypt's Role in the Events of 701 B.C.," 219–34) attempts to show that Hezekiah was never directly involved in seeking assistance from Egypt by claiming that Isaiah gives no direct condemnation of the matter and that Hezekiah is elsewhere praised for his piety (2 Kgs 18:5). However, he gives no attention to the Assyrian Rabshakeh's taunts about Hezekiah's dependency on Egypt in 2 Kgs 18:19–21 (//Isa 36:4–6), and he interprets Isa 30:1–5; 31:1–3 as references to the Israelite king Hoshea's interest in aid from king So of Egypt (2 Kgs 17:4), following Hayes and Irvine (*Isaiah, the Eighth-Century Prophet*, 336–52). See also James K. Hoffmeier, "Egypt's Role in the Events of 701 B.C.: A Rejoinder to J. J. M. Roberts," in *Jerusalem in Bible and Archaeology: The First Temple Period* (ed. Andrew G. Vaughn and Ann E. Killebrew; SBLSymS 18; Atlanta: Society of Biblical Literature, 2003), 285–9. Against Hoffmeier's position, see Roberts, "Egypt, Assyria, Isaiah, and the Ashdod Affair," 282–3.

[24] Those who view the Cush oracle against the background of 701 include Duhm, *Jesaia*, 136; August Dillmann, *Der Prophet Jesaia* (Leipzig: Hirzel, 1890), 164–5; Cheyne, *Isaiah*, 96; Gray, *Isaiah*, 309; Herbert Donner, *Israel unter den Völkern: Die Stellung der klassischen Propheten des 8. Jahrhunderts v. Chr. zur Aussenpolitik der Könige von Israel und Juda* (VTSup 11; Leiden: Brill, 1964), 123–4; Eichrodt, *Jesaja 13–23 und 28–39*, 59–63; Gonçalves, *L'expédition de Sennachérib*, 139–45; Nadav Na'aman, "Hezekiah and the Kings of Assyria," *TA* 21 (1994): 242–3; Joseph Blenkinsopp, *Isaiah 1–39* (AB 19; New York: Doubleday, 2000), 310.

specifically denounce such alliances (30:1–5; 31:1–3). These oracles scold Judah for failing to "look to the Holy One of Israel" (31:1) and for carrying out a plan other than Yhwh's plan (30:1). Similarly, the oracle in 18 condemns seeking aid from Cush, because Judah should wait for Yhwh's timing (18:4). Thus, Sennacherib's attack on Jerusalem provides a background when Hezekiah is known to have sought military assistance and when Egypt and Cush came to the aid of Palestinian cities, while the denunciation of Cushite messengers aligns with similar Isaianic protests against Hezekiah's apparent attempts to acquire military assistance from Egypt.

3. Isaiah 18:1–2, 4–6

Although the insertion of Isa 18:3 divides the present form of the Cush oracle into two main parts, the original oracle contained verses 1–2, 4–6 as a single literary unit. Verses 1–2 give a detailed description of messengers from Cush, while verses 4–6 use agricultural metaphors to depict Yhwh observing the situation quiescently before becoming involved. Before considering the unity of these verses, we may first observe that the literary characteristics of Isa 18 resonate with other texts from the book of Isaiah that are thought to originate from the eighth century B.C.E. The introductory particle הוֹי occurs twenty-one times in the book, and such oracles often appear in series, for example, at 5:8, 11, 18, 20, 21, 22 (also 10:1, 5), and 28:1; 29:1, 15; 30:1; 31:1 (cf. Hab 2:6, 9, 12, 15, 19, possibly also 2:5). In both of these groupings, much of the content is widely viewed in relation to the eighth century, which may indicate that the Cush oracle also stems from the same period. In addition, two other הוֹי oracles, 30:1–5; 31:1–3, express similar injunctions against dependency on Egyptian military assistance, with specific denunciation of foreign ambassadors (cf. 30:4). Moreover, if הוֹי oracles are normally presented in series, the fact that Isa 18 is one of only two הוֹי passages among the מַשָּׂא oracles in Isa 13–23 (also 17:12–14) suggests that it has probably been transposed from a prior literary setting among other הוֹי oracles. The discussion below will propose that the Cush oracle was originally located in the collection of הוֹי oracles in Isa 28–31.

At this point, it is also worth noting that the Cush oracle contains a number of terms and expressions that are unique in the Hebrew Bible. If secondary material is often identified by the reapplication of earlier words and motifs, the occurrence of unusual expressions at least does not speak against early origins within the Isaianic tradition. For example, Cush is singularly described as אֶרֶץ צִלְצַל כְּנָפָיִם, a land of 'winged boats' (or 'whirring wings'; 18:1).[25] Additional examples, from 18:2, include כְּלֵי־גֹמֶא ('vessels of papyrus') and the description of Cushites as מְמֻשָּׁךְ ('drawn out'; possibly meaning 'tall').[26] These literary characteristics, combined with strong resonance with historical circumstances of the eighth century, contribute to the likelihood of Isaianic origins for this oracle about Cush.

However, the extent of the Cush oracle in its earliest formation remains to be determined. As stated in the initial comments and explored more thoroughly below, both verses 3 and 7 have probably been added secondarily to the oracle. With the insertion of verse 3, it is not immediately obvious whether verses 1–2, 4–6 formed a single oracle or are two separate literary units. It is to the details of both of these sections and the elements that unite them as a single composition that we should now turn.

Despite vivid descriptors, the identity and aim of the delegates in the first two verses is not immediately clear, since the 'envoys' (צִירִים) could be perceived as a different group from the 'swift messengers' (מַלְאָכִים קַלִּים).[27] Verses 1–2a give the impression that the land 'beyond the rivers of Cush' is sending the צִירִים in vessels, while the last part of verse 2 directs the מַלְאָכִים קַלִּים to go to a nation tall and smooth, a people feared near and far, and so on. Thus, it is claimed that Cush is sending the צִירִים, while an unnamed group (perhaps Judah) is sending the מַלְאָכִים קַלִּים. This view is supported by the assertion that the command in 18:2 should be understood to mean 'go' (הלך), rather than 'turn back' or 'return,' which would imply either that a different

[25] Meir Lubetski ("Beetlemania of Bygone Times," *JSOT* 91 [2000]: 3–26) argues that צִלְצַל could be related to 'whirring' or 'buzzing' like a cricket (cf. Deut 28:42). However, the LXX interprets צִלְצַל כְּנָפָיִם as πλοίων πτέρυγες ('winged boats') and the Targum has ספינה ('ship'). In support of the latter option, G. R. Driver ("Isaiah I–XXXIX: Textual and Linguistic Problems," *JSS* 13 [1968]: 45) cites the Aramaic צלצל, 'ship,' which would parallel 'vessels of papyrus' in Isa 18:2; see also J. V. Kinnier Wilson, "A Return to the Problems of Behemoth and Leviathan," *VT* 25 (1975): 11.

[26] Herodotus (*Hist.* 3.20) describes Ethiopians as "the tallest and most handsome" of all people.

[27] This view is advanced by Marta Høyland Lavik, *A People Tall and Smooth-Skinned: The Rhetoric of Isaiah 18* (VTSup 112; Leiden: Brill, 2006), 68–70.

group of messengers is being sent to Cush (e.g., Judean messengers),[28] or that messengers (possibly also Cushite) are commanded to go, in which case, the 'people feared near and far,' to whom they are directed, refers to Assyrians, rather than to Cushites.[29] Put simply, the alternative interpretations are that 18:1–2 describes either two different groups of messengers or two different locales.[30]

Despite these arguments, there is a solid basis of evidence to view both descriptions as referring to the same group of Cushite messengers, and to interpret the command to 'go' as a dismissal back to their homeland.[31] First, regarding the messengers, the context gives no indication that the perspective has shifted in such a way that a different group is being addressed. Without any evidence to the contrary, it is more natural to interpret מַלְאָכִים קַלִּים simply as an explication of the previous reference to צִירִים.[32] Lavik has determined that the מַלְאָכִים קַלִּים should be understood as Judeans because the adjective קַל ('swift, light') is used in Isa 30:16 to describe swift horses, which are ridden by the people of Yhwh.[33] Of course, the comparison is not quite the same, since the adjective modifies horses in 30:16, but messengers in 18:2. More significantly, however, the assertion that the term should be used in 18:2 to describe *Judean* messengers on the basis of its presumed reference to Judeans in 30:16 can be sustained only by an illegitimate transfer of meaning from one passage to another without regard for the context of 18:2. By way of illustration, we may cite two additional occurrences of the adjective קַל in Isaiah: one refers to Yhwh riding a swift cloud (19:1), and the other speaks of an army coming swiftly

---

[28] Lavik, *A People Tall and Smooth-Skinned*, 68–70; Sweeney, *Isaiah 1–39*, 257; Blenkinsopp, *Isaiah 1–39*, 309–10; Childs, *Isaiah*, 138.

[29] Waldemar Janzen, *Mourning Cry and Woe Oracle* (BZAW 125; Berlin: de Gruyter, 1972), 60–1; Vermeylen, *Du prophète Isaïe*, 1:317; Clements, *Isaiah 1–39*, 164; Hayes and Irvine, *Isaiah, the Eighth-Century Prophet*, 254–5; John D. W. Watts, *Isaiah 1–33* (WBC 24; Dallas: Word, 1985), 245–6; Niccacci, "Isaiah XVIII–XX," 216. Kissane (*Isaiah*, 1:198) proposes that the Cushite messengers are being sent to the Medes.

[30] In addition, some have suggested that the 'messengers' are to be understood figuratively (Oswalt, *Isaiah, Chapters 1–39*, 361), or that these are messengers from Yhwh's divine council (Janzen, *Mourning Cry and Woe Oracle*, 60–1; Hermann Barth, *Die Jesaja-Worte in der Josiazeit: Israel und Assur als Thema einer produktiven Neuinterpretation der Jesajaüberlieferung* [WMANT 48; Neukirchen-Vluyn: Neukirchener Verlag, 1977], 13–14; cf. Ezek 30:9).

[31] Gray, *Isaiah*, 308; Wildberger, *Isaiah 13–27*, 216–17; Naʾaman, "Hezekiah and the Kings of Assyria," 242.

[32] מַלְאָךְ and צִיר are also paralleled in Prov 13:17.

[33] Lavik, *A People Tall and Smooth-Skinned*, 70.

from the ends of the earth (5:26). It would be equally inappropri-
ate to suggest that the messengers in 18:2 should be identified with
either of these, merely on the basis of the common occurrence of the
adjective.

   Another objection against identifying the messengers with the envoys
is that the reference to Cush as a 'nation tall and smooth' in verse 2
would seem to be redundant if they are being instructed to return to
their own homeland.[34] In response to this point, however, it should be
observed that the primary rhetorical aim of the oracle is not to address
foreigners directly, but to proclaim a message concerning Cush to a
Judean audience.[35] On this basis, there is no logical inconsistency with
providing a detailed description of Cush in verse 2 for the benefit of
a Judean audience, even while ostensibly addressing Cushite messengers. Moreover, precisely this same rhetorical approach is adopted in
18:1–2a, in which the land 'beyond the rivers of Cush,' as well as its
envoys, are 'directly' addressed by the prophet.

   Finally, there is no reason why the imperative of הלך cannot be used
to direct the messengers back to their homeland. Admittedly, a different verb, such as שוב ('turn back, return'), would communicate the
direction of motion more explicitly, but sufficient indication is given
in 18:2 that the intent is to send them away. While הלך does not always
mean 'to go back,' it can be used in this way in the Hebrew Bible, and
even appears occasionally as a parallel to שוב (e.g., Gen 32:1 [31:55];
Exod 4:18–19, 21; Num 24:25; Deut 20:5–8; 1 Sam 3:5; 29:7; Isa 37:37;
Jer 41:14). Furthermore, the meaning of the verb is clarified by the
description of the land that follows the command. The use of הלך to
instruct the swift messengers to go back home can be confirmed by
determining that the 'nation tall and smooth' refers to Cush and its
inhabitants, as the following discussion will aim to demonstrate.

   An additional interpretational difficulty in 18:1–2 is the identity of
those being described at the end of the second verse. There, the swift
messengers are commanded to go to a nation that is described in the
NRSV as 'tall and smooth' (מְמֻשָּׁךְ וּמוֹרָט), 'feared near and far' (נוֹרָא
מִן־הוּא וָהָלְאָה), 'mighty and conquering' (קַו־קָו וּמְבוּסָה), and 'whose

---

   [34] Sweeney, Isaiah 1–39, 257.
   [35] John H. Hayes ("The Usage of Oracles against Foreign Nations in Ancient Israel,"
JBL 87 [1968]: 81–92) observes, "the importance of the speeches must not be sought,
therefore, in what they 'said' to the enemy but rather in the function which they per-
formed within the context of Israelite society" (p. 81).

land the rivers divide' (אֲשֶׁר־בָּזְאוּ נְהָרִים אַרְצוֹ).[36] Aside from their recurrence in 18:7, many of these descriptors are never used elsewhere in reference to a group of people in the Hebrew Bible, so while they offer a very vivid portrait, the intended referent is not immediately obvious.

Of these characterizations, the designation 'land that the rivers divide' in connection with the portrayal of an imposing military invites the most confusion, since it could be understood to recall the geography of Assyria. However, a closer examination suggests that Cush is in view.[37] The verb בזא only occurs in Isa 18:2, 7, but it is often interpreted to mean 'to divide, cut through,' as a possible by-form of Aramaic בזע, which can have this meaning.[38] The same notion of opening or splitting land with rivers can be found in Gen 2:13 (סבב; 'to encircle') and Hab 3:9 (בקע; 'to split'), but never in reference to Mesopotamia. Habakkuk 3:9 speaks of Yhwh splitting the land with rivers[39] following language that may echo the exodus from Egypt,[40] while Gen 2:13 describes the Gihon river encircling the land of Cush.

Furthermore, Isa 18:7 also interprets 18:2 in reference to Cushites. This later addition to the Cush oracle does not specifically name Cush, but it borrows the distinct expressions from the latter half of verse 2. It describes a time when tribute will be brought (יוּבַל־שַׁי) to Yhwh in Zion, using a particular phrase borrowed from Ps 68:29–32 (28–31), which explicitly names Cush and Egypt bringing gifts to Jerusalem (see discussion below).[41] Since Cushites bring tribute in Ps 68, the

---

[36] Anna Kiesow ("Schwarz, stark, schon: Schwarze Menschen in alttestamentlichen Texten," in *Körperkonzepte im Ersten Testament: Aspekte einer Feministischen Anthropologie* [ed. Ulrike Bail, Gerlinde Baumann, and Isa Breitmaier; Stuttgart: Kohlhammer, 2003], 144–52) asserts that Cushites are characterized in the Hebrew Bible primarily by their military strength. In the case of Isa 18:1–2, the unique description of Cushites includes no explicit reference to the color of their skin (cf. Jer 13:23).

[37] Hayes and Irvine, *Isaiah, the Eighth-Century Prophet*, 254–5.

[38] "בָּזָא," BDB 102.

[39] See John Day, *God's Conflict with the Dragon and the Sea: Echoes of a Canaanite Myth in the Old Testament* (COP 35; Cambridge: Cambridge University Press, 1985), 104–9. Francis I. Andersen (*Habakkuk* [AB 25; New York: Doubleday, 2001], 317) points out that the plural of נָהָר ('river') is normally נְהָרוֹת, with a feminine plural ending. It appears with a masculine plural ending (נְהָרִים) twice in Hab 3:8 (but not in 3:9), and also in Isa 18:2, 7; 33:21 (cf. the masculine plural construct form נַהֲרֵי in Job 20:17; Isa 18:1; Zeph 3:10).

[40] Andersen, *Habakkuk*, 340–1; Ralph L. Smith, *Micah-Malachi* (WBC 32; Waco, Tex.: Word, 1984), 115–16.

[41] Isaiah 45:14 refers to Egypt, Cush, and the Sabeans (סְבָאִים), who are called 'men of stature' (אַנְשֵׁי מִדָּה), all bringing their wealth and paying homage. Cush is associated with Sheba/Seba elsewhere in the Hebrew Bible at Gen 10:7; 1 Chr 1:9; Isa 43:3.

application of the rare phrase יוּבַל־שַׁי to Isa 18:7 indicates that the redactor of this verse has Cushites in mind.[42]

Finally, Lavik posits a chiastic arrangement in Isa 18:1–2 to support the unity of these verses, but in actuality, this structural scheme argues against her view of the envoys and messengers as two different groups. According to Lavik, the chiasm is formed by the elements of 'land,' 'rivers,' and 'messengers':[43]

> A: אֶרֶץ צִלְצַל כְּנָפָיִם; 'land of winged boats (18:1a)
>   B: מֵעֵבֶר לְנַהֲרֵי־כוּשׁ; 'beyond the rivers of Cush' (18:1b)
>   C: צִירִים; 'envoys' (18:2a)
>   C': מַלְאָכִים; 'messengers' (18:2b)
>   B': נְהָרִים; 'rivers' (18:2c)
> A': אַרְצוֹ; 'its land' (18:2c)

From this structural arrangement, Lavik draws the conclusion that 'land' (A/A') and 'rivers' (B/B') both refer to Cush, but that 'envoys' (C) refers to Cushites, while 'messengers' (C') refers to Judeans.[44] However, a consistent interpretation of the supposed chiastic structure would maintain that each of these elements is identical to its respective counterpart. If so, Isa 18:1–2 would depict a scene in which the Cushite ambassadors are being sent back to their own homeland, as we have proposed.

Despite a shift in imagery and the subsequent insertion of verse 3, 18:4–6 should be understood as part of the original oracle concerning Cush. In these verses, Yhwh is initially inactive, merely looking on from his dwelling (18:4), but according to his timing he will cut off the shoots and branches, which will be left for the birds and animals to consume (18:5–6). Viticultural imagery is familiar within the book of Isaiah (e.g., 5:1–7) and agricultural devastation is a common metaphorical expression of judgment in prophetic literature (e.g., Isa 5:5–7; 16:8–10; Jer 5:10–11, 17; 12:10–11; Hos 2:12).[45]

---

[42] The discussion of Isa 18:7 below will argue for the direction of influence from Ps 68. However, even if Ps 68 had borrowed from Isa 18:7, the explicit naming of Cush in Ps 68:32 (31) would nonetheless demonstrate that the contributor to Ps 68 has understood the description of Isa 18:7 (and thereby 18:2) to refer to Cushites.

[43] Lavik, *A People Tall and Smooth-Skinned*, 61–2.

[44] Lavik, *A People Tall and Smooth-Skinned*, 68–70.

[45] Carey Ellen Walsh (*The Fruit of the Vine: Viticulture in Ancient Israel* [HSM 60; Winona Lake, Ind.: Eisenbrauns, 2000], 120–2) observes that pruning was an essential part of tending the vineyard and that its negligence could also be detrimental (cf. Isa 5:6).

While there may be little doubt that Isa 18:5–6 speaks about some kind of judgment, the object of that judgment is ambiguous. As a result, commentators usually propose that these verses denounce Assyria, Cush/Egypt, or Judah. In the end, it is difficult to place great confidence in any of these proposals without additional historical data. Each of these possibilities will be considered briefly before positing an alternative.

Some have proposed that while Yhwh may quietly observe the oppression of Judah for a period (18:4), verses 5–6 proclaim that Yhwh will eventually bring about Assyria's destruction.[46] Any potential alliances with Cush are ultimately futile, since only Yhwh can provide deliverance from such a foe. Assyria was indeed the dominant threat to Judah during the last part of the eighth century B.C.E., and a prophecy about its destruction certainly would have been most welcome by the royal court.

Others often interpret 18:4–6 as judgment against Cush or Egypt on the basis of the rejection of the Cushite messengers in 18:1–2.[47] According to this understanding, Judah should avoid alliances with Cush because these potential allies are themselves facing imminent destruction. This could also be supported by associating the Cush oracle with Isa 20, which describes the captivity of Egypt and Cush in conjunction with the Ashdod rebellion of 711 B.C.E.

The third main possibility is that 18:5–6 issues judgment against Judah.[48] This reading supposes that although the oracle addresses Cush, the rebuke is really directed against the Judeans for seeking

---

[46] Duhm, *Jesaia*, 138–9; Cheyne, *Isaiah*, 95–6; Gray, *Isaiah*, 315–16; Kissane, *Isaiah*, 1:199–200; Donner, *Israel unter den Völkern*, 125–6; Childs, *Isaiah and the Assyrian Crisis*, 44–6; Oswalt, *Isaiah, Chapters 1–39*, 362–3; Blenkinsopp, *Isaiah 1–39*, 311.

[47] Fohrer, *Jesaja*, 1:223–4; Gottwald, *All the Kingdoms of the Earth*, 163; Hans Werner Hoffmann, *Die Intention der Verkündigung Jesajas* (BZAW 136; Berlin: de Gruyter, 1974), 71–3; Kaiser, *Isaiah 13–39*, 91–2, 95–6; Clements, *Isaiah 1–39*, 165–6; Shemaryahu Talmon, "Prophetic Rhetoric and Agricultural Metaphora," in *Storia e Tradizioni di Israele: Scritti in onore di J. Alberto Soggin* (ed. Daniele Garrone and Felice Israel; Brescia: Paideia, 1991), 272; Christopher R. Seitz, *Isaiah 1–39* (IBC; Louisville: John Knox, 1993), 148–9; Wildberger, *Isaiah 13–27*, 218–19; Kenton L. Sparks, *Ethnicity and Identity in Ancient Israel: Prolegomena to the Study of Ethnic Sentiments and their Expression in the Hebrew Bible* (Winona Lake, Ind.: Eisenbrauns, 1998), 204.

[48] Procksch, *Jesaja I*, 241; Hayes and Irvine, *Isaiah, the Eighth-Century Prophet*, 255–6; Jesper Høgenhaven, *Gott und Volk bei Jesaja: Eine Untersuchung zur biblischen Theologie* (ATDan 24; Leiden: Brill, 1988), 132–4; Childs, *Isaiah*, 138; Lavik, *A People Tall and Smooth-Skinned*, 184–5, 208–10.

such alliances.[49] A defense of this view has been sustained recently by Lavik, who emphasizes the rhetorical force of juxtaposing this proclamation against the initial cry of הוֹי at the beginning of the oracle. In her view, the oracle is shaped by a 'rhetoric of entrapment':[50] in light of the first two verses, the Judean audience anticipates a condemnation against Cush, but they soon discover in verses 5–6 that the finger of accusation is pointed at themselves.[51] This reading of the oracle is not impossible, but such a rhetorical device requires an explicit indication that Judah is the intended object of wrath. For example, Nathan is unequivocal in his confrontation against David in 2 Sam 12:7, and the book of Amos heaps condemnation on various foreign nations before finally leveling criticism directly against Israel.[52] In these instances, the rhetorical impact is felt only as long as the object of the injunction is clearly identified. Since this is not the case in Isa 18:5–6, this particular rhetorical device is unlikely.

While there are merits to each of these three options (Assyria, Cush, Judah), the ambiguous language suggests that none of these nations is directly intended as the object of condemnation. An alternative interpretation of 18:5–6 might be to consider the possibility that these verses do not depict the destruction of any particular nation. If the metaphorical pruning of the tendrils and branches is viewed alongside the exchange of political envoys, it would seem that this imagery should be applied specifically to Judah's policies of seeking ill-conceived alliances with foreign nations. According to this view, it is such attempts to forge precarious treaties that will be cut down even before they have come to fruition.

---

[49] Karl Marti (*Jesaja*, 149–50) views Isa 18:5–6 as a condemnation against the northern kingdom of Israel on the assumption that these verses originally followed 17:11, which also uses agricultural imagery, and on the basis of the shift from first to third person between verses 4–5 as evidence that 18:5–6 has been relocated to its present position. However, similar grammatical features can be found elsewhere in Isaiah (e.g., 8:11–14; 21:6–10), and Hans Wildberger (*Isaiah 13–27*, 210) points out that 18:4 requires further development beyond the description of Yhwh's quiescent observance. Marvin Sweeney (*Isaiah 1–39*, 257) interprets 18:5–6 against Israel on the assumption that the Cush oracle is a continuation of the מַשָּׂא unit that begins at 17:1. Against this, however, see Chapter 2, above.

[50] Lavik borrows this expression from Robert Alter, *The Art of Biblical Poetry* (Edinburgh: T. & T. Clark, 1990), 144.

[51] Lavik, *A People Tall and Smooth-Skinned*, 184–5, 208–10.

[52] See John Barton, *Amos's Oracles against the Nations: A Study of Amos 1:3–2:5* (SOTSMS 6; Cambridge: Cambridge University Press, 1980).

This interpretation can be supported by comparing 18:1–2, 4–6 with the הוֹי oracles in Isa 30:1–5 and 31:1–3, which similarly denounce alliances with Egypt. In the latter passages, there is never any assurance given that Yhwh will bring about the destruction of Assyria. Neither is a threat of judgment directed against any specific nation, other than a warning of destruction as the natural outcome of futile treaties. As Hans Wildberger notes,

> Isaiah never uses a woe-oracle in conjunction with a threat of judgment. The woe signals actions that are contradictory to orderly behavior, and such activity will bring on disaster by its very nature.[53]

In 31:3, for example, both the helper and the helped will perish because of Egypt's incapability. Even here, however, the point of Yhwh stretching out his hand is not simply to pronounce judgment or destruction specifically on Judah or Egypt. Instead, the alliance with Egypt is condemned as futile because the Egyptians are human and not God. Therefore, in 30:1–5; 31:1–3, and also 18:1–2, 4–6, the message of these oracles is that by seeking alliances with Egypt (or Cush), Judah is carrying out a plan that is different from Yhwh's plan and is neglecting to seek Yhwh for deliverance. Such a plan, whether with Egypt or Cush, is doomed to certain failure for all of those who are involved.

A comparison of the Cush oracle in Isa 18:1–2, 4–6 with the Egypt oracles in 30:1–5 and 31:1–3 also supports the cohesion of these two sections in Isa 18 as a single literary unit. Although הוֹי oracles have no single formal structure, each of these oracles is introduced by the particle הוֹי followed by a participial phrase (18:1; 30:1–2; 31:1).[54]

---

[53] Hans Wildberger, *Isaiah 28–39* (trans. Thomas H. Trapp; Minneapolis: Fortress, 2002), 688.

[54] The form-critical background of הוֹי oracles has received much discussion. Claus Westermann (*Basic Forms of Prophetic Speech* [trans. H. C. White; Philadelphia: Westminster, 1967; repr. Cambridge: Lutterworth; Louisville: Westminster/John Knox, 1991], 190–8) suggested that הוֹי oracles derived from covenant curses (cf. Erhard Gerstenberger, "The Woe-Oracles of the Prophets," *JBL* 81 [1962]: 249–63), but recent study commonly traces the origin of the prophetic use of הוֹי to funeral laments (cf. Jer 22:18); see Richard J. Clifford, "The Use of *hôy* in the Prophets," *CBQ* 28 (1966): 458–64; Gunther Wanke, "אוֹי und הוֹי," *ZAW* 78 (1966): 215–18; James G. Williams, "The Alas-Oracles of the Eighth-Century Prophets," *HUCA* 38 (1967): 75–91; Janzen, *Mourning Cry and Woe Oracle*; Vermeylen, *Du prophète Isaïe*, 2:603–52; Delbert R. Hillers, "*Hôy* and *Hôy*-Oracles: A Neglected Syntactic Aspect," in *The Word of the Lord Shall Go Forth: Essays in Honor of David Noel Freedman* (ed. Carol L. Meyers and M. O'Connor; Winona Lake, Ind.: Eisenbrauns, 1983), 185–8; H.-J. Zobel, "הוֹי," *TDOT* 3:359–64. Concerning Isa 30:1–5; 31:1–3, see also Jesper Høgenhaven,

Furthermore, in each of these examples, the oracle consists of two main parts: the initial condemnation of foreign dependency, followed by a statement about the failed outcome on all sides that will result from it. In 30:1–5, taking refuge in Pharaoh's protection will result in all parties coming to shame, and in 31:1–3, the helper and the helped will perish together. Likewise, the description in 18:5–6 of shoots and branches being cut away and left to be ravaged by wild animals is the result of attempts at diplomacy between Judah and Cush.

At the same time, the affinities with Isa 30:1–5; 31:1–3 also suggest that the Cush oracle was originally included with these other passages as part of the collection of הוֹי oracles in Isa 28–31.[55] The observation that הוֹי oracles in Isaiah are usually grouped together in series (e.g., Isa 5:8, 11, 18, 20, 21, 22 [also 10:1, 5]; cf. Hab 2) supports this possibility, and an original literary setting within Isa 28–31 would help to explain the conspicuous appearance of this הוֹי oracle among many מַשָּׂא oracles in Isa 13–23. If this is the case, we may conclude that the Cush oracle has been deliberately relocated to its present location to correspond with the material about Egypt and Cush in the chapters that now follow it. This proposal will be given further consideration in Chapter 6, below.

4. Isaiah 18:7

Many critical scholars view Isa 18:7 as a secondary addition to the original Cush oracle.[56] This conclusion is supported by the reiteration of the distinct description of the Cushites from verse 2 ('a people tall and smooth,' etc.), a switch to prose that contrasts with the poetry of the beginning part of the chapter, and the initial phrase בָּעֵת הַהִיא

"Prophecy and Propaganda: Aspects of Political and Religious Reasoning in Israel and the Ancient Near East," *SJOT* 3 (1989): 125–41.

[55] This possibility is suggested briefly by Harold L. Ginsberg, "Reflexes of Sargon in Isaiah after 715 B.C.E.," *JAOS* 88 (1968): 47 n. 2. Lisa A. Heidorn ("The Horses of Kush," *JNES* 56 [1997]: 105–14) argues that Cush was known to be an important center for horse breeding, which may provide an additional point of association with the Egypt oracles (cf. Isa 31:1–3; 36:6–8).

[56] For example, Duhm, *Jesaia*, 139–40; Cheyne, *Isaiah*, 98–9; Marti, *Jesaja*, 149–50; Gray, *Isaiah*, 316; Procksch, *Jesaja I*, 242–3; Kissane, *Isaiah*, 1:200; Fohrer, *Jesaja*, 1:224; Donner, *Israel unter den Völkern*, 123; Eichrodt, *Jesaja 13–23 und 28–39*, 63; Kaiser, *Isaiah 13–39*, 92; Høgenhaven, *Gott und Volk bei Jesaja*, 132; Wildberger, *Isaiah 13–27*, 209; Clements, *Isaiah 1–39*, 166.

('at that time'), which often introduces editorial additions in prophetic literature.[57] As the following discussion shows, additional elements in this verse provide links with material pertaining to a later historical period and incorporate new perspectives into the oracle about Cush.

The fact that much of Isa 18:7 is borrowed directly from verse 2 suggests that Cushites are still in view, but echoes from other passages produce a shift in the outlook of the oracle. This can be seen in the first part of 18:7, which uses the phrase יוּבַל־שַׁי ('tribute will be brought') to speak of Cushites bearing gifts to Zion. Only two other passages in the Hebrew Bible have the verb יבל ('to bring') with the noun שַׁי ('gift, present'): Pss 68:30 (29) and 76:12 (11).[58] In addition to these, יבל is collocated with מִנְחָה ('gift') rather than שַׁי in Zeph 3:10, a text that similarly describes tribute from Cush. Since this expression in Zeph 3 is joined by a verbatim quotation of the phrase 'beyond the rivers of Cush' (מֵעֵבֶר לְנַהֲרֵי־כוּשׁ) from Isa 18:1, it would appear that this passage in Zeph 3 has been influenced by Isa 18 and need not be given further consideration here.[59]

Of greater interest for the present inquiry is Ps 68:30 (29), which uses יבל שַׁי in connection with Cush and Egypt bringing gifts to Jerusalem (68:32 [31]). The dating of this particular psalm is notoriously difficult, in large part because of its apparently fragmentary nature;[60] any evidence for dating one portion may not necessarily apply to the entire psalm in its current form. J. J. M. Roberts, for example, cites the reference to the temple in verse 30 (29) and the archaic use of זוּ as a relative pronoun in the preceding verse (cf. Exod 15:13, 16) to support the possibility that these verses date to the Solomonic era,[61] while reference to northern tribes in verse 28 may also indicate an early perspective. In the end, Ps 68 need not necessarily be dated as

---

[57] De Vries, *From Old Revelation to New*, 64–74.

[58] Hosea 10:6; 12:2 (1) use יבל (without שַׁי) to depict similar scenes of bringing tribute.

[59] Kissane (*Isaiah*, 1:200) thinks that Isa 18:7 may have been influenced by Zeph 3:10, but offers no support for the suggestion.

[60] William F. Albright, "A Catalogue of Early Hebrew Lyric Poems (Psalm LXVIII)," *HUCA* 23 (1950–51): 1–40.

[61] J. J. M. Roberts ("Zion in the Theology of the Davidic-Solomonic Empire," in *The Bible and the Ancient Near East: Collected Essays* [Winona Lake, Ind.: Eisenbrauns, 2002], 331–47, esp. 344–5; repr. from *Studies in the Period of David and Solomon and Other Essays* [ed. T. Ishida; Winona Lake, Ind.: Eisenbrauns, 1982], 93–108); see also J. M. Allegro, "Uses of the Semitic Demonstrative Element z in Hebrew," *VT* 5 (1955): 309–12.

early as the tenth century B.C.E., since the present concern is simply to demonstrate that the relevant portion of this psalm at least antedates Isa 18:7.

While Wildberger accepts the antiquity of much of Ps 68, he assumes that verses 31–33 (30–32) are post-exilic on the basis that 'everyone' shares this view.[62] Accordingly, he proposes that the composition of these verses may be dependent on Isa 18:7. However, the opposite direction of influence can be asserted by observing that Isa 18:7 combines two specific textual elements from distinct sources: the unique description of the Cushites is taken from 18:2, while the rare phrase for bringing tribute comes from Ps 68:30 (29). In the latter verse, it is specifically kings, rather than Cushites, who bring the tribute, whereas the Cushites are only mentioned at a later point (Ps 68:32 [31]). Since Cushites are directly associated with יבל שַׁי only at Isa 18:7, it is likely that Isa 18:7 has borrowed from Ps 68:30 (29) in addition to Isa 18:2. Thus, even if Wildberger is right that verses 31–33 (30–32) constitute a later addition to Ps 68, this does not preclude the present assertion that the rare expression יבל שַׁי has been borrowed from Ps 68:30 (29) and applied to the Cushites in Isa 18:7.

Despite some thematic and linguistic similarities with Ps 68:29–32 (28–31), Isa 18:7 offers a few key points of departure. This section of Ps 68 refers to God only as אֱלֹהִים,[63] while Isa 18:7 prefers יְהוָה צְבָאוֹת ('Yhwh of hosts') and שֵׁם יְהוָה צְבָאוֹת ('the name of Yhwh of hosts').[64] Also, the people bring gifts to the 'temple' and 'Jerusalem' in Ps 68:29–32, whereas Isa 18:7 makes no mention of either of these; rather, it has 'Mount Zion,' and 'the place of the name,' both of which are absent from this psalm. In Isa 18:7, therefore, we find that the

---

[62] Wildberger, *Isaiah 13–27*, 224–5; cf. Hermann Gunkel, *Die Psalmen* (2d ed.; HKAT; Göttingen: Vandenhoek & Ruprecht, 1926), 2:286–7.

[63] יהוה is named only three times in Ps 68 (verses 17, 21, 27; also יָהּ in verse 5), while אֱלֹהִים appears as many times in verses 29–32 and twenty-six times in the entire psalm.

[64] It is commonly assumed that subsequent to the destruction of the temple, the Deuteronomistic writers perceived the deity as more transcendent than in earlier times, and so referred to the divine presence as 'the name,' rather than 'Yhwh of hosts'; Tryggve N. D. Mettinger, *The Dethronement of Sabaoth: Studies in the Shem and Kabod Theologies* (trans. Frederick H. Cryer; ConBOT 18; Lund: Gleerup, 1982), 15–17; but see Sandra L. Richter, *The Deuteronomistic History and the Name Theology* (BZAW 318; Berlin: de Gruyter, 2002). In this regard, however, it is notable that Isa 18:7 combines both elements: 'the name of Yhwh of hosts' (cf. 1 Sam 17:45; 2 Sam 6:2, 18). See also A. D. H. Mayes, *Deuteronomy* (NCB; London: Marshall, Morgan & Scott; Grand Rapids: Eerdmans, 1981), 59–60.

earlier vision of kings bringing tribute in response to the power of God has been reapplied to envision the pilgrimage of a mighty and powerful nation to Zion.

These linguistic and thematic ties between Isa 18:7 and Ps 68 suggest the influence of the Psalter on the development of Isa 18:7. Similar expressions can be found elsewhere in the Psalms. In Ps 72:10–11, 15, for example, kings from Tarshish, Sheba, and Seba bring tribute to the righteous king, which is not unlike the depiction in Ps 68 of kings bringing tribute to Jerusalem and gifts being brought by Egypt and Cush. Foreign kings bearing gifts are also mentioned in Ps 76:12–13 (11–12), which happens to contain the only other occurrence of the expression יבל שׁי besides those in Ps 68:30 (29) and Isa 18:7.

The suggestion that previous expectations from the Psalms are applied to Cush in Isa 18:7 is further supported by a similar proposal advanced by Ronald Clements, which focuses on earlier expressions in the Psalter as the basis for the development of the theme of foreign nations paying homage to Israel in Isaiah 40–66.[65] Among other points, he claims that Isa 44:24–45:1 names Cyrus as the means by which the Davidic promise in Ps 72 is fulfilled.[66] Similarly, Ps 72:15–17 provides the basis for the anticipation in Isa 49:7–26 that foreign kings will bring gifts in homage to Israel.[67] In the case of Isa 18:7, we have already observed a similar dependence on the Psalms, particularly Ps 68, and it may be no coincidence that the same theme of foreign tribute being brought to Jerusalem is depicted.

Similarly, Isa 18:7 resonates with Isa 2:2–4 (//Mic 4:1–3), which envisions foreign nations streaming peacefully to Zion. Like 18:7, these verses also reflect considerable influence from the Psalms.[68] By contrast, however, several texts in Isa 56–66 speak less favorably of foreign nations, stressing the vindication of Israel and the subservience of other nations (e.g. 60:3–17; 61:5; 62:1–3; 64:1 [2]).[69] Also, Isa 45:14

---

[65] Ronald E. Clements, "Psalm 72 and Isaiah 40–66: A Study in Tradition," *PRSt* 28 (2001): 333–341.

[66] Clements, "Psalm 72 and Isaiah 40–66," 336–8; see also Benjamin D. Sommer, *A Prophet Reads Scripture: Allusion in Isaiah 40–66* (Standford: Standford University Press, 1988), 115.

[67] Clements, "Psalm 72 and Isaiah 40–66," 338–9.

[68] John T. Willis, "Isaiah 2:2–5 and the Psalms of Zion," in *Writing and Reading the Scroll of Isaiah* (ed. Craig C. Broyles and Craig A. Evans; 2 vols.; VTSup 70; Leiden: Brill, 1997), 1:295–316.

[69] Graham I. Davies, "The Destiny of the Nations in the Book of Isaiah," in *The Book of Isaiah—Le Livre de Isaïe: Les oracles et leurs relecture. Unité et complexité de*

seems to reflect the latter view, and has more in common with Isa 60 than 40–55.[70]

In any event, it would appear that such verses represent a subsequent development in attitudes toward foreign nations from the expectation of foreigners bearing tribute to Zion. Although foreigners are viewed more positively in Isa 56:3, 6–8; 66:18–21, such texts may indicate yet another shift in perspective, since these seem to be oriented toward the foreigners for their own sake, rather than concern for the centrality of Jerusalem. It may be possible to use this continuum of perspectives toward foreigners to ascertain an approximate relative chronology for the addition of Isa 18:7. As we have shown, this verse reflects the influence of earlier expectations from the Psalms, but is substantially different from the post-exilic expressions of hostility toward foreigners. On this basis, Isa 18:7 can be plausibly dated toward the end of the exilic period.

5. ISAIAH 18:3

Several factors suggest that Isa 18:3 is also a secondary addition to the Cush oracle, but is distinct from 18:7.[71] Rather than referring only to Cushites, the message of this verse is directed more broadly toward inhabitants of the entire world, using terminology that is characteristic of later texts. תֵּבֵל ('world'), for example, occurs only in passages that are generally taken to be secondary additions to the book of Isaiah (e.g., 13:11; 14:17, 21; 24:4; 26:9),[72] and נָשָׂא נֵס ('to raise a signal') is also very frequently found in later passages (e.g., 11:12; 13:2; 49:22).[73]

---

l'ouvrage (ed. Jacques Vermeylen; BETL 81; Leuven: Peeters, 1989), 93–120; Joseph Blenkinsopp, "Second Isaiah: Prophet of Universalism," *JSOT* 41 (1988): 83–103.

[70] Not only is Isa 45:14 arguably disconnected from the surrounding material, the motif of Egypt and Cush coming in chains, bearing gifts, and paying obeisance, and also the second-person feminine pronominal suffixes, closely resemble Isa 60; see Claus Westermann, *Isaiah 40–66* (trans. David M. G. Stalker; OTL; London: SCM, 1969), 169–70; cf. Matthew J. Lynch, "Zion's Warrior and the Nations: Isaiah 59:15b–63:6 in Isaiah's Zion Traditions," *CBQ* 70 (2008): 244–63.

[71] Marti, *Jesaja*, 148–9; Gray, *Isaiah*, 312–13; Vermeylen, *Du prophète Isaïe*, 1:319; Wildberger, *Isaiah 13–27*, 212; Clements, *Isaiah 1–39*, 165.

[72] Wildberger, *Isaiah 13–27*, 209–10.

[73] One exception is the occurrence of נָשָׂא נֵס in 5:26, which is generally considered authentic. For discussion of this expression in the book of Isaiah, see the discussion below and also H. G. M. Williamson, *The Book Called Isaiah: Deutero-Isaiah's Role in Composition and Redaction* (Oxford: Oxford University Press, 1994), 63–7.

Similarly, תקע שׁוֹפָר ('to blow a horn') recurs in Isaiah only at 27:13, which seems to be an editorial addition to the conclusion of Isa 24–27, arguably one of the latest portions of the book. The discussion that follows will attempt to identify specific intertextual influences on the composition of 18:3 as well as factors that might have contributed to the insertion of this verse into the oracle about Cush.

A helpful point of departure is an examination of the expressions נשׂא נֵס ('to raise a signal') and תקע שׁוֹפָר ('to blow a horn'). These phrases are collocated in the book of Isaiah only at 18:3, with only two additional occurrences in the Hebrew Bible, both of which are in Jeremiah (4:5–6; 51:27).[74] In book of Jeremiah, the נֵס is a military standard that signals the place of assembly or attack[75] and the blowing of the שׁוֹפָר serves a similar function. In Jer 4:5–6, the signal and the horn herald an impending invasion of Judah and Jerusalem, whereas 51:27 redirects the expressions to announce the destruction of Babylon and the execution of divine vengeance on the oppressors of Israel (cf. 51:10–11, 24).[76] Thus, the former harbingers of judgment are invoked to proclaim the good news of the fall of Babylon. Despite this reversal of circumstances between Jer 4:5–6 and 51:27, both texts refer to נשׂא נֵס and תקע שׁוֹפָר within the context of the battlefield to convey an announcement of an imminent military strike.[77]

However, the occurrence of these same phrases in Isa 18:3 points to a subsequent stage of development beyond Jer 51:27. By contrast with the instances in Jeremiah, the signal and the horn in Isa 18:3 alert the entire world to Yhwh's activity, but with no evident military setting.[78]

---

[74] A variant can be found at Jer 6:1, which parallels תקע שׁוֹפָר with נשׂא מַשְׂאֵת ('to raise a [smoke] signal'). For מַשְׂאֵת as 'smoke signal', cf. Judg 20:38, 40; Lachish Ostracon 4.10. In addition, Victor Sasson ("An Unrecognized 'Smoke Signal' in Isaiah xxx 27," *VT* 33 [1983]: 90–95) interprets מַשְׂאָה in MT Isa 30:27 in relation to this understanding of מַשְׂאֵת.

[75] Heinz-Joseph Fabry, "נֵס," *TDOT* 9:440.

[76] For discussion of Jer 51, see David J. Reimer, *The Oracles against Babylon in Jeremiah 50–51: A Horror Among the Nations* (San Francisco: Mellen Research University Press, 1993), 80–3; also Miklós Kőszeghy, *Der Streit um Babel in den Büchern Jesaja und Jeremia* (BWANT 13; Stuttgart: Kolhammer, 2007).

[77] The collocation of תקע שׁוֹפָר and נשׂא מַשְׂאֵת at Jer 6:1 also involves a military setting.

[78] Konrad D. Jenner ("The Big Shofar [Isaiah 27:13]: A *Hapax Legomenon* to be Understood Merely as a Metaphor or as a *Crux Interpretum* for the Interpretation of Eschatological Expectation?," in *Studies in Isaiah 24–27* [ed. Hendrik Jan Bosman et al.; OtSt 43; Leiden: Brill, 2000], 173–4) distinguishes two applications of שׁוֹפָר, but he interprets Isa 18:3 as a warning signal on the presupposition that נשׂא נֵס

Thus, Isa 18:3 indicates a subsequent step in the joint use of these phrases along a trajectory of development from a negative military sense (Jer 4:5–6), to a positive military sense (Jer 51:27), and finally to a positive non-military sense (Isa 18:3). Since these are the only instances in which the two phrases are used together in the Hebrew Bible, it is likely that Isa 18:3 has been influenced by the texts in Jeremiah, even if it applies the expressions in a different direction.

While תקע שׁוֹפָר is a rare expression in Isaiah (18:3; 27:13), נשׂא נֵס is slightly more common (Isa 5:26; 11:12; 13:2; 18:3).[79] In the Hebrew Bible, the only other occurrences of נשׂא נֵס are limited to the book of Jeremiah (Jer 4:6; 50:2; 51:12, 27), two of which are combined with תקע שׁוֹפָר (Jer 4:5–6; 51:27), as we have noted. It is significant that the same line of development that was identified in the combined use of תקע שׁוֹפָר and נשׂא נֵס in Jeremiah can also be detected in the use of נשׂא נֵס by itself in Isaiah. In Isa 5:26, the raising of the signal summons attackers against Jerusalem (cf. Jer 4:5–6), while the expression is reapplied in Isa 13:2 to announce the downfall of Babylon (cf. Jer 51:27), both of which involve the contextual setting of the battlefield. By contrast, Isa 11:12 reflects a further stage of development in the use of נשׂא נֵס, since it imparts good news without a military application. Thus, both phrases have been developed along the same path of reinterpretation, from military harbingers of doom to military signals of redemption, and finally, to reapplication as positive messages in non-military settings. Whereas the development of only נשׂא נֵס can be traced in Isaiah, the progression of both phrases can be observed in Jer 4:5–6; 51:27; Isa 18:3.

With regard to the collocation of raising the signal and blowing the horn, Isa 18:3 is especially significant because it is the only text in Isaiah that incorporates both elements (cf. Jer 4:5–6; 51:27) and it represents a subsequent stage in their application. This would lead to

---

is consistently used this way in Isaiah. Donald C. Polaski (*Authorizing an End: The Isaiah Apocalypse and Intertextuality* [BIS 50; Leiden: Brill, 2001], 325–6) insists on negative undertones in Isa 27:13 on the basis of threshing and gleaning imagery in 27:12 and description of the שׁוֹפָר as גָּדוֹל ('great'), which is apparently reminiscent of Yhwh's great sword in 27:1. Against this likelihood, it should be noted that none of the other adjectives modifying the sword in 27:1 (קָשֶׁה, 'harsh'; חָזָק, 'strong') has been carried over to verse 13.

[79] In addition, Isa 49:22 expresses a similar idea using the phrases נשׂא יָד ('to lift the hand') and הרים נֵס ('to raise a signal').

the conclusion that Isa 18:3 reflects the direct influence of Jer 51:27, although additional intertextual influences can be detected.

As in Jer 51:27, the raising of the signal in Isa 13:2 represents the second stage in the development of the phrase, since it summons attackers against Babylon, rather than Jerusalem (cf. Isa 5:26). Although Isa 18:3 represents a later (positive non-military) development, it seems to reflect the direct influence of 13:2 by virtue of the fact that these are the only instances in the Hebrew Bible in which the signal is raised specifically on a mountain.[80] The observation that 13:2 appears as an integral literary unit with what follows,[81] whereas 18:3 is a secondary insertion, provides additional support for the latter verse being influenced by the former.

The significance of the mountain setting as an intertextual link between Isa 13:2 and 18:3 becomes more apparent when these verses are compared with 27:13, which refers to blowing the trumpet (תקע שׁופר) within the context of the mountain of Jerusalem. Moreover, while 18:3 represents the only instance in which the two phrases are combined in the book of Isaiah (cf. Jer 4:5–6; 51:27; also 6:1), the raising of the signal at 13:2 and the blowing of the trumpet at 27:13 conspicuously form an inclusio around two consecutive sections in the current form of the book (Isa 13–23; 24–27).[82] In this case, it is clear that Isa 27:13 is a later development from 18:3.[83] Isaiah 27:13 envisions the lost being gathered to Jerusalem from Assyria and Egypt,

---

[80] Isaiah 30:17 similarly refers to remaining 'like a flagstaff on top of the mountain, like a signal on a hill' (כַּתֹּרֶן עַל־רֹאשׁ הָהָר וְכַנֵּס עַל־הַגִּבְעָה), although the notion of fleeing in this verse may be understood to imply a military context.

[81] Clements (*Isaiah 1–39*, 132–3), for example, argues that Isa 13:2–22 is a series of five separate prophetic utterances rather than a compositional unity. Still, this proposal does not view 13:2–3 as a later addition to the other utterances.

[82] Wildberger, *Isaiah 13–27*, 445–51; 598–602; Williamson, *The Book Called Isaiah*, 177–83. Since both 27:12 and 27:13 speak about gathering the people of Yhwh from Egypt and Assyria and both are introduced by the phrase וְהָיָה בַּיּוֹם הַהוּא ('and it will be on that day'), it would appear that these two verses are separate additions to Isa 27; in any event, our present concern is that 27:13, at least, is secondary. See also Marvin A. Sweeney, "New Gleanings from an Old Vineyard: Isaiah 27 Reconsidered," in *Early Jewish and Christian Exegesis: Studies in Memory of William Hugh Brownlee* (ed. Craig A. Evans and William F. Stinespring; Atlanta: Scholars Press, 1987), 51–66; idem, "Textual Citations in Isaiah 24–27: Toward an Understanding of the Redactional Function of Chapters 24–27 in the Book of Isaiah," *JBL* 107 (1988): 39–52.

[83] J. Todd Hibbard (*Intertextuality in Isaiah 24–27: The Reuse and Evocation of Earlier Texts and Traditions* [FAT 2/16; Tübingen: Mohr Siebeck, 2006], 193 n. 116) dismisses the possibility of intertextual dependency between Isa 27:13 and 18:3 without offering any basis for this rejection.

while there is no hint of either a gathering or a return to Jerusalem in
18:3. Furthermore, the parallel use of הַנִּדָּחִים ('those who were driven
out') and הָאֹבְדִים ('those who were lost') in 27:13 suggests the influence of other texts on 27:13 (cf. Jer 23:1–2; 27:10, 15; Ezek 34:4, 16),
which have played no discernible role in the composition of 18:3.[84] For
our purposes, the fact that 27:13 has picked up from 18:3 both the
mountain locale and the phrase תקע שׁוֹפָר, suggests that the mountain
motif is no coincidence, but rather, is an essential element linking 13:2
and 18:3.

By way of summary, both Jer 51:27 and Isa 13:2 have directly influenced the composition of Isa 18:3. On one hand, Isa 18:3 develops
נשׂא נֵס and תקע שׁוֹפָר beyond their usage in the book of Jeremiah
(4:5–6; 51:27), but the literary influence from Jeremiah is made clear
by the fact that the phrases never appear together elsewhere in Isaiah,
or the rest of the Hebrew Bible, for that matter. On the other hand,
18:3 has also borrowed from 13:2, since in no other instance is the
signal raised on a mountain. Moreover, in both Isa 13:2 and Jer 51:27,
the raising of the signal, which previously beckoned enemy troops for
the punishment of Jerusalem (Isa 5:26; Jer 4:5–6), now announces the
gathering of armies to turn against Babylon. These texts presumably
reflect a period when the fall of Babylon was on the near horizon.
By contrast, however, the raising of the signal in Isa 18:3 has been
removed from the milieu of the battlefield and this verse gives no
indication of being set against the historical background of Babylon's
demise. Nevertheless, since we have established direct influence from
those passages that pertain to deliverance from Babylon, it is possible
that Isa 18:3 provides a further reflection on those momentous circumstances. From this perspective, the insertion of this verse within
the oracle about Cush may reflect an interest in drawing far-reaching,
worldwide attention to Yhwh's activity during the early post-exilic
period. Given the literary placement of the insertion, it would appear
that 18:3 anticipates Yhwh's involvement along the lines of that which
is described in 18:4–6.

It may be possible to discern additional literary influences on the
composition of Isa 18:3. As this verse describes, the alert is extended to
the inhabitants of the world, so that when the signal is raised, they look,
and when the horn is blown, they listen. The joint theme of seeing and

---

[84] Williamson, *The Book Called Isaiah*, 179–80.

hearing in Isaiah has been the subject of several studies, particularly by Ronald Clements, who identifies at least four stages in its development in the book.[85] According to his analysis, the subject first appears in Isa 6:9–10 as a metaphor to describe Judah's failure to respond to Yhwh's warnings through the prophet. The recurrence of the theme in 32:1–8 is thought to reflect the work of editors during the reign of Josiah in the late seventh century B.C.E., although Clements does not explain precisely how this represents a different line of development. In the third stage, several passages in Deutero-Isaiah demonstrate further reflection on this theme during the Babylonian exile (42:16, 18–20, 21–25; 43:8; 44:18). Clements initially suggested that the writer perceived captivity to Assyria and Babylon as a general experience of blindness and deafness,[86] but later reformulated his view by examining occurrences of the theme within contexts that describe the practice of idolatry (42:16–20; 44:9–20)[87] and the failure to heed Yhwh's teaching

---

[85] Clements, "The Unity of the Book of Isaiah," 125–6; idem, "Beyond Tradition-History: Deutero-Isaianic Development of First Isaiah's Themes," *JSOT* 31 (1985): 95–113; idem, "Patterns in the Prophetic Canon: Healing the Blind and the Lame," in *Canon, Theology, and Old Testament Interpretation: Essays in Honor of Brevard S. Childs* (ed. Gene M. Tucker, David L. Petersen, and Robert R. Wilson; Philadelphia: Fortress, 1988), 189–200. Clements undertakes a similar study of the theme of light as a metaphor for salvation in "A Light to the Nations: A Central Theme of the Book of Isaiah," in *Forming Prophetic Literature: Essays on Isaiah and the Twelve in Honor of John D. W. Watts* (ed. James W. Watts and Paul R. House; JSOTSup 235; Sheffield: Sheffield Academic Press, 1996), 57–69; see also Craig A. Evans, *To See and Not Perceive: Isaiah 6:9–10 in Early Jewish and Christian Interpretation* (JSOTSup 64; Sheffield: JSOT Press, 1989), 17–52. Additional work has been done on seeing and hearing in Isaiah, but is less informative for our present purposes: Rolf Rendtorff, "Isaiah 6 in the Framework of the Composition of the Book," in *Canon and Theology: Overtures to an Old Testament Theology* (trans. and ed. Margaret Kohl; Edinburgh: T. & T. Clark, 1994), 170–80; repr. from "Jesaja 6 im Rahmen der Komposition des Jesajabuches," in *The Book of Isaiah—Le Livre de Isaïe: Les oracles et leurs relecture. Unité et complexité de l'ouvrage* (ed. Jacques Vermeylen; BETL 81; Leuven: Peeters, 1989), 73–82; K. T. Aitken, "Hearing and Seeing: Metamorphoses of a Motif in Isaiah 1–39," in *Among the Prophets: Language, Image and Structure in the Prophetic Writings* (ed. Philip R. Davies and David J. A. Clines; JSOTSup 144; Sheffield: JSOT Press, 1993), 12–41; Philip Stern, "The 'Blind Servant' Imagery of Deutero-Isaiah and Its Implications," *Bib* 75 (1994): 224–32; Geoffrey D. Robinson, "The Motif of Deafness and Blindness in Isaiah 6:9–10: A Contextual, Literary, and Theological Analysis," *BBR* 8 (1998), 167–86.

[86] Clements, "The Unity of the Book of Isaiah," 125.

[87] Incidentally, the words for 'engraver' (i.e., one who makes idols) and 'deaf' share the same root in Hebrew (חרשׁ), but despite the juxtaposition of these themes, there is no clear indication of wordplay. References to idol makers in 40:19–20, for example, are followed by the topic of hearing in 40:21 without the use of חרשׁ, while references to deafness in 42:18–19 follow a verse about idols in which חרשׁ does not occur.

(42:21–25).[88] Thus, he concluded that seeing and hearing for Deutero-Isaiah involve a call to abandon idols and heed Yhwh's instruction. In later stages in the formation of the book, as exemplified by 35:5 (possibly also 29:18), deafness and blindness are no longer viewed metaphorically, but rather, the concepts describe a new era of anticipated salvation. Reference to the weak becoming strong (35:3) and the lame leaping (35:6) confirms that the expectation of future salvation in 35:5 is characterized by those who were literally blind and deaf being made to see and hear.

Clements' discussions of the subject make no mention of the combined seeing and hearing in Isa 18:3, but according to his rubric, the application of the theme in this verse would most closely align with Deutero-Isaiah. His examples from earlier periods (6:9–10; 32:1–8) involve Judah's failure to respond to the prophetic message, while the post-exilic occurrences (29:18; 35:5) anticipate physical healing from blindness and deafness. In contrast to these perspectives, seeing and hearing in Isa 18:3 seem to describe the realization of pre-exilic expectations without conveying any sense of physical healing.

We may also observe that Isa 18:3 addresses the inhabitants of the entire world, which suggests a far-reaching application of the theme of seeing and hearing that may be shared by Deutero-Isaiah. In 42:6–7, for example, the 'light to the nations' will open blind eyes and release captive prisoners,[89] while 43:8–9 assembles the blind and deaf together with the nations.[90] From this perspective, the insertion of 18:3 into the Cush oracle could theoretically serve to single out this nation among those to which the 'light' has been sent. However, despite broad thematic similarities, Isa 18:3 contains none of the typically Deutero-Isaianic expressions for foreign peoples, such as 'nations,' 'coastlands,' or 'ends of the earth'. This does not preclude common authorship, of

---

[88] Clements, "Beyond Tradition-History," 101–3.

[89] There is considerable disagreement about whether Isa 40–55 expresses a universalistic expectation of salvation of people from other nations, particularly because passages in these chapters seem to speak of the nations both positively (e.g., 42:4; 45:22–23; 49:6; 51:4–6) and negatively (43:3–4; 45:14; 49:23; 54:3). For a thorough discussion of the issue, see Joel S. Kaminsky and Anne Stewart, "God of All the World: Universalism and Developing Monotheism in Isaiah 40–66," *HTR* 99 (2006): 139–63.

[90] The blind and deaf in Isa 43:8 should probably be interpreted as Israelites, considering the reference to 'my sons' and 'my daughters' in 43:6–7 and the descriptions of blindness and deafness in relation to 'my servant' in the previous chapter (42:18–20). All the same, they are juxtaposed as co-witnesses with the nations before Yhwh in 43:8–10; see Clements, "Beyond Tradition-History," 102.

course, but it would be safer to say that the writer of 18:3 may have been familiar with the content of Isa 40–55.

Before concluding the discussion of Isa 18:3 and Deutero-Isaiah, a few comments should be made about 11:12. This verse is relevant because it contains the only other positive non-military occurrence of נֵס נָשָׂא in the Hebrew Bible, aside from 18:3.[91] In addition to this characteristic, Cush is named in 11:11–12 among those nations that are intended recipients of the signal. At the same time, there are several close intertextual connections between Isa 11:11–16 and Isa 40–55.[92] For example, 49:22 speaks of Yhwh lifting the hand (יָד נָשָׂא) for the nations and raising a signal (נֵס הָרִים) to gather those who have been scattered (cf. 40:11; 49:5–6, 18; 54:7). Also, Deutero-Isaiah often alludes to the exodus, while 11:15–16 recalls the highway (מְסִלָּה) that enables deliverance (cf. 40:3; 49:11) and the drying up of the sea and the waterways (cf. 42:15; 43:16; 44:27; 50:2; 51:10). There is no need for our present interest to insist that 11:11–16 must have been written by Deutero-Isaiah,[93] but we may note that the echo of these verses in 18:3 coincides with our previous observations that the seeing and hearing motif also may have been influenced by Deutero-Isaiah. Despite any points of correspondence, however, it is unlikely that Isa 11:11–16 and 18:3 can be attributed to the same hand. Whereas 11:11–16 focuses primarily on gathering Yhwh's people from Cush and other lands, 18:3 broadens the scope and makes no mention of Diaspora Jews.

Finally, the widened scope of 'all the inhabitants of the world' (כָּל־יֹשְׁבֵי תֵבֵל) and 'those dwelling on the earth' (שֹׁכְנֵי אָרֶץ) in Isa 18:3 suggests some affinity with the material in Isa 24–27.[94] For example,

---

[91] A similar (positive non-military) expression can also be found in Isa 49:22, which parallels נָשָׂא יָד ('to lift up a hand') with נֵס הָרִים ('to raise a signal').

[92] Williamson, *The Book Called Isaiah*, 125–7; idem, "Isaiah xi 11–16 and the Redaction of Isaiah i–xii," in *Congress Volume: Paris, 1992* (ed. J. A. Emerton; VTSup 61; Leiden: Brill, 1995), 343–57.

[93] Marvin A. Sweeney ("Jesse's New Shoot in Isaiah 11: A Josianic Reading of the Prophet Isaiah," in *A Gift of God in Due Season* [ed. David M. Carr and Richard D. Weis; JSOTSup 225; Sheffield: Sheffield Academic Press, 1996], 103–18) asserts that 11:1–16 was contributed as part of the 'Josianic' redaction in the seventh century B.C.E., but he does not indicate why it could not be exilic, nor does he consider any literary connections with Deutero-Isaiah. See also idem, *King Josiah of Judah: The Lost Messiah of Israel* (Oxford: Oxford University Press, 2001), 235–40.

[94] H. G. M. Williamson ("On Getting Carried Away with the Infinitive Construct of נשא," in *Shai le-Sara Japhet: Studies in the Bible, its Exegesis and its Language* [ed. M. Bar-Asher, E. Tov, D. Rom-Shilony, and N. Wazana; Jerusalem: Bialik Institute, 2007], 364*–5*) suggests that the alliteration produced by the use of the rare infinitive

while we observed the centrality of the mountains in 18:3, the mountain of Yhwh serves as the venue for a great feast for all the earth
in 25:6–10. Moreover, the word תֵּבֵל ('world'), which nearly always
appears in late, universalistic texts,[95] never occurs in Deutero-Isaiah,
but the exact phrase יֹשְׁבֵי תֵבֵל ('inhabitants of the world') can be found
in 26:9, 18 (cf. 24:4; 27:6). If 18:3 offers a reflection on 11:11–12, the
insertion of this verse within the Cush oracle suggests that this nation
is viewed as one representative of people from all distant lands.

6. Conclusion

The present study has posited that the original oracle about Cush
consisted of the material that is now contained in verses 1–2, 4–6,
and that it can be plausibly viewed within the historical context of
Sennacherib's campaign against Judah in 701 B.C.E. While the appearance of this הוֹי oracle among the מַשָּׂא oracles in Isa 13–23 is unusual,
similarities in content and form with the הוֹי oracles in 28–31 suggest
that these latter chapters provided the original literary context for this
oracle. If this is the case, we may conclude that the relocation of the
Cush oracle to its present position is likely related to the oracle about
Egypt and the narrative about both nations in the following chapters,
a possibility that will be considered in Chapter 6, below.

It appears that verses 7 and 3 are separate additions to the Cush
oracle, offering two distinct reinterpretations of the original material.
The final verse repeats much of the singular language from verse 2 in
its description of Cushites bringing tribute to Zion, while the theme
of bearing gifts has likely been influenced by Ps 68. This image of foreign pilgrimage to Zion is similar to other passages in Isaiah (such
as 2:2–4), but it can be distinguished from the negative portrayal of
foreign nations that especially characterizes Isa 60–62.[96] Therefore, this

---

construct form in the phrase כְּנֵשֹׂא־נֵס in Isa 18:3 is characteristic of literary devices
featured in Isa 24–27. See also idem, "Sound, Sense and Language in Isaiah 24–27,"
JJS 46 (1995): 1–9; William H. Irwin, "Syntax and Style in Isaiah 26," *CBQ* 41 (1979):
240–61.

[95] H.-J. Fabry and N. van Meeteren, "תֵּבֵל," *TDOT* 15:559.

[96] In contrast to Isa 60–62, Isa 56:1–8 speaks favorably of foreign people, although
unlike 18:7, it seems to depict conversion of individual foreigners, rather than the
tribute of a nation (cf. also 66:18–21). Since 60–62 is often perceived as a 'core' of
early material within 56–66, 56:1–8 could be among the latest elements in the growth

perspective of the Cushites in 18:7 may indicate that the addition of this verse predates the material in the latter section of the book.

We have observed that the language of 18:3 has been directly influenced by Isa 13:2 and Jer 51:27, and it is possible that Isa 11:11–16 and 40–55 have also played some role in the development of the verse. In contrast to 18:7, which is specifically oriented toward Cush, the focus of 18:3 has been widened to refer to the entire world, in line with the perspective of much of the material in 24–27. Regarding these latter chapters, while a number of echoes from 13–23 and elsewhere in Isaiah indicate that this section probably has not been composed in isolation,[97] our analysis of 18:3 may provide an example in which 24–27 has contributed to the formation of other parts of the book.

---

of this section. On this subject, see Seizo Sekine, *Die Tritojesajanische Sammlung (Jes 56–66) redaktionsgeschichtlich untersucht* (BZAW 175; Berlin: de Gruyter, 1989), 31–42, 228–33; Willem A. M. Beuken, "Isaiah Chapters LXV–LXVI: Trito-Isaiah and the Closure of the Book of Isaiah," in *Congress Volume: Leuven, 1989* (ed. J. A. Emerton; VTSup 43; Leiden: Brill, 1991), 204–21; Odil Hannes Steck, *Studien zu Tritojesaja* (BZAW 203; Berlin: de Gruyter, 1991), 34–45.

[97] Some examples are discussed in Sweeney, "Textual Citations in Isaiah 24–27," 39–52.

CHAPTER FOUR

THE REDACTIONAL FORMATION OF ISAIAH 19

1. INTRODUCTION

In the current form of the book, Isa 19:1–25 comprises an oracle about Egypt that begins with a מַשָּׂא superscription, in common with many other oracles about foreign nations in Isa 13–23. This chapter is distinguished from the preceding Cush oracle by a מַשָּׂא title at 19:1, while a narrative about Cush and Egypt begins at 20:1. Although 19:1–4 may probably be attributed to the eighth century B.C.E. (see below), the following discussion will seek to demonstrate that the remainder of the chapter has been produced by later editorial additions to the original oracle. While most critical scholars agree that the five 'in that day' passages constituting verses 16–25 are probably secondary, we will show that there is also reason to doubt the authenticity of verses 5–15. Thus, much of Isa 19 is the product of various accretions that are held together by common interest in Egypt. In what follows, each of the major stages in the formation of the chapter will be surveyed, with particular regard to literary influences that have played some role in their development.

2. ISAIAH 19:1–4

The question of authorship stands among many uncertainties about Isa 19:1–4, not least because the vague historical allusions provide weak footing for a determination of the date of composition. The 'harsh master' and 'mighty king' in 19:4, for example, could refer to any number of rulers. While these epithets could be suitably applied to Assyrian kings of the eighth century B.C.E., the text makes no specific mention of Assyria, nor does it describe a foreign ruler over Egypt. The portrayal of internal conflict in 19:2 may also suggest various circumstances in Egypt's history, but significant doubt remains concerning what may be intended. Given the weak historical references in 19:1–4, a literary analysis of these verses provides a better indication of their origin.

From a literary standpoint, many critical scholars deny Isaianic authorship of Isa 19:1–4 on two main grounds. First, this oracle is one of nine in Isa 13–23 that begin with a 'מַשָּׂא GN' superscription (13:1; 15:1; 17:1; 21:1, 11, 13; 22:1; 23:1; cf. 14:28; 30:6). Since a few of the מַשָּׂא oracles seem to relate to events toward the end of the exile (especially 13:1–14:23; 21:1–10), some commentators assume that the collection of these oracles would not have been incorporated into the book until after that time (see Chapters 1–2, above). However, other מַשָּׂא material, such as 17:1–3; 22:1–8, seems to relate to the eighth century B.C.E., which suggests that the superscription does not necessarily preclude the authenticity of any oracle's contents.

Secondly, the authenticity of Isa 19:1–4 is often ruled out on the basis of a style that is thought to be a poor imitation of the genuine work of Isaiah ben Amoz.[1] For example, 'Egypt' is repeated eight times within the first four verses, and the appearance of Yhwh riding on the clouds in 19:1 is thought to be more characteristic of psalmic texts than prophetic material (cf. Pss 18:10–11 [9–10]; 68:5, 34 [4, 33]; 104:3).[2] Even if certain broad literary characteristics can be identified among texts for which there is a greater consensus, these cannot rule out the possibility of Isaianic authorship for a particular passage. In this particular case, there is no basis for the assertion that the prophet Isaiah could (or would) not have mentioned Egypt several times within a few lines or used certain poetic imagery.

On the contrary, several literary features of Isa 19:1–4 support the Isaianic origin of this passage. To begin, these verses contain a few terms and expressions that are found in other material widely recognized as Isaianic. אֱלִילִים ('idols'), for example, is especially common in Isaianic passages (cf. Isa 2:8, 18, 20 [twice]; 10:10, 11; 19:1, 3; 31:7; also Lev 19:4; 26:1; 1 Chr 16:26; Ps 96:5; 97:7; Ezek 30:13; Hab 2:18).[3]

---

[1] Bernhard Duhm, *Das Buch Jesaia* (4th ed; HKAT; Göttingen: Vandenhoeck & Ruprecht, 1922), 140–1; T. K. Cheyne, *Introduction to the Book of Isaiah* (London: Adam and Charles Black, 1895), 112; Karl Marti, *Das Buch Jesaja* (KHC 10; Tübingen: Mohr [Siebeck], 1900), 152, 155; George Buchanan Gray, *The Book of Isaiah: I–XXVII* (ICC; Edinburgh: T. & T. Clark, 1912), 322–3; Otto Kaiser, *Isaiah 13–39* (trans. R. A. Wilson; OTL; London: SCM, 1974), 99; Jacques Vermeylen, *Du prophète Isaïe à l'apocalyptique: Isaïe, I–XXXV* (2 vols.; Paris: Gabalda, 1977–78), 1:320–1.

[2] Cheyne (*Isaiah*, 112) lists several additional literary characteristics along these lines to dispute the authenticity of Isa 19:1–4.

[3] The etymology of אֱלִילִים is uncertain, although it may have developed as a disparaging pun on אֵל or אֱלֹהִים ('god, gods'). If the Isaianic passages account for the

The occurrence in Isa 2:8, for example, appears as part of a passage that addresses the 'house of Jacob' (2:5–6), and those in 10:10–11 compare the idols of Jerusalem and Samaria. Similarly, the rare *pilpel* verb סִכְסֵךְ ('to stir up, provoke'; 19:2) recurs only in Isa 9:10 (11), where it describes the provocation of enemy nations for the punishment of the northern kingdom of Israel.

Not only are there linguistic features in Isa 19:1–4 that resemble Isaianic material, it applies them in much the same way, which would suggest common authorship instead of subsequent development. This can be illustrated by observing several close similarities with 3:1–7, which pronounces judgment against Jerusalem. In particular, both 3:1 and 19:4 contain the rare title הָאָדוֹן יְהוָה צְבָאוֹת ('the Lord, Yhwh of hosts'),[4] which occurs elsewhere in the Hebrew Bible only at Isa 1:24; 10:16, 33. Both passages also share more common expressions, including אִישׁ בְּרֵעֵהוּ ('each against another'; Isa 3:5; 19:2) and מֹשֵׁל + בְּ ('to rule over'; Isa 3:4; 19:4). More significantly, 3:1–7 relates to Jerusalem and 19:1–4 is about Egypt, but both of these texts address divination in various forms and both are principally concerned with the upheaval of national leadership. In 3:1–7, powerful officials will be replaced by children resulting in conflict among the people, while 19:1–4 describes Egyptians fighting against Egyptians, with a fierce ruler set in power over them.

In addition to these common elements, 3:1–7 and 19:1–4 share the same literary form, as both are written as announcements of judgment.[5] According to Claus Westermann, an announcement of judgment usually contains two main parts: a first-person statement of the intervention of the deity followed by a third-person description of the result of the intervention as punishment. Isaiah 19 begins with the introductory particle הִנֵּה, followed by the divine name (יְהוָה) plus the participial phrase רֹכֵב עַל־עָב קַל ('riding on a swift cloud'). After this, the first-person intervention speech continues through verse 4a,

---

earliest occurrences, it is possible that Isaiah may have even coined the term; see Horst Dietrich Preuss, "אֱלִיל," *TDOT* 1:285–7.

  [4] *BHS* proposes the deletion of הָאָדוֹן in 19:4 (also 10:16) since it is absent from the Greek and Syriac versions. However, the word is retained in 1QIsaᵃ as well as other passages in MT Isaiah.

  [5] Claus Westermann, *Basic Forms of Prophetic Speech* (trans. H. C. White; Philadelphia: Westminster, 1967; repr. Louisville: Westminster John Knox, 1991), 169–76; cf. Marvin Sweeney, *Isaiah 1–39* (FOTL 16; Grand Rapids: Eerdmans, 1996), 108–9, 268.

followed by a brief statement of the result in the third person: וּמֶ֣לֶךְ
עַ֖ז יִמְשָׁל־בָּֽם ('a strong king will rule over them'). In Isa 3:1–7, the
beginning of the announcement of judgment is syntactically identical
to 19:1: הִנֵּה is followed by the name of the deity and the participial
phrase מֵסִיר מִירוּשָׁלַ֙ם וּמִיהוּדָה ('removing from Jerusalem and Judah').
As in Isa 19, the main part of the announcement in Isa 3 consists of
the intervention in the first person (3:4), followed by a third-person
description of the result (3:5–7).

In his survey of prophetic judgment speech, Westermann explains
that the announcement of judgment is normally preceded by a reason for the judgment,[6] but on a few occasions no reason is given to
accompany the announcement of judgment.[7] In addition to the formal similarities that we have already identified, it is noteworthy that
Isa 19:1–4 and 3:1–7 share this unusual characteristic of the absence
of a reason for judgment in the original formulation of the speech.[8]
The final form of Isa 3 now contains a reason for judgment in verses
8–9a, which some have taken as an original component with the preceding verses.[9] However, 3:8 does not really constitute a reason for
the judgment ('Jerusalem has stumbled and Judah has fallen'), and
3:8–9a seems to imply that the judgment has already been carried out,
which would suggest that these verses are a later addition to the original announcement.[10] In summary, Isa 3:1–7 and 19:1–4 address the
same theme using identical terminology and literary form. Since many
critical scholars agree on the general authenticity of Isa 3:1–7,[11] the

---

[6] Westermann, *Basic Forms*, 176–7.

[7] Westermann, *Basic Forms*, 171.

[8] H. G. M. Williamson (*Isaiah 1–27* [3 vols; ICC; London: T. & T. Clark, 2006],
1:240) points out that Isa 10:33–34 likewise begins with הִנֵּ֤ה הָאָדוֹן יְהוָ֣ה צְבָא֔וֹת +
participle, and that it also lacks a reason for judgment.

[9] For example, Hans Wildberger, *Isaiah 1–12* (trans. Thomas H. Trapp; Minneapolis: Fortress, 1991), 126–7; Ronald E. Clements, *Isaiah 1–39* (NCB; Grand Rapids:
Eerdmans; London: Marshall, Morgan & Scott, 1980), 46–7; Sweeney, *Isaiah 1–39*,
108; Joseph Blenkinsopp, *Isaiah 1–39* (AB 19; New York: Doubleday, 2000), 199; cf.
Otto Kaiser, *Isaiah 1–12* (trans. John Bowden; 2d ed.; OTL; London: SCM, 1983),
68, 72–3. Westermann (*Basic Forms*, 176–7) specifically cites Isa 3:1–9a (+ 9b–11)
as an example in which he believes the announcement (3:1–7) precedes the reason
(3:8–9a).

[10] Williamson, *Isaiah 1–27*, 1:240.

[11] Duhm, *Jesaia*, 44–6; Gray, *Isaiah*, 62; Edward J. Kissane, *The Book of Isaiah*
(2 vols.; rev. ed.; Dublin: Browne and Nolan, 1941), 1:32–3; Wildberger, *Isaiah 1–12*,
127–8; Clements, *Isaiah 1–39*, 46–8; Sweeney, *Isaiah 1–39*, 109; Blenkinsopp, *Isaiah
1–39*, 198–9; Williamson, *Isaiah 1–27*, 1:242.

occurrence of the same literary features suggests that this is the case for 19:1–4 as well.

Some attention should also be given to the possibility of intertextual influence between Isa 19:3 and 8:19, which refers to various forms of divination and is often viewed as a later addition to the book.[12] However, a close comparison of the terminology speaks against the likelihood of direct influence between these verses. Both 8:19 and 19:3 refer to consulting אֹבוֹת ('ghosts') and יִדְּעֹנִים ('familiar spirits'),[13] but the frequent and widespread collocation of these terms in the Hebrew Bible suggests a widely used idiomatic expression rather than borrowing between these two passages (cf. Lev 19:31; 20:6, 27; Deut 18:11; 1 Sam 28:3, 7–9; 2 Kgs 21:6; 23:24; 2 Chr 33:6).[14] At the same time, Isa 19:3 uses two additional terms that are absent from 8:19. אִטִּים ('spirits') is a *hapax legomenon*,[15] and it has already been noted that אֱלִילִים ('idols') is frequently featured in Isaianic texts.

In light of the previous observations, therefore, the literary characteristics of Isa 19:1–4 support the possibility of including these verses among those that can likely be attributed to Isaiah ben Amoz. Certainly, the indistinct historical elements of this pericope can be applied to the eighth century without difficulty, even if they cannot confirm the origins of the passage. For example, the internal conflict described in 19:1–4 could plausibly relate to circumstances during the rise of the 25th Dynasty, when the Nubian king Piankhy sought to extend his empire further north along the Nile.[16] However, while Isa 19:4 mentions a certain 'harsh ruler,' it seems unlikely that the oracle about Egypt relates to Sennacherib's campaign against Jerusalem in 701.[17] Egypt plays a central role in that event, but there is no mention of

---

[12] Duhm, *Jesaia*, 141; Marti, *Jesaja*, 152; Kaiser, *Isaiah 13–39*, 101; Hermann Barth, *Die Jesaja-Worte in der Josiazeit: Israel und Assur als Thema einer produktiven Neuinterpretation der Jesajaüberlieferung* (WMANT 48; Neukirchen-Vluyn: Neukirchener Verlag, 1977), 152–6; Vermeylen, *Du prophète Isaïe*, 1:321; Wildberger, *Isaiah 1–12*, 364–5, 371; Clements, *Isaiah 1–39*, 101–3; Blenkinsopp, *Isaiah 1–39*, 244–5.

[13] Wildberger (*Isaiah 13–27*, 237) views 19:1–4 as generally Isaianic, but takes וְאֶל־הָאֹבוֹת וְאֶל־הַיִּדְּעֹנִים in Isa 19:3 as a later gloss influenced by 8:19.

[14] The terms never appear separately, with the exception of אוֹב in 1 Chr 10:13; Isa 29:4.

[15] A. S. Yahuda ("Hebrew Words of Egyptian Origin, 6," *JBL* 66 [1947]: 85–6) suggests that אִטִּים has been borrowed from Egyptian.

[16] For discussion of Cushite rule in Egypt, see Chapter 3, above.

[17] *Contra* Matthijs J. de Jong, *Isaiah among the Ancient Near Eastern Prophets: A Comparative Study of the Earliest Stages of the Isaiah Tradition and the Neo-Assyrian Prophecies* (VTSup 117; Leiden: Brill, 2007), 150–1.

an exchange of messengers in 19:1–4, a key theme in other texts that can be plausibly connected with that crisis (cf. Isa 18:1–2; 30:1–5; 31:1–3; 36:6).

3. ISAIAH 19:11–14

There is general agreement among critical scholars that Isa 19:5–10 contrasts sharply with the surrounding material, since these intervening verses use unusual terminology to emphasize environmental and economic devastation in Egypt as a result of the drying up of the Nile (see below). There is less of a consensus about the relationship between verses 1–4 and 11–14. Since both sections speak negatively of Egypt, some commentators suppose that verses 11–14 were composed as part of a single literary unit with verses 1–4.[18] Despite any points of contact between these units, however, it is difficult to view the latter verses as a compositional unit with the initial oracle of verses 1–4, especially since the formal characteristics of an announcement of judgment are limited to the first four verses of the chapter.[19]

In addition, the secondary nature of 19:11–14 is suggested by the reapplication of certain themes and terms from verses 1–4. For example, 19:3 speaks of the 'spirit of Egypt within it' (רוּחַ־מִצְרַיִם בְּקִרְבּוֹ) being emptied out and the confounding of Egypt's plans by Yhwh, whereas 19:14 states that Yhwh will 'mix (or pour) into it' (מָסַךְ בְּקִרְבָּהּ) a 'spirit of confusion' (רוּחַ עִוְעִים).[20] Similarly, 19:11 picks up the topic of Egypt's plan (עֵצָה) from verse 3 and mocks the purported wisdom of Egypt's sages (חֲכָמִים; cf. 1 Kgs 5:10 [4:30]).[21] Although it involves some of the same topics from the initial oracle, 19:11–14 extends them along a slightly different trajectory. Whereas the original message depicts a theophany that brings about the internal upset

---

[18] Cheyne, *Isaiah*, 110–11; Gray, *Isaiah*, 320–3; Otto Procksch, *Jesaja I* (KAT 9/1; Leipzig: Deichert, 1930), 247; Vermeylen, *Du prophète Isaïe*, 1:320–1; Clements, *Isaiah 1–39*, 168; Blenkinsopp, *Isaiah 1–39*, 314.

[19] Marti (*Jesaja*, 155) and Kaiser (*Isaiah 13–39*, 99) view 19:11–14 as a later addition to verses 1–4.

[20] Willem A. M. Beuken, *Jesaja 13–27* (HTKAT; Freiburg: Herder, 2007), 185–6.

[21] See also Isa 29:14; 31:2; 44:25. For the subject of wisdom in Isaiah, see William McKane, *Prophets and Wise Men* (SBT 44; London: SCM, 1965), 69–73, 80; J. William Whedbee, *Isaiah and Wisdom* (Nashville: Abingdon, 1971), 115–16, 135–6.

of Egypt, verses 11–14 express a warning against those who might be lured into dependency on the wisest of Pharaoh's counselors.

In addition to the influence of the first four verses of the chapter, Isa 19:11–14 also reflects the condemnation of dependency on Egypt from Isa 30:1–5 (cf. also 31:1–3). Both passages focus on Egyptians, but of greater significance is the observation that 19:11–14 emphasizes their foolish plans, which echoes the accusation in Isa 30 that the Judeans are forming a plan (עֵצָה) to recruit Pharaoh's assistance.[22] Furthermore, 19:11–14 twice refers to the officials of Zoan, who are mentioned elsewhere in the Hebrew Bible only at Isa 30:4. Similarly, with one exception (36:6), Isa 19:11 and 30:2–3 contain the only references to Pharaoh by name in the book of Isaiah. Also, whereas the 'rebellious children' of Judah are formulating a plan against Yhwh in 30:1, this behavior is attributed to Pharaoh's supposedly wise counselors in 19:11–14. Thus, 19:11–14 draws several elements from 30:1–5 to echo the message about Egypt's inadequacy, while directing criticism specifically against the leaders of Egypt.

In addition to the Egypt material from Isa 30:1–5, 19:11–14 shows signs of influence from other passages among the group of הוֹי oracles in Isa 28–31. In particular, 19:11–14 echoes the theme of drunkenness and confusion that is prominent in 28:7–8; 29:9–10.[23] In 28:7–8, the priests and prophets wander (תעה, *qal*) in their own drunkenness, and in 19:13–14, the leaders of Egypt cause its citizens to wander (תעה, *hip'il*) like a drunkard (cf. 9:15 [16]). Similarly, 29:9–10 also addresses the leadership of Jerusalem using the metaphor of drunkenness. Whereas 29:10 has the phrase נָסַךְ עֲלֵיכֶם יְהוָה רוּחַ תַּרְדֵּמָה ("Yhwh has poured out upon you a spirit of deep sleep"), 19:14 uses a very similar expression: יְהוָה מָסַךְ בְּקִרְבָּהּ רוּחַ עִוְעִים ("Yhwh has poured/ mixed within it a spirit of confusion"). All three of these texts employ the theme of drunkenness to admonish leadership. In both 28:7–8 and 29:9–10 the leaders of Jerusalem are in view, while 19:13–14 applies similar sentiments to the Egyptian leaders of Zoan and Memphis.

---

[22] For studies on the motif of Yhwh's plan in Isaiah, see Johannes Fichtner, "Jahves Plan in der Botschaft des Jesaja," *ZAW* 63 (1951): 16–33; Hans Wildberger, "Jesajas Verständnis der Geschichte," in *Congress Volume: Bonn, 1962* (VTSup 9; Leiden: Brill, 1962), 83–117; Joseph Jensen, "Yahweh's Plan in Isaiah and in the Rest of the Old Testament," *CBQ* 48 (1986): 443–55; Wolfgang Werner, *Studien zur alttestamentlichen Vorstellung vom Plan Jahwes* (BZAW 173; Berlin: de Gruyter, 1988), 37–53.

[23] Kaiser, *Isaiah 13–39*, 103–4; Brevard S. Childs, *Isaiah* (OTL; Louisville: Westminster John Knox, 2001), 143.

The basic critique of Isa 19:11–14 against societal leadership also resonates strongly with material in the book of Jeremiah.[24] It has already
been noted that Isa 19:13–14 describes the Egyptian authorities leading the nation astray (תעה) by invoking an expression from 28:7–8
that critiques Judean priests and prophets. The same verb also appears
several times in Jeremiah (23:13, 32; 42:20; 50:6), always within the
context of certain leaders misguiding the people.[25] Of these, the two
occurrences in Jer 23 refer to prophets misleading the people, as also
in Isa 28:7 (cf. Mic 3:5). In Jer 42:20 the prophet attempts to persuade
the commanders and people not to go to Egypt, with the assertion
that they are leading themselves astray (reading with the Qere, הִתְעֵתֶם
בְּנַפְשׁוֹתֵיכֶם). Along similar lines, Jer 50:6 compares the people to sheep
that have been caused to wander by their shepherds (cf. Isa 53:6; Jer
10:21). The fact that Isa 19:13–14 uses the same terminology to express
the same concern suggests the possibility of intertextual influence from
the literature of Jeremiah. In this case, however, the critique is leveled
against the leadership of Egypt rather than Judah.

Furthermore, it was previously observed that in Isa 19:11–14 and
28:7–8, the notion of leading astray (תעה) is combined with the
metaphor of drunkenness (שכר/שכור), a theme that is prominent
in 29:9–10. At the same time, drunkenness is associated specifically
with vomit (קיא) only in Isa 19:11–14; 28:7–8, and two occurrences
in the book of Jeremiah (25:27; 48:26). The occurrence in Jer 25:27 is
especially noteworthy because the prophet commands various nations,
among them Judah and Egypt (including Pharaoh and his officials, cf.
25:19), to drink from the cup of wrath, to become drunk, and to vomit
(cf. Isa 29:9).

There are additional literary ties between Isa 19:11–14 and the book
of Jeremiah. For example, the rhetorical question 'how can you say…'
(אֵיךְ תֹּאמְרוּ) in Isa 19:11 is only used elsewhere in the Hebrew Bible
in this condemnatory fashion in Jer 2:23; 8:8; 48:14.[26] The phrase in

---

[24] None of the following textual connections is discussed in Ute Wendel, *Jesaja und
Jeremia: Worte, Motive und Einsichten Jesajas in der Verkündigung Jeremias* (BibTS
25; Neukirchen-Vluyn: Neukirchener-Verlag, 1995).

[25] In addition to general roles (e.g., prophets, officials), Christopher R. Seitz (*Theology in Conflict: Reactions to the Exile in the Book of Jeremiah* [BZAW 176; Berlin: de
Gruyter, 1989], 10–11) counts twenty-nine distinct professional offices in Jer 20–45;
51–52.

[26] The example from Jer 48:14 is applied within an oracle against Moab, which also
denounces its leaders (cf. Isa 16:6–8). Also, it is worth noting that the oracle about

Isa 19:11 is linked particularly with Jer 8:8, since both texts use this rhetorical question to condemn those who claim to be wise. In addition, the term describing the advice of Pharaoh's counselors as 'foolish' (בער) occurs most often in the book of Jeremiah (10:8, 14, 21; 51:17; also Ps 94:8; Ezek 21:36 [31]). Of these, there is very close similarity between the portrayal in Jer 10:7–8 of 'the wisest of the nations' (חַכְמֵי הַגּוֹיִם) as being foolish and the criticism in Isa 19:11 against 'the wisest of Pharaoh's counselors' (חַכְמֵי יֹעֲצֵי פַרְעֹה). The occurrence of בער in Jer 10:21 is similar in some respects, as it denounces the leaders of Judah, who are characterized as shepherds whose flock is scattered because they have failed to consult Yhwh.

The portrayal of the rulers of Memphis as 'deceived' (נשא) in Isa 19:13 is also closely tied to material in Jeremiah.[27] Aside from the serpent's deception of the woman (Gen 3:13) and references to Sennacherib's attack against Hezekiah (2 Kgs 18:29//Isa 36:14//2 Chr 32:15; 2 Kgs 19:10//Isa 37:10), all other occurrences of the word are located in Jeremiah and related passages (Jer 4:10; 29:8; 37:9; 49:16; cf. Obad 3, 7).[28] Some of the texts in Jeremiah also address the matter of deceptive leaders. For example, 29:8 refers to the deception of the people by 'prophets and diviners' in their midst, a theme that was previously noted to be echoed in Isa 28:7; 29:10. In Jer 37:9, the prophet addresses King Zedekiah's messengers, who have deceived themselves into presuming that Pharaoh will be able to rescue Judah from impending destruction. As a final element for comparison, it should be noted that Isa 19:13 represents one of the very few references to the Egyptian city of Memphis (נֹף) outside of the book of Jeremiah (Jer 2:16; 44:1; 46:14, 19; also Ezek 30:13, 16).

In summary, the preceding discussion has posited three main sources of influence for the composition of Isa 19:11–14. Given that 19:11–14 has been set forth as an expansion of verses 1–4, it is not surprising to discover that some of the themes from the earlier section have been extended by way of *Fortschreibung* in verses 11–14. In addition,

---

Moab in Jer 48 provides the only collocation of drunkenness with vomit (48:26) in addition to those already mentioned in Isa 19:11–14; 28:7–8; Jer 25:27.

[27] Several occurrences of נשא in the MT are dubious on account of potential confusion with the more common root נשא ('to raise up'), including Num 21:30; Pss 55:16 (15); 89:23 (22); Jer 23:39. For discussion of the form וְשִׁשֵּׁאתִיךָ in MT Ezek 39:2, see Mitchell Dahood, "Hebrew-Ugaritic Lexicography XI," *Bib* 54 (1973): 365.

[28] Since Obadiah is closely linked with Jer 49, it is likely that the occurrences of נשא in Obad 3, 7 have been borrowed from Jer 49:16.

19:11–14 has borrowed from a selection of specific passages within the collection of הוֹי oracles in Isa 28–31 (28:7–8; 29:9–10; 30:1–5). Finally, the general theme and also some specific expressions of Isa 19:11–14 are distinctly characteristic of portions of the book of Jeremiah.

As an additional observation Isa 19:11–14 and the related influential texts can also be categorized according to their interest in one of two broad themes. First, many of the passages concern the topic of inadequate leadership, most often in reference to Jerusalem. This is illustrated in different ways, such as drunkenness (Isa 28:7–8; 29:9–10) or the folly of those who purport to be wise (Jer 10:7–8). In addition, the critique against leadership is directed toward various groups of influential people, including prophets (Isa 28:7–8; 29:9–10; Jer 23:13, 32; 29:8), priests (Isa 28:7–8), and officials (Jer 25:18–19; cf. 1:18; 2:26; 4:9; 8:1; 26:11).

The second group of texts deals with Egypt in some way. This is the central focus of the verses from Isa 19, of course, as well as 30:1–5. However, most of the texts relating to inept leadership in the previously mentioned group address influential Judeans with no mention of Egypt's leaders. Thus, Isa 19:11–14 represents a convergence of these two broad elements, which are rarely brought together elsewhere (see below). Since 19:11–14 serves as an expansion of an earlier oracle about Egypt, the redactor has apparently drawn from various expressions of critique against Jerusalem to formulate a similar reproof of Pharaoh's officials. In other words, whatever may be said about the leaders of Jerusalem can also be applied in some way to their counterparts in Egypt.

While most of the passages that we have surveyed deal with either inept Judean leadership or Egypt, the occasional convergence of these two themes in Jeremiah suggests a possible background for the composition of Isa 19:11–14. For example, Jer 25:15–29 depicts the cup of wrath that Jeremiah is to give to various nations to drink. At the head of the list, Judah, with its 'kings and officials,' and Pharaoh, with his officials, are directed to drink from the cup. In this example, both Judah and Egypt are linked by virtue of having officials who surround the head of state, while references to the other nations in this text involve only the king.

Similarly, Jer 37:1–10 relates an episode in which the Egyptian army had attacked the Babylonians during the reign of Zedekiah. The king sent two messengers, one of them Zephaniah the priest, to ask Jeremiah whether the outcome would be favorable for Judah, but the prophet replied that Jerusalem would still fall to Babylon. In connection with the same circumstances, 37:11–16 describes direct conflict between court officials and Jeremiah as they accuse him of desertion to the Babylonians. Then, when the king asks Jeremiah for a word from Yhwh in 37:17–21, Jeremiah explicitly condemns Zedekiah's official prophets who had been predicting deliverance from Babylon. Each of these panels in Jer 37 features the prophet at odds with various officers who serve the king.[29]

The combination of the themes of poor leadership and Egypt in Isa 19:11–14 suggests that this section may also reflect Zedekiah's diplomatic relations with Egypt prior to the fall of Jerusalem. The critique in Isa 19:11–14 is clearly directed against Pharaoh and his officials rather than the Judean court, but many of the same elements are used to characterize the advisers of Pharaoh. Moreover, 19:11–14 draws from an earlier reproof of Egypt in 30:1–5, which was probably composed in relation to Hezekiah's foreign policy with Egypt during Sennacherib's siege of Jerusalem in 701 B.C.E. (cf. 31:1–3; 36:6). Undoubtedly, Hezekiah's pursuit of Egyptian aid provides a particularly apt historical parallel to Zedekiah's hopes that Egypt might provide the necessary military force to overcome the sort of Babylonian oppression that is depicted in Jer 37. Although Isa 19:11–14 is directed against Egypt, the message is essentially the same as that in the examples from Jeremiah. While Zedekiah's officials are leading the nation astray by placing their hope in Egypt, their Egyptian counterparts can only offer foolish advice.

4. Isaiah 19:5–10

Despite points of connection in Isa 19 between verses 1–4 and 11–14, the latter section gives no indication of any awareness of the intervening material that now occupies verses 5–10. Furthermore, the portrayal of environmental and economic devastation in 19:5–10 injects a very

---

[29] Christopher R. Seitz ("The Crisis of Interpretation over the Meaning and Purpose of the Exile: A Redactional Study of Jeremiah XXI–XLIII," *VT* 35 [1985]: 86–7) identifies the association between Zedekiah and his officials in rebellion against Jeremiah as a characteristic of a 'Golah-redaction,' which he dates during 597–555 B.C.E.

different perspective, which leads many commentators to suspect that
these verses are a later interpolation.[30]

Many of the linguistic features of 19:5–10 are unique to this section.
Most notably, rather than the usual term מִצְרַיִם, Egypt is identified in
19:6 using the rare term מָצוֹר, which is found elsewhere only at 2 Kgs
19:24//Isa 37:25; Mic 7:12.[31] The absence of מִצְרַיִם in Isa 19:5–10 is
especially striking in light of its occurrence eight times in verses 1–4
and twenty-six times in the entire chapter. This section uses a variety
of terms to focus on Egypt's waterways, but there is no direct reference
to Egypt itself, aside from יְאֹרֵי מָצוֹר ('the streams of Egypt') in 19:6.
Similarly, Yhwh is naturally a central figure in the oracle about Egypt
and some reference to the deity occurs seventeen times in the chapter,
without a single occurrence in verses 5–10.

Another distinguishing characteristic of 19:5–10 is the description
of catastrophic circumstances specific to Egypt, which could indicate
an intimate familiarity with the land and those who are dependent on
it.[32] Many of the terms are uniquely applicable to Egypt, such as the
hapax legomena עָרוֹת ('reed'; 19:7)[33] and שָׂתֹת ('weavers'; 19:10), which
may be influenced by the Egyptian language.[34] Other terms are more

---

[30] Duhm, *Jesaia*, 140–1; Cheyne, *Isaiah*, 110; Marti, *Jesaja*, 155; Gray, *Isaiah*, 325;
Procksch, *Jesaja I*, 246; Kaiser, *Isaiah 13–39*, 99; Vermeylen, *Du prophète Isaïe*, 1:322;
Wildberger, *Isaiah 13–27*, 234–5; Clements, *Isaiah 1–39*, 168; Blenkinsopp, *Isaiah
1–39*, 314–15.

[31] Of these, LXX Mic 7:12 has ἀπὸ Τύρου ('from Tyre'), which indicates that it is
interpreting the form as מָצוֹר. It should be noted that a few scholars do not interpret
מָצוֹר as Egypt. P. J. Calderone ("The Rivers of 'Maṣor,'" *Bib* 42 [1961]: 423–32) proposes an enclitic *mêm* on the construct noun יארי, which results in יארים צור ('chan-
nels of rock'), but maintains the phrase as a reference to the Nile. By contrast, Hayim
Tawil, ("The Historicity of 2 Kings 19:24 [Isaiah 37:25]: The Problem of *Yeʾōrê Maṣôr*,"
JNES 41 [1982]: 195–206) attempts to identify the occurrence in 2 Kgs 19:24 (//Isa
37:25) with Sennacherib's operations at Mount Muṣri in Mesopotamia, but he gives
little consideration to the occurrence in Isa 19:6 within the context of Egypt, except to
note that the usual term for Egypt (מִצְרַיִם) is not used (201 n. 34).

[32] On the environmental impact of the Nile, see Douglas J. Brewer and Renée F.
Friedman, *Fish and Fishing in Ancient Egypt* (NHE 2; Warminster: Aris & Phillips,
1989); Daniel Hillel, *The Natural History of the Bible: An Environmental Exploration of
the Hebrew Scriptures* (New York: Columbia University Press, 2006), 87–117; Douglas
J. Brewer and Emily Teeter, *Egypt and the Egyptians* (2d ed.; Cambridge: Cambridge
University Press, 2007), 17–29.

[33] Joseph Reider ("Etymological Studies in Biblical Hebrew," *VT* 2 [1952], 113–30)
emends the text to וערו תעלי יאור ('and the growths of the Nile will be laid bare'),
which requires the use of a verb derived from Arabic that does not recur in the
Hebrew Bible.

[34] For studies on the influence of Egyptian language and culture on these verses and
on Hebrew more generally, see N. Herz, "Isaiah 19,7," *OLZ* 15 (1912): 496–7; Israel
Eitan, "An Egyptian Loan Word in Is. 19," *JQR* 15 (1925): 419–20; T. W. Thacker, "A

widely recognized as Egyptian loanwords, including יְאוֹר ('stream, the Nile'; 19:6–8) and סוּף ('reed'; 19:6).[35] Because these characteristics are unique to this section of Isa 19, they suggest a perspective that is intimately familiar with the environment, the language, and possibly even the literature of Egypt and its inhabitants.[36] In particular, these verses contain some thematic similarities with the prophecy of Neferti (Neferrohu), given during the reign of the Egyptian king Amen-emhet I (ca. 1990–1960 B.C.E.).[37] Both texts describe the desiccation of rivers with devastating consequences for the environment, the fish, and those whose livelihood is directly dependent on Egypt's waterways.[38]

Despite these distinctive linguistic and thematic features of 19:5–10, this section contains a few similarities with other biblical texts. Among these, Job 14:11 contains a phrase that is identical to the last half of Isa 19:5: וְנָהָר יֶחֱרַב וְיָבֵשׁ ("and the river will waste away and dry up").[39] Due to the lack of historical referents, however, it is difficult to determine the date of either text or the direction of influence.[40] Nevertheless, the occurrence in Job 14:11 is applied universally without any restriction to Egypt, which may suggest influence from Isaiah 19.

Note on עָרוֹת (Is. xix 7)," JTS 34 (1933): 163–5; Yahuda, "Hebrew Words of Egyptian Origin," 85–6; Thomas O. Lambdin, "Egyptian Loan Words in the Old Testament," JAOS 73 (1953): 145–55; Maximilian Ellenbogen, Foreign Words in the Old Testament: Their Origin and Etymology (London: Luzac, 1962), 80; William A. Ward, "The Semitic Biconsonantal Root sp and the Common Origin of Egyptian čwf and Hebrew sûp: 'Marsh(-Plant),'" VT 24 (1974): 339–49; Alviero Niccacci, "Isaiah XVIII–XX from an Egyptological Perspective," VT 48 (1998): 214–38; Yoshiyuki Muchiki, Egyptian Proper Names and Loanwords in North-West Semitic (SBLDS 173; Atlanta: Society of Biblical Literature, 1999), 205–73. Additional discussion of Egyptian influence on Isa 19:5–10 is offered in Sarah Israelit-Groll, "The Egyptian Background to Isaiah 19.18," in Boundaries of the Ancient Near Eastern World: A Tribute to Cyrus H. Gordon (ed. Meir Lubetski, Claire Gottlieb, and Sharon Keller; JSOTSup 273; Sheffield: Sheffield Academic Press, 1998), 300–3.

[35] Wildberger, Isaiah 13–27, 234–5.

[36] Kaiser, Isaiah 13–39, 102–3; Oswald Loretz, "Der ugaritische Topos b'l rkb und die 'Sprache Kanaans' in Jes 19,1–25," UF 19 (1987): 112. Since Shmuel Aḥituv ("Egypt that Isaiah Knew," in Jerusalem Studies in Egyptology [ed. Irene Shirun-Grumach; ÄAT 40; Wiesbaden: Harrassowitz, 1998], 3–7), for example, views these verses as authentic, such knowledge of Egypt is attributed to the prophet Isaiah.

[37] "The Prophecy of Neferti," translated by John A. Wilson (ANET, 444–6); "The Prophecies of Neferti," translated by Nili Shupak (COS 1.45:106–10); "The Prophecies of Neferti" (AEL 1:139–45).

[38] Wildberger, Isaiah 13–27, 244–5; Edda Bresciani, "Oracles d'Égypte et prophéties bibliques," MdB 45 (1986): 44–45; Hilary Marlow, "The Lament over the River Nile—Isaiah xix 5–10 in Its Wider Context," VT 57 (2007): 229–42.

[39] The verbs חרב and יבש are paralleled also in Isa 42:15; 44:27; Jer 51:36; Nah 1:4; cf. Gen 8:13–14.

[40] David J. A. Clines, Job 1–20 (WBC 17; Dallas: Word, 1998), 329–30.

Similarly, Isa 24 refers generally to the devastation of land and the reaction of its inhabitants.[41] The influence of Isa 19:5–10 on this chapter can be detected in its pairing of the verb אבל (I: 'to mourn'; II: 'to dry up') with אמל ('to wither, dry out') in 24:4, 7 (cf. 19:8; 33:9).[42] One widely recognized characteristic of Isa 24–27, and 24:1–20 in particular, is the tendency to apply previous judgment oracles against Israel and other nations more universally to the entire world.[43] This appears to be the case with regard to the dependency of Isa 24 on 19:8–10, since these latter verses describe the despair of those who live and work beside the waterways of Egypt, whereas 24:4 speaks of the condition of the earth (אֶרֶץ) and the whole world (תֵּבֵל).[44] Thus, the direction of influence probably stems from Isa 19, as the scene of devastation in Egypt is reinterpreted to address a broader vision concerning the entire world. Because these occurrences in Isa 24 and Job 14 have probably been influenced by Isa 19, they have little bearing on the formation of the latter chapter.

However, some very close textual links can be identified between Isa 19:5–10 and 2 Kgs 19:21–28 (//Isa 37:22–29).[45] For example, the phrases וְנִשְּׁתוּ־מַיִם ('the waters are dried up') in Isa 19:5 and וְשָׁתִיתִי מָיִם ('I drank waters') in 2 Kgs 19:24 (//Isa 37:25) refer to identical themes using similar-sounding verbs.[46] Moreover, both texts deal with the same topic of environmental catastrophe followed by the despair and shame of the citizens (Isa 19:9–10; 2 Kgs 19:26//Isa 37:27).

The strongest evidence for direct textual influence between Isa 19:5–10 and 2 Kgs 19:21–28 (//Isa 37:22–29) is the use of the rare

[41] Vermeylen, *Du prophète Isaïe*, 1:323.

[42] Donald C. Polaski (*Authorizing an End: The Isaiah Apocalypse and Intertextuality* [BIS 50; Leiden: Brill, 2001], 105 n. 142) acknowledges similar imagery in Isa 19:8–10 and 24:4, but gives no indication of any direct influence between these texts.

[43] J. Todd Hibbard, *Intertextuality in Isaiah 24–27: The Reuse and Evocation of Earlier Texts and Traditions* (FAT 2/16; Tübingen: Mohr Siebeck, 2006), 37. Unfortunately, Hibbard makes no mention of 19:5–10 in his study, nor is this particular intertextual connection surveyed by Marvin A. Sweeney in "Textual Citations in Isaiah 24–27: Toward an Understanding of the Redactional Function of Chapters 24–27 in the Book of Isaiah," *JBL* 107 (1988): 39–52.

[44] תֵּבֵל is nearly always used in the Hebrew Bible within the context of early Jewish expressions of universalism; H.-J. Fabry and N. van Meeteren, "תֵּבֵל," *TDOT* 15:559, 561–2. See also the discussion in Chapter 3, above, of the occurrence of this term in Isa 18:3.

[45] Vermeylen, *Du prophète Isaïe*, 1:322–3.

[46] 2 Kgs 19:24 includes the adjective זָרִים ('*foreign* waters'), which is not in Isa 37:25.

term מָצוֹר to refer to Egypt in both passages. The phrase כֹּל...וְאַחְרִב
יְאֹרֵי מָצוֹר ('I dried up...all the streams of Egypt') in 2 Kgs 19:24
(//Isa 37:25) is nearly identical to וְחָרְבוּ יְאֹרֵי מָצוֹר ('the streams of
Egypt are dried up') in Isa 19:6. In addition to these textual similarities, the redactional insertion of Isa 19:5–10 is very similar to the current placement of 2 Kgs 19:21–28 (//Isa 37:22–29). This latter poem is
widely viewed as a secondary insertion into the surrounding narrative,
with the result that these arrogant claims are attributed to Sennacherib
(2 Kgs 19:20//Isa 37:21).[47] By comparison, the portrayal of devastation
in Isa 19:5–10 is not associated with any specific ruler, but the insertion of these verses following Isa 19:4 produces the effect of linking
the disaster in Egypt with the reign of the 'harsh master' and 'powerful ruler' in that verse. Along these lines, Gray argues for Isa 19:5–10
as a secondary addition by noting that the drying up of the river does
not proceed naturally from the accession of the harsh master in 19:4.[48]
While his observation may be valid, these elements are likewise joined
in 2 Kgs 19 (//Isa 37) so that Sennacherib boasts that his own military
efforts have produced such environmental devastation in Egypt. Thus,
while it may not reflect a natural progression, both passages have been
contrived for the same effect. In summary, since Isa 19:5–10 and 2 Kgs
19:21–28 (//Isa 37:22–29) serve similar redactional purposes, share
much of the same language, and invoke the same imagery of environmental devastation in Egypt, we may conclude that both passages have
been composed and inserted by the same hand.

Finally, there are a few points of correspondence between Isa 19:5–10
and the oracles against Egypt in Ezek 29–32 and especially 30:1–19.
These include the desolation and drying up of the water in Egypt (cf.
Isa 19:5; Ezek 29:9–10, 12; 30:7, 12), specific mention of the rivers in

[47] B. Stade, "Miscellen," *ZAW* 6 (1886): 177–8; Karl Budde, "The Poem in 2 Kings
xix 21–28 (Isaiah xxxvii 22–29)," *JTS* 35 (1934): 307–13; Brevard S. Childs, *Isaiah and
the Assyrian Crisis* (SBT Second Series 3; London: SCM, 1967), 96–7; Kaiser, *Isaiah
13–39*, 376; Francolino J. Gonçalves, *L'Expédition de Sennachérib en Palestine dans
la littérature hébraïque ancienne* (EBib 7; Paris: Gabalda, 1986), 449–51; Mordechai
Cogan and Hayim Tadmor, *II Kings* (AB 11; New York: Doubleday, 1988), 236; Stephen L. McKenzie, *The Trouble with Kings: The Composition of the Book of Kings in
the Deuteronomistic History* (VTSup 42; Leiden: Brill, 1991), 105; Arie van der Kooij,
"The Story of Hezekiah and Sennacherib (2 Kings 18–19): A Sample of Ancient Historiography," in *Past, Present, Future: The Deuteronomistic History and the Prophets*
(ed. Johannes C. de Moor and Harry F. van Rooy; OtSt 44; Leiden: Brill, 2000), 115;
Blenkinsopp, *Isaiah 1–39*, 476.
[48] Gray, *Isaiah*, 325.

Egypt (יְאֹר; Isa 19:6–8; Ezek 29:3–5, 9–10; 30:12), and concern for fish and fishing (דִּיג/דָּגָה; Isa 19:8;[49] Ezek 29:4–5). Especially noteworthy is the close similarity between 'I will make the streams dry' (וְנָתַתִּי יְאֹרִים חָרָבָה) in Ezek 30:12 and 'the streams of Egypt will dry up' (וְחָרְבוּ יְאֹרֵי מָצוֹר) in Isa 19:6. Of course, both of these resonate strongly with the phrase 'I dried up...all the streams of Egypt' (וָאַחְרִב...כֹּל יְאֹרֵי מָצוֹר), which was previously observed in 2 Kgs 19:24 (//Isa 37:25), indicating a close literary relationship among all three texts.

The relationship between Isa 19:5–10 and Ezek 30:1–19 seems to be especially informative. In addition to the close literary ties between these two texts, Ezek 30:1–19 has the distinction of being the only undated oracle about Egypt among those that are collected in the book of Ezekiel (Ezek 29–32). Despite the lack of an explicit date, Ezek 30:1–19 seems to correspond to the same period as 29:17–20, since both portray Nebuchadrezzar as Yhwh's instrument of judgment against Egypt.[50] Moreover, these two units are separated only by a single verse (29:21), which may very well be a later insertion. The oracle at 29:17–20 stands out among the rest because it contains the latest date in Ezekiel (571 B.C.E.), whereas all other dates in this group are associated with the fall of Jerusalem. Thus, it would appear that both 29:17–20 and 30:1–19 reflect the viewpoint that despite their inability to capture Tyre after a lengthy siege, the Babylonians would nonetheless press on toward a successful attack against Egypt.

The relationship between the Egypt oracles of Ezekiel and Isa 19:5–10 will be taken up in greater detail in Chapter 6, below. It may suffice for the present to point out that in addition to the linguistic links between Isa 19:5–10 and Ezek 30:1–19, it may be possible to detect the same expectation of a Babylonian attack against Egypt in Isa 19. As previously observed, the insertion of 19:5–10 following the reference to domination by a harsh master in 19:4 produces the effect of depicting environmental devastation in Egypt as an immediate consequence. In Ezek 30:10–12, this connection is made explicit by the expressed

---

[49] 1QIsa[a] has הדגים rather than MT's הַדַּיָּגִים.

[50] Walther Zimmerli, *Ezekiel 2* (trans. James D. Martin; Hermeneia; Philadelphia: Fortress, 1983), 127–8; Herculaas F. van Rooy, "Ezekiel's Prophecies against Egypt and the Babylonian Exiles," in *Proceedings of the Tenth World Congress of Jewish Studies, Div. A* (Jerusalem: Magnes, 1990), 115–22.

anticipation that the arrival of Nebuchadrezzar in Egypt would result in the drying up of the waterways and the desolation of the land.

On one hand, it has already been noted that Isa 19:5–10 shares several thematic and linguistic connections not only with Ezek 30, but also with the Egypt material that surrounds it. This would indicate that these verses in Isa 19 have been influenced by the material in Ezekiel. On the other hand, Ezek 30:1–19 also reflects the influence of textual material surrounding Isa 19:5–10. For example, Isa 19:1–4 contains two references to idols using the term אֱלִילִים (19:1, 3), which was noted above as a word that is somewhat common in Isaiah, but which is relatively rare elsewhere in the Hebrew Bible. This term occurs only once in the book of Ezekiel, at 30:13, where it refers to idols specifically in the land of Egypt, as is the case with Isa 19. Similar observations could be made regarding rare references to specific Egyptian cities in Isa 19:11–14 and Ezek 30:1–19.[51] Thus, while there are common elements in the Egypt material at Isa 19:5–10 and Ezek 30:1–19, each of these texts seems to be familiar with the material surrounding the other passage. Since both of texts are arguably secondary additions to their current literary settings, it would appear that they were composed by the same hand. As indicated by the reference to 571 B.C.E. at Ezek 29:17, it is possible that the contribution of Isa 19:5–10 occurred around the same time period, when the anticipation of a Babylonian invasion of Egypt was on the near horizon.

5. ISAIAH 19:15

Isaiah 19:15 does not seem to be part of the same compositional unit as verses 11–14.[52] This verse picks up the reference to Egypt's deeds (מַעֲשֶׂה) from 19:14 and extends it by declaring that neither 'head nor tail' will be able to perform (עשׂה) a deed (מַעֲשֶׂה) for Egypt. The phrase 'head and tail, palm and reed' is borrowed directly from Isa 9:13–14 (14–15), where it refers to elders and dignitaries who have

---

[51] For example, Memphis (נֹף) is mentioned in Jer 2:16; 44:1; 46:14, 19, and only also in Isa 19:13; Ezek 30:13, 16. Tanis (צֹעַן) is found in Num 13:22; Ps 78:12, 43; Isa 19:11, 13; 30:4; 33:20; Ezek 30:14.

[52] Procksch, *Jesaja I*, 248; Wildberger, *Isaiah 13–27*, 256–7; Clements, *Isaiah 1–39*, 169.

led the people of Judah astray. The application of the phrase following 19:11–14 extends the critique of those verses against the rulers of Egypt.[53]

The incorporation of the saying in 19:15, with its reference to a palm branch and reed, echoes the description of Egypt's waterside vegetation in verses 5–10, and the hopeless outlook expressed in 19:15 resonates strongly with that section of the chapter.[54] This leads to the conclusion that the addition of 19:15 coincides with the insertion of 19:5–10. Not only would its addition after verses 11–14 round off the extant Egypt oracle at that point in time, it would also serve as an appropriate extension of the theme of failed leadership. Thus, the portrayal of the impotence of Egypt's leaders in 19:15 following 19:11–14 correlates with the depiction of environmental devastation in 19:5–10 as the outcome of Egypt's rule by a harsh master in 19:4.

6. ISAIAH 19:16–17

Some commentators associate Isa 19:16–17 with the first fifteen verses of the chapter on account of its negative portrayal of Egypt, which contrasts sharply with the verses that follow.[55] However, a negative attitude toward Egypt is insufficient in itself to support the compositional unity of 19:1–17. To the contrary, we have already posited that 19:1–15 contains at least three strata of material that speak negatively of Egypt, which are best understood as separate contributions to the book on account of their diverse perspectives and aims. Moreover, the anticipated terrorization of Egypt by the land of Judah in 19:16–17 is significantly different from any other anti-Egypt material in the book of Isaiah.[56] The prophecies against Egypt in 30:1–5; 31:1–3, for example, warn that ill-advised treaties with Egypt will only result in failure

---

[53] Beuken (*Jesaja 13–27*, 190) views 'head and tail, branch and reed' as a merism for the entirety of Upper and Lower Egypt, but the contexts of both Isa 9:13–14 (14–15) and 19:11–14 suggest that societal leaders are more likely in view. Similarly, Mirjam Croughs ("Intertextuality in the Septuagint: The Case of Isaiah 19," *BIOSCS* 34 [2001]: 91–2) interprets the phrase as a metaphor for high and low social strata.

[54] Clements, *Isaiah 1–39*, 169.

[55] Cheyne, *Isaiah*, 99–100; Sweeney, *Isaiah 1–39*, 269–73; Hallvard Hagelia, "A Crescendo of Universalism: An Exegesis of Isa 19:16–25," *SEÅ* 70 (2005): 74–6.

[56] Wildberger *Isaiah 13–27*, 265–6.

for the helper and helped alike (31:3), whereas 19:16–17 depicts Judah in an extraordinary position of dominance over Egypt.

Additional factors in 19:16–17 indicate that this section is probably a later addition to the previous material.[57] These verses appear as the first in a series of five units (19:16–17, 18, 19–22, 23, 24–25), each of which is introduced by the formula בַּיּוֹם הַהוּא ('in that day'), a common indicator of editorial expansion.[58] Also, the prose style of verses 16–25 contrasts with the poetic form of verses 1–15.[59] Furthermore, the theme of Yhwh's 'plan' in 19:16–17 is a subsequent development of earlier material. In 19:3, Yhwh intends to confound the plans of the Egyptians, while 19:11–14 contrasts the foolish plans of Pharaoh's counselors with Yhwh's plans against Egypt. Verses 16–17 still anticipate Yhwh's plan against Egypt as a future reality, but the plan now includes the land of Judah in its execution and instills great fear in the Egyptians,[60] two particular elements that are lacking from previous manifestations of the theme.

Echoes from other biblical texts can also be detected in Isa 19:16–17. The twin themes of Yhwh stretching out his hand and planning a

---

[57] This view is held by Duhm, *Jesaia*, 140; Gray, *Isaiah*, 331; Vermeylen, *Du prophète Isaïe*, 1:323; Wildberger, *Isaiah 13–27*, 263; Clements, *Isaiah 1–39*, 169–70; Christopher R. Seitz, *Isaiah 1–39* (IBC; Louisville: John Knox, 1993), 150–1; Ernst Haag, "'Gesegnet sei mein Volk Ägypten' (Jes 19:25): Ein Zeugnis alttestamentlicher Eschatologie," in *Aspekte spät-ägyptischer Kultur: Festschrift für Erich Winter zum 65. Geburtstag* (ed. Martina Minas and Jürgen Zeidler; AegT 7; Mainz: von Zabern, 1994), 139–41; Blenkinsopp, *Isaiah 1–39*, 317–18; Childs, *Isaiah*, 142. A few commentators maintain that 19:16–25 (along with 19:1–15) is Isaianic, including Kissane, *Isaiah*, 1:211; Seth Erlandsson, *The Burden of Babylon: A Study of Isaiah 13:2–14:23* (ConBOT 4; Lund: Gleerup, 1970), 76–80; John N. Oswalt, *The Book of Isaiah, Chapters 1–39* (NICOT; Grand Rapids: Eerdmans, 1986), 372–81; John H. Hayes and Stuart A. Irvine, *Isaiah, the Eighth-Century Prophet: His Times and His Preaching* (Nashville: Abingdon, 1987), 263. J. J. M. Roberts ("Isaiah's Egyptian and Nubian Oracles," in *Israel's Prophets and Israel's Past: Essays on the Relationship of Prophetic Texts and Israelite History in Honor of John H. Hayes* [ed. Brad E. Kelle and Megan Bishop Moore; LHBOTS 446; London: T. & T. Clark, 2006], 206) dates Isa 19:16–25 to 720 B.C.E., but admits some unspecified elements of later editing.

[58] Simon J. De Vries, *From Old Revelation to New: A Tradition-Historical and Redaction-Critical Study of Temporal Transitions in Prophetic Prediction* (Grand Rapids: Eerdmans, 1995), 38–55, 118, 122–3.

[59] Wildberger, *Isaiah 13–27*, 263.

[60] For the comparison of the frightened Egyptians to women, cf. Jer 50:37; 51:30; Nah 3:13. This subject is discussed in Kevin J. Cathcart, "Treaty-Curses and the Book of Nahum," *CBQ* 35 (1973): 184–5; Cynthia R. Chapman, *The Gendered Language of Warfare in the Israelite-Assyrian Encounter* (HSM 62; Winona Lake, Ind.: Eisenbrauns, 2004), 71–2; Claudia Bergmann, "We Have Seen the Enemy, and He Is Only a 'She': The Portrayal of Warriors as Women," *CBQ* 69 (2007): 651–72.

plan are similarly paralleled in Isa 14:26–27. In addition, the waving
of Yhwh's hand in 11:15 dries up the river to enable the return of
exiles, with explicit reference to the first exodus from Egypt. Despite
such thematic resonance, however, 19:16–17 makes no mention of the
exodus motif and seems unconcerned with the return of exiles.[61]
Instead, the primary interest of 19:16–17 is in a future expectation
of some terrible event against Egypt in the course of the unfolding of
Yhwh's plan.

Although the circumstances of Isa 19:16–17 theoretically could be
applied to any number of historical events,[62] the invasion of Egypt by
the Persian king Cambyses in 525 B.C.E. provides a particularly apt
background.[63] Many details in the record of his campaign by Herodotus are dubious,[64] but there is little doubt about the general fact of
the invasion itself (*Hist.* 3.1–38). Before moving into Egypt, Cambyses
stopped along the coast of Palestine in Acco, where he set up a military
staging area (Strabo, *Geogr.* 16.2.25).[65] From there he advanced swiftly

---

[61] Kaiser (*Isaiah 13–39*, 106) supposes that the writer of Isa 19:16–17 might have
been reminded of the exodus by the drying up of the Nile in 19:5–10 (cf. Zech 10:11;
Exod 14–15; Isa 51:10), but there is no specific indication that the devastation in those
verses is meant to be understood as a reference to the exodus. Jože Krašovec ("Healing
of Egypt Through Judgement and the Creation of a Universal Chosen People [Isa-
iah 19:16–25]," in *Jerusalem Studies in Egyptology* [ed. Irene Shirun-Grumach; ÄAT
40; Wiesbaden: Harrassowitz, 1998], 297–8) also detects echoes of the exodus in Isa
19:16–17.

[62] Otto Kaiser, "Der geknickte Rohrstab: Zum geschichtlichen Hintergrund der
Überlieferung und Weiterbildung der prophetischen Ägyptensprüche im 5. Jahrhundert," in *Wort und Geschichte: Festschrift für Karl Elliger zum 70. Geburtstag* (ed.
Hartmut Gese and Hans Peter Rüger; AOAT 18; Neukirchen-Vluyn: Neukirchener,
1973), 99–106.

[63] Procksch, *Jesaja I*, 254; Wildberger, *Isaiah 13–27*, 267; Clements, *Isaiah 1–39*,
171; Blenkinsopp, *Isaiah 1–39*, 318.

[64] For discussion, see Edwin Yamauchi, "Cambyses in Egypt," in *Go to the Land
I Will Show You: Studies in Honor of Dwight W. Young* (ed. Joseph E. Coleson and
Victor H. Matthews; Winona Lake, Ind.: Eisenbrauns, 1996), 371–92. See also Wil-
helm Spiegelberg, *The Credibility of Herodotus' Account of Egypt in the Light of the
Egyptian Monuments* (trans. Aylward M. Blackman; Oxford: Blackwell, 1927); Erich
Lüddeckens, "Herodot und Ägypten," *ZDMG* 104 (1954): 330–46; Thomas W. Africa,
"Herodotus and Diodorus on Egypt," *JNES* 22 (1963): 254–8; Seth Benardete, *Herodo-
tean Inquiries* (The Hague: Nijhoff, 1969), 32–68; Kimball Armayor, "Did Herodotus
Ever Go to Egypt?," *JARCE* 15 (1978): 59–73; Truesdell S. Brown, "Herodotus' Portrait
of Cambyses," *Historia* 31 (1982): 387–403; Alan B. Lloyd, "Herodotus on Cambyses:
Some Thoughts on Recent Work," in *Achaemenid History III: Method and History* (ed.
Amélie Kuhrt and Heleen Sancisi-Weerdenburg; Leiden: Nederlands Instituut voor
het Nabije Oosten, 1988), 55–66; David Asheri, et al., *A Commentary on Herodotus
Books I–IV* (Oxford: Oxford University Press, 2007), 381–437.

[65] J. Maxwell Miller and John H. Hayes, *A History of Ancient Israel and Judah*
(London: SCM, 1986), 449.

to capture the strategic city of Memphis, after which he encountered little additional resistance from the Egyptians.[66]

One reaction to Cambyses' entry into Egypt is recorded in an inscription from the statue of Udjahorresnet, who was both a priest of the Saite goddess Neith and an Egyptian naval admiral who defected to the Persians.[67] According to Udjahorresnet's testimony, Cambyses restored the temple of Neith to its original service for the goddess,[68] and then prostrated himself before her as previous pharaohs had done.[69] These actions were probably motivated by a desire to portray himself as the legitimate successor to the throne of the Egyptian pharaoh Apries, rather than any genuine interest in the preservation of Egyptian religions or cultures. On the contrary, Cambyses reportedly destroyed a number of cultic centers in Egypt, and is accused of killing a sacred Apis bull.[70] A decree from Cambyses also describes a reduction in the government allotment for local temple offerings.[71] Similarly, a letter from the Jewish community at Elephantine to Bagohi, the Persian governor in Judah, refers to Cambyses destroying several temples in Egypt, although the temple to Yhw was apparently undamaged (*TAD* A4.7//A4.8). In any case, despite Udjahorresnet's favorable assessment of Cambyses, the Persian conquest of Egypt would

---

[66] Yamauchi, "Cambyses in Egypt," 373.

[67] "Statue Inscription of Udjahorresne" (*AEL* 3:36–41); Georges Posener, *La première domination perse en Égypt* (BE 11; Cairo: Imprimerie de l'Institut Français d'Archéologie Orientale, 1936), 1–26, 164–91; Eberhard Otto, *Die biographischen Inschriften der Ägyptischen Spätzeit: Ihre geistesgeschichtliche und literarische Bedeutung* (Leiden: Brill, 1954), 169–73; Alan B. Lloyd, "The Inscription of Udjahorresnet: A Collaborator's Testament," *JEA* 68 (1982): 166–80.

[68] This 'cleansing' of the temple has been compared with Nehemiah's expulsion of Tobiah in Neh 13:8–9. See Joseph Blenkinsopp, "The Mission of Udjahorresnet and Those of Ezra and Nehemiah," *JBL* 106 (1987): 409–21; and responses from Lester L. Grabbe, "What Was Ezra's Mission?," in *Second Temple Studies* (vol. 2 of *Temple Community in the Persian Period*; ed. Tamara C. Eskenazi and Kent H. Richards; JSOTSup 175; Sheffield: JSOT Press, 1994), 286–99; David Janzen, "The 'Mission' of Ezra and the Persian-Period Temple Community," *JBL* 119 (2000): 619–43.

[69] Yamauchi, "Cambyses in Egypt," 374–5.

[70] Yamauchi, "Cambyses in Egypt," 381–7.

[71] Francis Llewellyn Griffith, *Catalogue of the Demotic Papyri in the John Rylands Library, Manchester with Facsimiles and Complete Translations* (3 vols.; Manchester: Manchester University Press, 1909), 3:26–7; Wilhelm Spiegelberg, *Die sogenannte demotische Chronik des Pap. 215 der Bibliothèque Nationale zu Paris; nebst den auf der Rückseite des Papyrus stehenden Texten* (DS 7; Leipzig: J. C. Hinrichs, 1914), 32–3; Lester L. Grabbe, *Yehud: A History of the Persian Province of Judah* (vol. 1 of *A History of the Jews and Judaism in the Second Temple Period*; LSTS 47; London: T. & T. Clark, 2004), 209–14.

not have been welcomed by all Egyptians and certainly could have imposed the kind of fear upon Egypt that Isa 19:16–17 describes.

To be sure, there is no documentary evidence relating to Cambyses' invasion of Egypt and the Jews living in Palestine. However, there can be no doubt that he passed through the region on his way to Egypt and that his presence would have been keenly felt by Judeans as he assembled his troops in Acco. These circumstances correspond nicely with Isa 19:16–17, which anticipates an attack against Egypt and interprets imminent defeat of the Egyptians as the execution of Yhwh's plan against them. It should be noted that Isa 19:17 does not envision Judah attacking Egypt as such, but strictly speaking, it is 'the land of Judah' (אַדְמַת יְהוּדָה) that plays the central role in producing fear among the Egyptians. It is possible, therefore, that this unique expression refers literally to the land of Palestine in service of the Persian empire, as Cambyses used the area to prepare for the invasion. While Judah may never have seriously threatened Egypt, a Jewish onlooker may be emphasizing or even exaggerating in these verses the role of the region as an accessory to the downfall of Egypt.[72]

Admittedly, this interpretation of the historical background of Isa 19:16–17 is somewhat speculative, even if it is not implausible. While certainty about these verses remains elusive, it should be noted that the Persian invasion of Egypt in 525 B.C.E. coincides with our proposed chronology for the formation of the other sections of Isa 19. It has already been posited that 19:1–15 was probably in place by the mid-sixth century B.C.E., so the addition of 19:16–17 shortly thereafter is not at all improbable. Furthermore, there is every reason to expect that the dramatic circumstances of the Persian conquest of Egypt would be reflected in an oracle about that nation in the book of Isaiah.

7. ISAIAH 19:18

With Isaiah 19:18, the outlook toward Egypt takes a distinctly positive turn, which continues through the remainder of the chapter. Whereas 19:16–17 resumes the threatening tone against Egypt and seems to

---

[72] By way of analogy, Herodotus (*Hist.* 3.7–9) reports that Arabic tribes provided water and other assistance to Cambyses, which enabled him to pass through the Sinai desert, and furthermore, that without this help, he never would have made it to Egypt (*Hist.* 3.88).

anticipate Yhwh's plan for the nation in catastrophic terms, 19:18 envisions five cities in Egypt speaking the language of Canaan and swearing allegiance to Yhwh of hosts. In addition to this contrast, the introductory בַּיּוֹם הַהוּא ('in that day') suggests that 19:18 is a subsequent addition to the preceding material.

Some commentators relate the mention of five cities in Egypt in Isa 19:18 to the four localities listed in Jer 44:1.[73] This latter verse lists Migdol, Tahpanhes, Memphis, and Pathros, and the addition of Heliopolis, named in the preceding verse (Jer 43:13), would conveniently round out a list of five Jewish communities in Egypt. However, despite the uncertain reference to Heliopolis (see below) and the sum of five cities in Isa 19:18, there is no evidence for any direct influence between this verse and the verses in Jeremiah. Moreover, Pathros is not actually the name of a city (Jeremiah 44:1 calls it 'the land of Pathros'), but refers to the entire region of Upper Egypt.[74] Furthermore, we may surmise that if Isa 19:18 intended to make reference to five specific cities, it would have listed them, as in Jer 44:1. In fact, however, the cities of Isa 19:18 are unnamed, and the one that is singled out is described only as the 'city of righteousness' (LXX; see discussion below). Rather than making direct reference to the locations in Jeremiah, Isa 19:18 seems to be deliberately ambiguous, giving no indication that five particular cities are in mind.[75]

According to the MT, one of these cities is designated as עִיר הַהֶרֶס ('city of destruction'), a reading that has been followed by the Peshitta, but by few Hebrew manuscripts. Although הֶרֶס ('destruction') occurs nowhere else in the Hebrew Bible as a noun, its meaning could be inferred from the verb הרס, which can mean 'to destroy.' This reading makes little sense in a context that speaks very positively about the allegiance of the five cities to Yhwh of hosts, but it could reflect a later negative reaction against Jewish communities in Egypt.

---

[73] Kaiser, *Isaiah 13–39*, 106–8; Wildberger, *Isaiah 13–27*, 270–1; Clements, *Isaiah 1–39*, 171; Sweeney, *Isaiah 1–39*, 272; Blenkinsopp, *Isaiah 1–39*, 318.

[74] In Isa 11:11, Pathros is listed between Egypt and Cush; David W. Baker and Donald B. Redford, "Pathros," *ABD* 5:178. A similar arrangement can be found in an inscription from Esarhaddon, in *ARAB* 2 §758; "Texts from Hammurabi to the Downfall of the Assyrian Empire," translated by A. Leo Oppenheim (*ANET*, 290). Also, the localities in Jer 44:1 are listed in geographical order, beginning from Migdol in the far north and ending with Pathros in Upper Egypt.

[75] Bezalel Porten, *Archives from Elephantine: The Life of an Ancient Jewish Military Colony* (Berkeley: University of California Press, 1968), 119.

Alternatively, a number of manuscripts, including 1QIsa[a] and 4QIsa[b], have עיר החרס, 'the city of the sun,' which is also reflected in the Vulgate.[76] References in such textual witnesses to Heliopolis (= 'city of the sun') in Isa 19:18 have probably been influenced by Jer 43:13, which mentions the four additional Egyptian communities in the next verse (44:1). Jeremiah 43:13 also refers to the destruction of pillars (מַצְּבוֹת) in Egypt, which corresponds to the pillar (מַצֵּבָה) at the border of Egypt in Isa 19:19. The Targum of Isa 19:18 (קרתא בית שמש דעתידא למחרב; 'the city Beth Shemesh, which will be destroyed') harmonizes the two readings ('city of the sun' and 'city of destruction'), and its use of בֵּית שֶׁמֶשׁ reflects the direct influence of Jer 43:13, which also has בֵּית שֶׁמֶשׁ ('house/temple of the sun'). Despite these points of contact, the reference to the pillar in Isa 19:19 is contained within the next בַּיוֹם הַהוּא section, which is presumably a later addition to the work, so any link with Jer 43:13 on this basis would have come about only after Isa 19:18 had received further expansion.

Even if Jer 43:13 has not influenced the textual tradition, there are additional difficulties with reading a reference to Heliopolis in Isa 19:18. First, Heliopolis is nowhere else described as עיר החרס. Usually, the Hebrew Bible refers to Heliopolis as אוֹן ('On'; Gen 41:45, 50; 46:20; Ezek 30:17),[77] except at Jer 43:13, which has בֵּית שֶׁמֶשׁ. In addition, the reluctance to identify the other cities in Isa 19:18 rules against naming the city of Heliopolis here.[78] Moreover, this verse would make little sense if it were bestowing on the city a name that was already commonly used and recognized in Egypt.[79] The confusion between the

---

[76] This reading is advocated by Wildberger, *Isaiah 13–27*, 262–3; Clements, *Isaiah 1–39*, 171; L. Monsengwo-Pasinya, "Isaïe XIX 16–25 et universalisme dans la LXX," in *Congress Volume: Salamanca, 1983* (ed. J. A. Emerton; VTSup 36; Leiden: Brill, 1985), 201; Dominique Barthélemy, ed., *Critique textuelle de l'Ancien Testament* (3 vols.; OBO 50; Göttingen: Vandenhoeck & Ruprecht, 1982–1986), 2:143–50; Sweeney, *Isaiah 1–39*, 272; Israelit-Groll, "Egyptian Background," 302; Niccacci, "Isaiah XVIII–XX," 221; Blenkinsopp, *Isaiah 1–39*, 318; Childs, *Isaiah*, 144; Beuken, *Jesaja 13–27*, 176–7.

[77] Probably אוֹן in Ezek 30:17 rather than MT אָוֶן; cf. LXX ἡλίου πόλεως.

[78] Gray, *Isaiah*, 334.

[79] J. Glen Taylor, *Yahweh and the Sun: Biblical and Archaeological Evidence for Sun Worship in Ancient Israel* (JSOTSup 111; Sheffield, JSOT Press, 1993), 188. Rather than Heliopolis, Taylor (189) argues for a generic reference to a 'city of the sun' here, which he takes as evidence of solar Yahwism. He dismisses the reading of the LXX ('city of righteousness'), but even if 'city of the sun' were correct, there is no indication that it refers to sun worship in this context. He identifies a parallel in Isa 60:14, in which 'city of Yhwh' specifies Yhwh as the object of worship. However, since there is no other contextual indication that the sun is being worshipped in Isa 19:18, 'city of

textual variants עיר החרס ('city of the sun'; 1QIsaᵃ, 4QIsaᵇ) and עִיר
הַהֶרֶס ('city of destruction'; MT) in Isa 19:18 can easily be attributed
to the similarity of the words. The reference to 'city of the sun,' even if
influenced by Jer 43:13, is probably the earlier of the two readings. The
later reference to the destruction of the city (עִיר הַהֶרֶס) also echoes
Jer 43:13, but as a negative reaction, since Jer 43:13 is concerned with
the destruction of pillars in Egypt (cf. Exod 23:24).

Rather than naming Heliopolis (ἡλίου πόλεως), the LXX version
of Isa 19:18 has πόλις-ασεδεκ, which is a transcription of the Hebrew
עִיר הַצֶּדֶק ('city of righteousness').[80] Because ασεδεκ in LXX Isa 19:18
is a transcription rather than a translation of its Hebrew *Vorlage*, this
provides clear evidence of a Hebrew textual basis for עִיר הַצֶּדֶק, even if
no manuscripts have survived.[81] עִיר הַצֶּדֶק also echoes Isa 1:26, which
calls Jerusalem the city of righteousness. However, by way of comparison, LXX Isa 1:26 has πόλις δικαιοσύνης whereas 19:18 has πόλις-
ασεδεκ, which provides additional confirmation that the reading at
19:18 is a transcription of an actual Hebrew *Vorlage*, rather than a
Greek intertextual echo.

Therefore, עִיר הַצֶּדֶק ('city of righteousness'), as indicated by the
LXX, is the preferred reading for Isa 19:18.[82] In support of this, Gray

---

the sun' would more likely describe a characteristic of the city, rather than the object
of worship (cf. 'city of righteousness' in Isa 1:26).

[80] Aquila and Theodotion have αρες, which could be a transcription of either הרס
or חרס. Codex Sinaiticus has ασεδ, which could be from חֶסֶד ('faithfulness'), or possibly a mistranscription of חרס/הרס.

[81] Gray, *Isaiah*, 335; Arie van der Kooij, *Die alten Textzeugen des Jesajabuches* (OBO
35; Freiburg: Universitätsverlag, 1981), 54; idem, "The Old Greek of Isaiah 19:16–25:
Translation and Interpretation," in *VI Congress of the International Organization for
Septuagint and Cognate Studies, Jerusalem 1986* (ed. by C. E. Cox; SBLSCS 23; Atlanta:
Scholars Press, 1987), 136–37; idem, "'The Servant of the Lord': A Particular Group
of Jews in Egypt According to the Old Greek of Isaiah—Some Comments on LXX
Isa 49,1–6 and Related Passages," in *Studies in the Book of Isaiah: Festschrift Willem
A. M. Beuken* (ed. J. van Ruiten and M. Vervenne; BETL 132; Leuven: Leuven Uni-
versity Press, 1997), 392.

[82] Gray, *Isaiah*, 335; A. van Hoonacker, "Deux passages obscurs dans le chap.
XIX d'Isaïe (versets 11, 18)," *RBén* 36 (1924): 302–6; W. Vogels, "L'Égypte mon
peuple: L'Universalisme d'Is 19,16–25," *Bib* 57 (1976): 501–3; Isac Leo Seeligmann,
The Septuagint Version of Isaiah and Cognate Studies (ed. Robert Hanhart and Hermann Spieckermann; FAT 40; Tübingen: Mohr Siebeck, 2004), 220. John F. A. Sawyer ("'Blessed Be My People Egypt' [Isaiah 19:25]: The Context and Meaning of a
Remarkable Passage," in *A Word in Season: Essays in Honour of William McKane* [ed.
James D. Martin and Philip R. Davies; JSOTSup 42; Sheffield: JSOT Press, 1986], 62–3)
observes that the LXX's reticence to translate עִיר הַצֶּדֶק at Isa 19:18 (cf. Isa 1:26) may
have produced a deliberately cryptic rendering that would have been comprehended

observes that the expression 'to be called' (נֶאֱמַר לְ) identifies a quality of something, rather than merely its name (cf. Isa 1:26; 4:3; 32:5; 62:4).[83] If so, we should not expect the name of a city in Isa 19:18, but rather a descriptive characteristic, such as that which is indicated by 'city of righteousness.'

Because the only other occurrence of עִיר הַצֶּדֶק is at Isa 1:26 in reference to the restored city of Jerusalem, the designation of an Egyptian city as a 'city of righteousness' in 19:18 seems to draw a comparison between the worship of Yhwh among the communities of Egypt and the religion of Jerusalem. Since none of the cities is specifically named, however, the purpose is not to posit any particular Egyptian city as a new 'Jerusalem,' but to refer in general terms to the adherents of Yahwism in Egypt.

Additional elements in verse 18 contribute to the affirmation of the Egyptian centers of Yhwh worship. For example, the five Egyptian cities in Isa 19:18 are said to speak 'the language (or "lip") of Canaan' (שְׂפַת כְּנַעַן). Because of the obscurity of the phrase, some commentators have supposed that this must be a reference to the Hebrew language.[84] This could be supported by the focus on Yhwh worship in this verse, since Hebrew may have continued to be used in certain cultic functions.[85] Alternatively, the phrase could be taken to refer to

---

by readers with knowledge of Hebrew, which may correspond with the 'language of Canaan' in the same verse. In addition, he notes that none of the Greek versions, which would have been sympathetic to Jews in Egypt (cf. the insertion of ἐν Αἰγύπτῳ ['in Egypt'] at 19:25), offers the criticism reflected in the Hebrew variants 'city of the sun/destruction.'

[83] Gray, Isaiah, 334.

[84] Marti, Jesaja, 156; Gray, Isaiah, 334; Kaiser, Isaiah 13–39, 106; Eduard Yechezkel Kutscher, A History of the Hebrew Language (Jerusalem: Magnes, 1982), 71; Loretz, "Der ugaritische Topos b'l rkb," 111; Wildberger, Isaiah 13–27, 270; Hayes and Irvine, Isaiah, 264; Blenkinsopp, Isaiah 1–39, 318; Beuken, Jesaja 13–27, 192.

[85] Wildberger, Isaiah 13–27, 270; Christopher T. Begg, "The Peoples and the Worship of Yahweh in the Book of Isaiah," in Worship and the Hebrew Bible: Essays in Honour of John T. Willis (ed. M. Patrick Graham, Rick R. Marrs, and Steven L. McKenzie; JSOTSup 284; Sheffield: Sheffield Academic Press, 1999), 40–1; Blenkinsopp, Isaiah 1–39, 318. For discussion of Hebrew during the Persian period, see Joseph Naveh, "Hebrew Texts in Aramaic Script in the Persian Period?," BASOR 203 (1971): 27–32; Edward Lipiński, "Géographique linguistique de la Transeuphratène à l'époque achéménide," Transeu 3 (1990): 95–107; Angel Sáenz-Badillos, A History of the Hebrew Language (trans. John Elwolde; Cambridge: Cambridge University Press, 1993), 112–16; André Lemaire, "Ashdodien et judéen à l'époque perse: Ne 13:24," in Immigration and Emigration within the Ancient Near East: Festchrift E. Lipiński (ed. K. van Lerberghe and A. Schoors; OLA 65; Leuven: Peeters, 1995), 153–63; Joseph Naveh and Jonas C. Greenfield, "Hebrew and Aramaic in the Persian Period," CHJ 1:115–29;

Aramaic, which was the *lingua franca* of the Persian period, and was used by the Jewish community of Elephantine for both religious and secular purposes.[86]

Against both of these interpretations, we may suggest that an intentional reference either to Hebrew or to Aramaic would name the language more explicitly, as in other biblical texts (Hebrew: 2 Kgs 18:26, 28//Isa 36:11, 13; Neh 13:24; Aramaic: 2 Kgs 18:26//Isa 36:11; Ezra 4:7; Dan 2:4). Moreover, since שְׂפַת כְּנַעַן is a unique expression, there is no basis on which to assume that any particular language was ever known as 'the language of Canaan.' On the contrary, it would appear that 'the language of Canaan' is deliberately nondescript.[87] This possibility is further supported by the observation that this verse contains similar ambiguity in the nameless five cities of Egypt, one of which is designated only vaguely as a 'city of righteousness.'

We may also observe that the text does not specify the ethnic identity of these people, whether dispersed Judeans or Egyptian converts. The reference to 'the language of Canaan' does little to clarify the matter, since it appears within the context of Yhwh worship. Furthermore, the fact that it is the *cities* in the land of Egypt speaking the language of Canaan serves only to conceal the ethnicity of the speakers. However, the specification of 'the land of Egypt' instead of simply 'Egypt' seems to suggest that Jews living in Egypt, rather than ethnic Egyptian converts, are in view. In any event, the central aim is not to specify the precise location, language, or ethnic background of the people, but to emphasize their worship of Yhwh and the basis of that worship in continuity with the religion of Judah.

William M. Schniedewind, "Aramaic, the Death of Written Hebrew, and Language Shift in the Persian Period," in *Margins of Writing, Origins of Cultures* (ed. Seth L. Sanders; 2d printing; OIS 2; Chicago: The Oriental Institute of the University of Chicago, 2007), 141–51; Ingo Kottsieper, "'And They Did Not Care to Speak Yehudit': On Linguistic Change in Judah during the Late Persian Era," in *Judah and the Judeans in the Fourth Century B.C.E.* (ed. Oded Lipschits, Gary N. Knoppers, and Rainer Albertz; Winona Lake, Ind.: Eisenbrauns, 2007), 95–124. Joachim Schaper ("Hebrew and Its Study in the Persian Period," in *Hebrew Study from Ezra to Ben-Yehuda* [ed. William Horbury; Edinburgh: T. & T. Clark, 1999], 16–17) asserts that the distinction between Hebrew and Aramaic was based on social status rather than literary or cultic function. That is, Aramaic infiltrated Judean society among the upper classes, while Hebrew remained in use among the lower classes for some time.

[86] Porten, *Archives from Elephantine*, 33 n. 27.

[87] Haag, "'Gesegnet sei mein Volk Ägypten,'" 142. See also Israelit-Groll, "Egyptian Background," 300–3.

Another key component in the portrayal of Yahwism in Isa 19:18 is that the five cities will 'swear allegiance to' (נשבע ל) Yhwh of hosts. This expression is often used to describe Israelites or Judeans in worship (Josh 23:7; 2 Chr 15:14; Zeph 1:5), although Isa 45:23 includes all the ends of the earth professing their allegiance to Yhwh. In either case, the phrase involves a deep level of commitment to the worship of Yhwh.[88] In 2 Chr 15:14, for example, the people of Judah swear their allegiance to Yhwh after removing abominations and repairing the altar of Yhwh (2 Chr 15:8), whereas Zeph 1:5 rebukes those who divide their allegiance between Yhwh and Milcom, and Josh 23:7 also warns against swearing allegiance to foreign deities. Therefore, the description of the cities of Egypt swearing allegiance to Yhwh of hosts implies an expression of worship beyond mere 'lip service,' so to speak.

Since the Hebrew Bible says very little about the Jewish communities in Egypt, it is difficult to determine the circumstances leading to the development of this verse.[89] The most relevant text for the matter of Jews living in Egypt is probably Jer 42–44 (cf. 2 Kgs 25:22–26), which speaks rather unfavorably of those who fled to Egypt after the fall of Jerusalem. These chapters of Jeremiah will be addressed in the following paragraphs, but it may suffice for the moment to observe that Isa 19:18 offers a portrayal of the Jews in Egypt that contrasts sharply with Jer 42–44. If anything, this verse seems to have an apologetic tone that seeks to defend the legitimacy of the worship of Yhwh among those who are living in Egypt.

8. ISAIAH 19:19–22

The introduction of Isa 19:19–22 with בַּיּוֹם הַהוּא suggests that this is another discrete addition to the series. Although this section extends the interest in Yhwh worship from the previous verse, the numerous echoes of the exodus from Egypt distinguish this section from verse 18. It would seem that the material relating to the exodus motif has been added to enhance the sentiment expressed in 19:18.

---

[88] Monsengwo-Pasinya, "Isaïe XIX 16–25," 194.
[89] See the survey of Egyptian Judaism in Bezalel Porten, "The Jews in Egypt," *CHJ* 1:372–400.

This section represents the first obvious reference to the exodus in this oracle about Egypt.[90] Thus, the description of people in Egypt crying out (צעק; cf. Exod 8:8; 14:10, 15; Num 20:16; Deut 26:7; Judg 10:11–12; Josh 24:7) from their oppression (לחץ; cf. Exod 3:9; Deut 26:7; Judg 6:9; 10:11–12; 1 Sam 10:18) in Isa 19:20 and pleading (עתר) to Yhwh (Exod 8:4, 5, 24–26; 9:28; 10:17–18; cf. Zeph 3:10) in 19:22 uses language that has been borrowed from the account in the book of Exodus of the plight of the Israelites in Egypt. In response to their cry, Yhwh will send a savior (Isa 19:20; cf. Exod 14:30; Ps 106:21; Hos 13:4) and will rescue them (נצל; cf. Exod 3:8; 6:6; 18:8–10). Another key exodus element is the Egyptians coming to knowledge of Yhwh (Isa 19:21; cf. Exod 5:2; 7:5; 14:4, 18; also Ezek 20:5; 29:6, 9; 30:8, 19, 25–26; 32:15), while both 'striking' (נגף; cf. Exod 7:27; 12:13, 23, 27) and 'healing' (רפא; Exod 15:26; Deut 28:27; 32:39) in 19:22 are also drawn from exodus traditions.[91]

With regard to its relationship to exodus texts, Isa 19:19–22 does not portray a reversal of the exodus from Egypt, nor is it an antitype for the return of exiles from Babylon, as is commonly found in Isa 40–55 (e.g., Isa 40:3–5; 41:17–20; 42:14–16; 43:1–3, 14–21; 48:20–21; 49:8–12; 51:9–10; 52:11–12; 55:12–13; cf. 11:15–16).[92] Instead, the language of oppression and crying out is applied to adherents of Yhwh who remain in Egypt.[93] The plague motif offers a clear example: Yhwh

---

[90] Vogels, "L'Égypte mon peuple," 505–8; Wildberger, *Isaiah 13–27*, 275–8; Clements, *Isaiah 1–39*, 172; Monsengwo-Pasinya, "Isaïe XIX 16–25," 195–6; Blenkinsopp, *Isaiah 1–39*, 319. However, Kaiser (*Isaiah 13–39*, 106) views the drying up of the Nile in 19:5–10 as an explicit exodus reference, and Beuken (*Jesaja 13–27*, 186–7) identifies exodus themes in 19:11–15.

[91] The concept of wounding and healing is expressed variously in the Hebrew Bible (Deut 32:39; Isa 30:26; 53:5; 57:17–18; Hos 6:1; cf. 2 Chr 7:13–14), but unfortunately, this particular example is not given specific attention in Zoltán Kustár, *"Durch seine Wunden sind wir geheilt": Eine Untersuchung zur Metaphorik von Israels Krankheit und Heilung im Jesajabuch* (BWANT 154; Stuttgart: Kohlhammer, 2002).

[92] See Bernhard W. Anderson, "Exodus Typology in Second Isaiah," in *Israel's Prophetic Heritage: Essays in Honor of James Muilenburg* (ed. Bernhard W. Anderson and Walter Harrelson; London: SCM, 1962), 177–95; idem, "Exodus and Covenant in Second Isaiah and Prophetic Tradition," in *Magnalia Dei, The Mighty Acts of God: Essays on the Bible and Archaeology in Memory of G. Ernest Wright* (ed. Frank Moore Cross, Werner E. Lemke, and Patrick D. Miller; Garden City, N.Y.: Doubleday, 1976), 339–60. Hallvard Hagelia (Coram Deo: *Spirituality in the Book of Isaiah, with Particular Attention to Faith in Yahweh* [ConBOT 49; Stockholm: Almqvist & Wiksell, 2001], 187) interprets the exodus motif here as possibly a reference to deliverance from Babylon on the basis of the appearance of the theme in Deutero-Isaiah.

[93] Michael Fishbane, "Torah and Tradition," in *Tradition and Theology in the Old Testament* (ed. D. A. Knight; 2d ed.; TBS; Sheffield: JSOT Press, 1990), 276–8. Similar

will strike in Isa 19:22, not to deliver Israelites out of Egypt as in the exodus, but to bring about the salvation of people within the land of Egypt. As Duane Christensen observes, "The picture presented here is indeed remarkable. Yahweh will one day send a Moses *redivivus* to deliver Egypt from bondage!"[94] While Deutero-Isaiah applies the exodus motif to the return from Babylonian exile, 19:19–22 refers to those who remain in Egypt and seems unconcerned with a return to Jerusalem.

In summary, the exodus motif in Isa 19:19–22 serves to address two main topics. First, these verses seem to presuppose that the people are permanent inhabitants of Egypt. The phrase 'the land of Egypt' (אֶרֶץ מִצְרַיִם) has been picked up from 19:18 and reapplied in verses 19–20 to emphasize the worship of Yhwh within the boundaries of that nation. The establishment of an altar and a pillar in the land further indicates that the worshippers have taken up permanent residence.[95]

The second main emphasis of Isa 19:19–22 is the legitimacy of the worship of Yhwh. This is communicated in a variety of ways, including the altar and pillar, knowing and returning (שׁוב) to Yhwh, and worship with sacrifices, offerings, and vows. The underlying message of this assemblage of religious practices is that the people are engaged in genuine worship of Yhwh, despite their geographic separation from Jerusalem.

These two elements of geography and legitimate worship resonate with 19:18, which speaks of five cities in Egypt swearing allegiance to Yhwh. However, verses 19–22 extend the sentiment by applying the exodus motif to the situation. It seems, therefore, that these verses set out to establish a case for the affirmation of legitimate Yhwh worship among the Jewish communities living in Egypt. On one hand, these verses potentially conflict with biblical texts that emphasize the centrality of worship in Jerusalem. On the other hand, other Jewish cultic centers are known to have existed,[96] including one at Mizpah,[97]

---

ideas are discussed, but without reference to Isa 19:19–22, in Ronald Hendel, "The Exodus in Biblical Memory," *JBL* 120 (2001): 601–22.

[94] Duane L. Christensen, *Prophecy and War in Ancient Israel: Studies in the Oracles against the Nations in Old Testament Prophecy* (Berkeley: BIBAL, 1989), 133.

[95] Wildberger, *Isaiah 13–27*, 274.

[96] Ephraim Stern, "The Religious Revolution in Persian-Period Judah," in *Judah and the Judeans in the Persian Period* (ed. Oded Lipschits and Manfred Oeming; Winona Lake, Ind.: Eisenbrauns, 2006), 199–205; Jill Middlemas, *The Templeless Age: An Introduction to the History, Literature, and Theology of the "Exile"* (Louisville: Westminster John Knox, 2007), 30–34.

[97] Jer 41:5 refers to a 'house of Yhwh' (בֵּית יְהוָה) in association with Mizpah, which

the Samaritan temple on Mount Gerizim,[98] and Egyptian temples at Elephantine[99] and Leontopolis.[100] In addition to these, a fourth-century Aramaic ostracon from Idumea, in southern Palestine, mentions a temple of Yhw (*byt yhw*).[101]

may be supported by recent archaeological analysis; see Jeffrey R. Zorn, "Mizpah: Newly Discovered Stratum Reveals Judah's Other Capital," *BAR* 23/5 (1997): 28–38, 66; Joseph Blenkinsopp, "The Judaean Priesthood during the Neo-Babylonian and Achaemenid Periods: A Hypothetical Reconstruction," *CBQ* 60 (1998): 25–43; Jeffrey R. Zorn, "Tell en-Naṣbeh and the Problem of the Material Culture of the Sixth Century," in *Judah and the Judeans in the Neo-Babylonian Period* (ed. Oded Lipschits and Joseph Blenkinsopp; Winona Lake, Ind.: Eisenbrauns, 2003), 413–47; Joel Weinberg, "Gedaliah, the Son of Ahikam in Mizpah: His Status and Role, Supporters and Opponents," *ZAW* 119 (2007): 356–68. Diana Edelman (*The Origins of the "Second" Temple: Persian Imperial Policy and the Rebuilding of Jerusalem* [BibleWorld; London: Equinox, 2005], 344–8) argues that the Jerusalem temple was rebuilt to replace the Yhwh temple at Mizpah as part of the establishment of a new provincial seat at Jerusalem during the reign of Artaxerxes I, around 440 B.C.E. Regarding the possibility of a similar temple at Bethel, see Joseph Blenkinsopp, "Bethel in the Neo-Babylonian Period," in *Judah and the Judeans in the Neo-Babylonian Period* (ed. Oded Lipschits and Joseph Blenkinsopp; Winona Lake, Ind.: Eisenbrauns, 2003), 93–107.

[98] Josephus's dating (*Ant.* 11.8.4) of the Samaritan temple on Mount Gerizim to the mid-fourth century B.C.E. has often been accepted as generally accurate, but recent archaeological evidence indicates that it was probably built about a century earlier. For discussion of the findings, see József Zsengellér, *Gerizim as Israel: Northern Tradition of the Old Testament and the Early History of the Samaritans* (UTR 38; Utrecht: Faculteit der Godgeleerdheid, Universiteit Utrecht, 1998), 150–8; Ephraim Stern and Yitzhak Magen, "Archaeological Evidence for the First Stage of the Samaritan Temple on Mount Gerizim," *IEJ* 52 (2002): 49–57; Yitzhak Magen, "The Dating of the First Phase of the Samaritan Temple on Mount Gerizim in Light of the Archaeological Evidence," in *Judah and the Judeans in the Fourth Century B.C.E.* (ed. Oded Lipschits, Gary N. Knoppers, and Rainer Albertz; Winona Lake, Ind.: Eisenbrauns, 2007), 157–211.

[99] Reinhard G. Kratz ("The Second Temple of Jeb and of Jerusalem," in *Judah and the Judeans in the Persian Period* [ed. Oded Lipschits and Manfred Oeming; Winona Lake, Ind.: Eisenbrauns, 2006], 247–64) compares the building of the Second Temple in Jerusalem with the reconstruction of the Yhw temple in Elephantine, although there is no record of the actual completion of the second temple at Elephantine; cf. *TAD* A4.7–10. See also the discussion of Elephantine that follows.

[100] Our knowledge about Onias's flight to Egypt and the construction of a temple in Leontopolis is limited to reports by Josephus (*Ant.* 13.3.1–3; *J.W.* 1.1.1; 7.10.2–3). Incidentally, Onias appeals to Isa 19:19 (*Ant.* 13.3.1; *J.W.* 7.10.3) in support of the construction of the temple. For discussion, see M. Delcor, "Le temple d'Onias en Égypte," *RB* 75 (1968): 188–205; Robert Hayward, "The Jewish Temple at Leontopolis: A Reconsideration," *JJS* 33 (1982): 429–43; Gideon Bohak, "CPJ III, 520: The Egyptian Reaction to Onias' Temple," *JSJ* 26 (1995): 32–41; Joseph M. Modrzejewski, *The Jews of Egypt: From Rameses II to Emperor Hadrian* (trans. Robert Cornman; Edinburgh: T. & T. Clark, 1995), 124–33; Erich S. Gruen, "The Origins and Objectives of Onias' Temple," *ScrCl* 16 (1997): 47–70; Jörg Frey, "Temple and Rival Temple: The Cases of Elephantine, Mt. Gerizim, and Leontopolis," in *Gemeinde ohne Tempel = Community without Temple: Zur Substituierung und Transformation des Jerusalemer Tempels und seines Kults im Alten Testament, antiken Judentum und frühen Christentum* (ed. Beate Ego, et al.; WUNT 118; Tübingen: Mohr Siebeck, 1999), 186–94.

[101] André Lemaire, *Collections Moussaïeff, Jeselsohn, Welch et divers* (vol. 2 of

Relatively few biblical texts speak directly to the matter of Jews living and worshipping in Egypt during the exilic and post-exilic periods. The most relevant material can be found in Jer 42–44, which describes Jeremiah's objections against the emigration of Jews to Egypt. According to the biblical accounts, Johanan and other Jewish leaders made plans to flee to Egypt in fear of retaliation from the Babylonians after the assassination of Gedaliah, whom Nebuchadnezzar had appointed over Judah (Jer 41:16–18; cf. 2 Kgs 25:22–26).[102] Jeremiah exhorted them to remain in Judah and serve Babylon, but the people left for Egypt anyway, bringing Jeremiah with them.

In light of the emphasis on worship in Isa 19:19–22, it is noteworthy that much of the Jeremiah material about Jews in Egypt also addresses their worship, but in denunciation of it.[103] In Jer 44 they are condemned for reverting to the idolatry of pre-exilic days (44:9–10, 17–19) and the

---

Nouvelles inscriptions araméennes d'Idumée; Supplément à *Transeuphratène* 9; Paris: Gabalda, 2002), 149–56; idem, "New Aramaic Ostraca from Idumea and Their Historical Interpretation," in *Judah and the Judeans in the Persian Period* (ed. Oded Lipschits and Manfred Oeming; Winona Lake, Ind.: Eisenbrauns, 2006), 416–17.

[102] Although many English translations add that Gedaliah was appointed as 'governor' (e.g., 2 Kgs 25:22; Jer 40:7, NRSV), Miller and Hayes (*A History of Ancient Israel and Judah*, 421–4) argue that Gedaliah's installation as king to replace Zedekiah over the people of Judah may have been suppressed because he was not of the Davidic line. Second Kings 25:22–26 makes no mention of any title, and Jer 41:1, 10 mention an unnamed 'king' in reference to Gedaliah. Compare also the seal from Mizpah (Tell en-Naṣbeh) that reads *ly'znyhw 'bd hmlk* ('belonging to Jaazaniah, servant of the king') with 2 Kgs 25:23 and Jer 40:8, which names Jaazaniah as a commander under Gedaliah; see William F. Badè, "The Seal of Jaazaniah," *ZAW* 51 (1933): 150–6.

[103] Among various proposals, the 'Queen of Heaven' in Jer 7:18; 44:17–19, 25 is often identified with the Canaanite goddess Astarte. Compare Moshe Weinfeld, "The Worship of Molech and of the Queen of Heaven and its Background," *UF* 4 (1972): 133–54; Susan Ackerman, *Under Every Green Tree: Popular Religion in Sixth-Century Judah* (HSM 46; Winona Lake, Ind.: Eisenbrauns, 2001), 5–35; and the surveys in Cornelius Houtman, "Queen of Heaven," *DDD* 678–80; John Day, *Yahweh and the Gods and Goddesses of Canaan* (JSOTSup 265; Sheffield: Sheffield Academic Press, 2000), 144–50. On the role of this expression in Jer 44, see William McKane, "Worship of the Queen of Heaven (Jer 44)," in *"Wer ist wie du, Herr, unter den Göttern?" Studien zur Theologie und Religionsgeschichte Israels für Otto Kaiser zum 70. Geburtstag* (Göttingen: Vandenhoeck & Ruprecht, 1994), 318–24. For discussion of this passage in relation to terracotta figurines, see P. R. S. Moorey, *Idols of the People: Miniature Images of Clay in the Ancient Near East* (Schweich Lectures; Oxford: Oxford University Press, 2003), 47–50. As it happens, the Arameans at Syene, a garrison near Elephantine, had a temple to the Queen of Heaven; see Bezalel Porten, "Settlement of the Jews at Elephantine and the Arameans at Syene," in *Judah and the Judeans in the Neo-Babylonian Period* (ed. Oded Lipschits and Joseph Blenkinsopp; Winona Lake, Ind.: Eisenbrauns, 2003), 451–70; Russell Hobson, "Jeremiah 41 and the Ammonite Alliance," *JHS* 10 (2010): 5–6.

prophet associates their behavior with the fall of Jerusalem (44:2–3). In fact, 44:21–23 explicitly holds the Jews in Egypt culpable for what has happened:

> Because you burned sacrifices and sinned against Yhwh and you did not heed the voice of Yhwh or walk in his instruction, his statutes and his laws, this disaster has happened to you, even today. (44:23)

Many scholars have recognized that the book of Jeremiah contains much of this type of material that resembles the language and theology of the Deuteronomistic History. The complexities of Deuteronomistic redactional activity in Jeremiah have been recently surveyed by Rainer Albertz,[104] who identifies three Deuteronomistic redactions of the book, arguing that all of these were formulated within Palestine, despite the presumed development of the Deuteronomistic History in Babylon.[105] The validity of his proposals need not be evaluated here, except to note that the texts denouncing the flight to Egypt in Jer 42–44 provide some of his strongest evidence in favor of a Judean viewpoint.

References to Judah as 'this land' (Jer 42:10, 13) suggest a Judean perspective,[106] and the urgency to remain in Palestine for the sake of preserving the Judean community there would have been irrelevant to Babylonian exiles.[107] Albertz supposes that the preservation of the dwindling Judean community is the primary impetus for the condemnation of the flight to Egypt in Jer 42:1–43:7; 44,[108] which he attributes

---

[104] Rainer Albertz, *Israel in Exile: The History of the Sixth Century* B.C.E. (trans. David Green; StBL 3; Atlanta: Society of Biblical Literature, 2003), 302–12.

[105] Albertz, *Israel in Exile*, 312–45. For the Judean setting of the Deuteronomistic redactions of Jeremiah, Albertz largely follows Winfried Thiel, *Die deuteronomistische Redaktion von Jeremia 26–45* (WMANT 52; Neukirchen-Vluyn: Neukirchener Verlag, 1981), 113. Those who argue for a Babylonian composition of the Deuteronomistic book of Jeremiah include Ernest W. Nicholson, *Preaching to the Exiles: A Study in the Prose Tradition in the Book of Jeremiah* (Oxford: Blackwell, 1970), 110–11; Seitz, *Theology in Conflict*, 213; Norbert Lohfink, "Gab es eine deuteronomistische Bewegung?" in *Jeremia und die 'Deuteronomistische Bewegung'* (ed. Walter Groß; BBB 98; Weinheim: Beltz Athenäum, 1995), 359; Hermann-Josef Stipp, "Probleme des redaktionsgeschichtlichen Modells der Entstehung des Jeremiabuches," in *Jeremia und die 'Deuteronomistische Bewegung'* (ed. Walter Groß; BBB 98; Weinheim: Betz Athenäum, 1995), 250.

[106] MT Jer 42:12 has 'he will restore (וְהֵשִׁיב) you to your land,' but Albertz (*Israel in Exile*, 324) proposes 'he will cause you to dwell (וְהֹשִׁיב),' in agreement with Aquila, the Peshitta, and the Vulgate. In support of the latter, Jer 42:10 also refers to 'dwelling/remaining' (ישב) in the land.

[107] Albertz, *Israel in Exile*, 323–5.

[108] Albertz, *Israel in Exile*, 336–7.

to the second Deuteronomistic redaction of Jeremiah, carried out in 545–540 B.C.E. (43:8–13 is from the third redaction, in 525–520).[109] While this may have been an actual concern of the Judeans, the text presupposes that the Jews were already living in Egypt (cf. 43:4–7; 44:24, 26), and the condemnation of idolatry in Egypt in Jer 44 suggests that the main issue is wider than simply maintaining a healthy population of Jews in Judah. The fact that 44:22–23 seeks to cast blame for the fall of Jerusalem on the idolatry of the Jews in Egypt may indicate that the Judeans sought to absolve themselves of any lingering culpability, and that the community already living in Egypt served as a convenient scapegoat.

It would be difficult to insist that Isa 19:19–22 responds to Jer 42–44 directly, but the portrayal of worship in these verses is certainly at odds with the message of Jer 44 (cf. Jer 44:26). For example, Jer 44:11–13 pronounces the destruction of those who have opted to live in Egypt, whereas Isa 19:19–22 speaks of a savior who will defend and deliver the oppressed in Egypt. Despite Jeremiah's broad condemnation of those who emigrated, a few texts hold out the possibility for a *golah* to return to Judah (Jer 44:14, 28), while Isa 19:19–22 uses exodus language to describe the deliverance of the people within the boundaries of Egypt, with no particular interest in relocation back to Judah. The permanency of the communities in Egypt in Isa 19:19–22 is underscored by the establishment of cultic centers, while Jer 44:7–8 expresses concern about the people cutting themselves off from the Judeans. In sum, the main emphasis of Jer 44 is the idolatry of those who fled to Egypt, while Isa 19:19–22 describes in considerable detail the devotion to Yhwh of the worshippers in that land. Even if Isa 19:19–22 does not react specifically against Jer 42–44, it provides a very different outlook toward Diaspora Jews in Egypt. These verses are unique in the Hebrew Bible, not only for their positive portrayal of Egypt, but also for their support for the religious devotion of those Jews who were living there.

The description of worship in Isa 19:19–22 also recalls the situation depicted in Josh 22:9–34. In that passage, the Transjordanian tribes built an altar at the border along the Jordan, which rivaled the one at the tabernacle in Israel. When the rest of the Israelites objected, the tribes settling east of the Jordan insisted that their altar was built only

---

[109] Albertz, *Israel in Exile*, 339–45.

as a witness (עֵד) of their fellowship with the other Israelites, rather than for sacrifices or offerings. Joshua 22:9–34 and Isa 19:19–22 are similar in their attention to the matter of Yhwh worship away from a centralized location. Also, the altar in Josh 22 has been erected at the border, while Isa 19:19–20 mentions a pillar at the border and an altar in the midst of Egypt, which serves as a witness (עֵד) to Yhwh.

At the same time, commentators have observed a number of terms in Josh 22 that are thought to be characteristic of Priestly writings.[110] Expressions like נָשִׂיא ('official'; Josh 22:14, 30, 32), עֵדָה ('assembly'; Josh 22:12, 16–18, 20, 30), מָעַל מַעַל ('to act faithlessly'; Josh 22:16, 20, 22, 31), and מָרַד ('to rebel'; Josh 22:16, 18–19, 22, 29) are especially common in texts that are supposedly influenced by P, and Phinehas the priest is a central figure in the story. While some hold to the antiquity of Josh 22:9–34,[111] others propose either that the entire account is a late composition by Priestly writers,[112] or that it is a Priestly reworking of an older narrative.[113] In view of the last suggestion, we may observe that despite the obvious similarities with Josh 22, Isa 19:19–22 is apparently unaware of any of the presumed Priestly elements, since they are absent from these verses. Kloppenborg points to the repeated emphasis on the function of the altar (מִזְבֵּחַ) in Josh 22 for a witness instead of sacrifice, an apparent contradiction in terms, as evidence

---

[110] Julius Wellhausen, *Die Composition des Hexateuchs und der historischen Bücher des Alten Testaments* (3d ed.; Berlin: Georg Reimer, 1899), 132–3; Martin Noth, *Das Buch Josua* (HAT 7; Tübingen: Mohr [Siebeck], 1938), 1:103–5. See the summary of supposed P elements in John S. Kloppenborg, "Joshua 22: The Priestly Editing of an Ancient Tradition," *Bib* 62 (1981): 347–71.

[111] For example, Kurt Möhlenbrink, "Die Landnahmesagen des Buches Josua," *ZAW* 56 (1938): 246–50; Jan Dus, "Der Brauch der Ladewanderung im alten Israel," *TZ* 17 (1961): 15–16; idem, "Die Lösung des Rätsels von Jos. 22," *ArOr* 32 (1964): 529–46.

[112] A. Menes, "Tempel und Synagoge," *ZAW* 50 (1932): 268–76. J. G. Vink ("The Date and Origin of the Priestly Code in the Old Testament," in *The Priestly Code and Seven Other Studies* [ed. P. A. H. de Boer; OtSt 15; Leiden: Brill, 1969], 73–77) proposes that Josh 22 was composed as an etiological explanation for the provision of cultic places for Diaspora Jews outside Jerusalem, and notes potential connection specifically with the community at Elephantine (see discussion below).

[113] For example, Otto Eissfeldt, *Hexateuch-Synopse: Die Erzählung der fünf Bücher Mose und des Buches Josua mit dem Anfange des Richterbuches* (Leipzig: Hinrichs, 1922), 79; J. Alberto Soggin, *Joshua* (trans. R. A. Wilson; OTL; London: SCM, 1972), 212–15; Kloppenborg, "Joshua 22," 347–71; Robert G. Boling, *Joshua* (AB 6; Garden City, N.Y.: Doubleday, 1982), 510. While Elie Assis ("The Position and Function of Jos 22 in the Book of Joshua," *ZAW* 116 [2004]: 528–41) observes both Deuteronomistic and Priestly influences on Josh 22, he is mainly concerned to demonstrate its literary coherence within the book.

that a Priestly editor has sought to eliminate various cultic impurities from the original account.[114] In this regard, however, we may observe that Isa 19:21 specifically mentions making sacrifices (זֶבַח) in addition to other offerings at the Egypt altar. Thus, while the altar and pillar of Isa 19:19–22 may clash with the Deuteronomistic prohibition,[115] this passage seems to impinge on Priestly sentiments as well.[116] In any event, the account in Josh 22 provides something of a paradigm for faithful Yahwists living beyond the boundaries of the main community.

Similarly, although there is no solid basis for linking these verses directly with the Elephantine community, the known evidence about Jewish life in that colony provides a historical analogy to Isa 19:19–22. If we are correct in relating 19:16–17 to Cambyses' invasion of Egypt in 525 B.C.E., the chronological position of 19:19–22 shortly thereafter would correspond to the fifth-century documents from this community. It is not known precisely when Jews first settled in Elephantine, but the migration may have been due to the movement of Jewish mercenaries and the establishment of a military colony on the southern border of Egypt, possibly as early as the seventh century B.C.E.[117] The *Letter of Aristeas* describes Judean soldiers assisting Egypt in military conflict against Ethiopia (*Let. Aris.* 13),[118] and the Elephantine texts

---

[114] Kloppenborg, "Joshua 22," 364.

[115] It is difficult to determine the precise relationship between the altar and pillar in Isa 19:19 and the Deuteronomic prohibition of these (cf. Exod 34:13; Lev 26:1; Deut 7:5; 12:3; 16:21–22; 2 Kgs 23:14–15; 2 Chr 14:2; 31:1; Jer 43:13; Hos 10:1–2). The ban can be understood to refer to the presence of a *single* altar in a particular location (Cheyne, *Isaiah*, 101–2; cf. Mal 1:11), or it could be viewed as applicable only within the limits of Judah (Blenkinsopp, *Isaiah 1–39*, 319). See also E. Stockton, "Sacred Pillars in the Bible," *ABR* 20 (1972): 16–32; Tryggve N. D. Mettinger, *No Graven Image?: Israelite Aniconism in Its Ancient Near Eastern Context* (ConBOT 42; Stockholm: Almqvist & Wiksell, 1995), 140–68.

[116] Since there is no evidence of Priestly influence in Isa 19:19–22, we cannot be certain that these verses take direct issue with a Priestly redaction of Josh 22. Alternatively, Isa 19:19–22 and the Priestly redaction of Josh 22:9–34 could represent two distinct interpretations of an earlier narrative.

[117] Bezalel Porten, "Settlement of the Jews," 457–61.

[118] *Aristeas* does not specify whether Psammetichus I (664–610) or II (595–589) is intended, and conflict with Nubia occurred during both reigns. Porten ("Settlement of the Jews," 459–61) argues for the former, but the latter may be more likely, considering the protests in Jeremiah (27:1–22; 37:1–10) and Ezekiel (17:1–21; cf. 8:17) against the military alliances of Zedekiah (597–586) with Egypt (see Abraham Malamat, "The Twilight of Judah: In the Egyptian-Babylonian Maelstrom," in *History of Biblical Israel: Major Problems and Minor Issues* [CHANE 7; Leiden: Brill, 2001], 299–321; repr. from VTSup 28 [1975]: 123–45). There is no reason to suppose that Judeans could not have settled in Egypt as early as the mid-seventh century, but at

imply that the community existed prior to the arrival of Cambyses in Egypt in 525 B.C.E.[119]

Although the description of Yhwh worship in Isa 19:19–22 could be interpreted merely as a utopian hope for the religion of Jews in Egypt, several points of contact can be identified with the Jewish community in Elephantine.[120] The mention of an altar and pillar to Yhwh in Isa 19:19 suggests a cultic site in Egypt, and letters from Elephantine are clear that there was a temple to Yhw, in addition to evidence of religious syncretism.[121] According to the Aramaic documents, the Yhw temple was destroyed in 410 B.C.E. by the priests of the neighboring Chnum temple (*TAD* A4.7–8), but the Yhw priests subsequently requested permission from Bagohi, the governor of Judah, to rebuild the temple (*TAD* A4.5; A4.7–8), which appears to have been granted (*TAD* A4.9–10).[122] In addition to the temple structure, the texts describe various types of offerings (*TAD* A4.7:19–21; A4.8:18–21)[123] and celebration of the Passover meal (*TAD* A4.1; cf. D7.6; D7.24). The latter element could indicate that the Jews in Elephantine were aware of the account of the exodus from Egypt, which, as we have observed, is a central theme of Isa 19:19–22.[124]

Despite any temptation to draw a direct line of connection between Isa 19:19–22 and the Elephantine community, there is insufficient

---

the same time, there is no evidence that the comments in the *Letter of Aristeas* refer specifically to the establishment of Elephantine, as Porten infers. E. C. B. MacLaurin ("Date of the Foundation of the Jewish Colony at Elephantine," *JNES* 27 [1968]: 89–96) suggests that the Elephantine colony was founded by Hebrews who were left behind from the time of the exodus. On the Jewish presence in Egypt, see also Edda Bresciani, "La sixième satrapie: L'Égypte perse et ses sémites," in *Le livre de traverse: De l'exégèse biblique à l'anthropologie* (ed. Olivier Abel and Françoise Smyth; Paris: Cerf, 2002), 87–99.

[119] *TAD* A4.7 (//A4.8) claims that Cambyses overthrew all of the temples of the deities of Egypt except the Yhw temple at Elephantine. Although probably an exaggeration, the statement at least serves to place the Jewish community in Elephantine prior to the invasion of Cambyses.

[120] Porten, "The Jews in Egypt," 1:372–400.

[121] Other deities mentioned at Elephantine include Eshem-Bethel and Anat Bethel (*TAD* C3.15.127–8), and Anat-Yhw (*TAD* B7.3.3). See Karel van der Toorn, "Anat-Yahu, Some Other Deities, and the Jews of Elephantine," *Numen* 39 (1992): 80–101; Grabbe, *Yehud*, 241–2.

[122] Without any extant Elephantine documents following the end of the fifth century B.C.E., no record is ever given of the actual reconstruction of the temple.

[123] *TAD* A4.7:28; A4.8:27 mention animal sacrifices (דבחן), but not specifically that they were ever offered at Elephantine.

[124] See Erich S. Gruen, *Heritage and Hellenism: The Reinvention of Jewish Tradition* (HCS 30; Berkeley: University of California Press, 1998), 60–64.

evidence to support it. Furthermore, our interpretation of these verses has argued against a reference to any particular community of Jews. Nonetheless, the texts from Elephantine bear witness of an actual Jewish community in the fifth century that corresponds with the themes of Isa 19:19–22.

9. Isaiah 19:23

The fourth בַּיּוֹם הַהוּא section describes a highway (מְסִלָּה) between Egypt and Assyria, which enables bi-directional travel and joint worship between these two nations.[125] This verse can be identified as a later addition to the previous section because it continues the interest in worship in Egypt, but is less concerned with the practices of worship and the community within the setting of Egypt, and instead depicts movement on an international scale.

Although Assyria is named four times, this is the first specific mention of that nation within the entire oracle about Egypt. According to our redactional chronology, however, the verse would not have been added to the book until several centuries after the fall of the Assyrian empire.[126] Because of this anachronism, various proposals have been offered to explain the references to Egypt and Assyria here and in the following verses.

First, some would view Egypt and Assyria as representations of the two main centers of exile.[127] The מְסִלָּה ('highway') is featured in Isa 40–55 as a way for the return of exiles (Isa 40:3; 49:11; cf. Jer 31:21), and the term appears specifically within the context of gathering exiles in Isa 11:16, which also includes exodus language (cf. Isa 27:13; Zech 10:10). The main difficulty with this view, however, is that unlike these examples, there is no mention of a return, a central locus of assembly, or any other indication that exiles are being described in Isa 19:23.

---

[125] The Hebrew clause וְעָבְדוּ מִצְרַיִם אֶת־אַשּׁוּר could be interpreted to mean 'Egyptians will serve Assyria' as advocated by Marvin Sweeney (*Isaiah 1–39*, 274) and Stephanie Dalley ("Recent Evidence from Assyrian Sources for Judaean History from Uzziah to Manasseh," *JSOT* 28 [2004]: 389). Given the context of worship in the previous verses, however, it is more likely that עבד refers to worship rather than servitude.

[126] Nonetheless, Dalley ("Evidence from Assyrian Sources," 389, 398) assumes that Isa 19:23–25 was composed in the eighth century B.C.E. by Isaiah ben Amoz.

[127] Marti, *Jesaja*, 158; Seitz, *Isaiah 1–39*, 151; Blenkinsopp, *Isaiah 1–39*, 319.

Furthermore, it would make little sense to introduce Assyria here for the first time in the oracle if the expression were intended to describe the Babylonian exile. With no previous reference to Assyria, a reference to the Babylonian exile would more naturally name Babylon.

A similar proposal has suggested that rather than speaking about exiles, Egypt and Assyria reflect an expectation of the entire world gathering together to worship Yhwh.[128] This view interprets the verse in correspondence with such passages as Isa 2:2–4 (//Mic 4:1–3), in which distant nations of the world assemble in Jerusalem. Unlike such obvious examples, however, Isa 19:23 makes no mention of Jerusalem as a central meeting place, either for exiles (cf. 27:13) or for foreign nations (cf. 2:2–4). On the contrary, the description of each nation entering into the other suggests a mutual interchange that is rather distinct from either the repatriation of exiles or the gathering of nations in Zion.

Alternatively, many commentators have suggested that 'Egypt' and 'Assyria' in Isa 19:23 are ciphers for the Ptolemaic and Seleucid kingdoms, respectively.[129] Under these circumstances, the verse expresses a hope for unity of worship, if not also political harmony between the divided empires. The main critique against this position is that it would require a date of composition no earlier than the third century B.C.E.[130] This is admittedly late, especially when compared with some portions of the book of Isaiah. Nevertheless, the inclusion of 19:23–25 in 1QIsaᵃ, which may be dated as early as 150–125 B.C.E.,[131] allows for

---

[128] Hagelia, "A Crescendo of Universalism," 84–5; Childs, *Isaiah*, 144–5.

[129] Duhm, *Jesaia*, 146–7; Cheyne, *Isaiah*, 107; Marti, *Jesaja*, 158–9; Gray, *Isaiah*, 341; Procksch, *Jesaja I*, 253–4; Kaiser, *Isaiah 13–39*, 109–10; Vermeylen, *Du prophète Isaïe*, 1:324; Clements, *Isaiah 1–39*, 172; G. I. Davies, "The Destiny of the Nations in the Book of Isaiah," in *The Book of Isaiah—Le livre de Isaïe: Les oracles et leurs relecture. Unité et complexité de l'ouvrage* (ed. Jacques Vermeylen; BETL 81; Leuven: Peeters, 1989), 98. Blenkinsopp (*Isaiah 1–39*, 319) proposes that 'Egypt' and 'Assyria' should be understood to refer to Diaspora localities as well as the Ptolemaic and Seleucid Empires. In addition, Kustár ('*Durch seine Wunden sind wir geheilt,*' 25) dates all of 19:18–25 to this period.

[130] Wildberger, *Isaiah 13–27*, 279.

[131] Emanuel Tov, "The Text of Isaiah at Qumran," in *Writing and Reading the Scroll of Isaiah* (ed. Craig C. Broyles and Craig A. Evans; 2 vols; VTSup 70/2; Leiden: Brill, 1997), 494; following Frank Moore Cross, *The Ancient Library of Qumran* (3d ed.; Sheffield: Sheffield Academic Press, 1995), 176; cf. Solomon A. Birnbaum, "The Dates of the Cave Scrolls," *BASOR* 115 (1949): 20–22; Frank Moore Cross, "The Development of the Jewish Scripts," in *The Bible and the Ancient Near East: Essays in Honor of William Foxwell Albright* (ed. G. Ernest Wright; London: Routledge & Kegan Paul, 1961), 135–6.

an interval of at least a century after the time of composition.[132] Furthermore, this period correlates with the relative chronology that we
have proposed for the development of this chapter. This interpretation
views the anachronistic mention of Assyria as a metaphorical reference to an actual geopolitical entity, which seems to be warranted by
the international travel on the מְסִלָּה and the emphasis on the land
of Egypt in the earlier sections of the oracle. In any event, the image
of harmony between Egypt and Assyria without any reference to the
centrality of Jerusalem is unlike any other passage in Isaiah, if not the
entire Hebrew Bible. In that case, 19:23, along with the verses that
follow, may very well reflect a relatively late development in the book
of Isaiah.

Despite this possible historical setting, it cannot be determined
whether this verse describes specific circumstances or a general eschatological hope for the future. Either way, this verse builds on the
previous description of worship in Egypt to add a wider-reaching perspective. If the kingdoms of the Ptolemies and Seleucids are in view,
verse 23 envisions peaceful relations among adherents of Yhwh from
both groups.

10. Isaiah 19:24–25

The final בַּיּוֹם הַהוּא section of Isa 19 expresses sentiments similar
to the previous verse and is probably an expansion of it. Along with
Egypt and Assyria, these verses incorporate Israel as a 'third,' and contain the only reference specifically to Israel in the entire Egypt oracle
(cf. 'the land of Judah' in 19:17). The mention of Israel as a third is
probably not meant to indicate its ranking in subordination to Egypt
and Assyria, since these verses also refer to Israel as a blessing in the
midst of the earth and Yhwh's heritage (cf. Deut 4:20; 9:26, 29; 1 Kgs
8:51, 53; Pss 28:9; 94:5; Mic 7:14). Rather, if verses 24–25 are an expansion of the previous verse, the designation may refer simply to the
added mention of Israel as the third in the group, proceeding from the
foregoing discussion of Egypt and Assyria. Since no specific mention
of Israel has been made until this point, it would appear that 19:24–25

---

[132] The same might be said regarding the LXX and Targum Pseudo-Jonathan; see
Blenkinsopp, *Isaiah 1–39*, 77–8.

has been supplied to ensure that Israel is assigned a role in the anticipated scheme of Yhwh's activity in the world.

These final verses of Isa 19 offer an extraordinary portrayal of Egypt and Assyria, two nations that are elsewhere epitomized in the role of harsh treatment of Israel (e.g., Isa 7:18; 10:24; 52:4; Jer 2:36; Hos 11:5; Zech 10:11). In verses 24–25 Egypt is called 'my people' (e.g., Lev 26:12; Jer 7:23; 11:4; Ezek 36:28; Hos 2:25 [23]), and Assyria is known as 'the work of my hands' (Isa 29:23; 60:21; 64:7 [8]; cf. Jonah 4:10–11), both of which are expressions otherwise reserved for Israel.[133] Therefore, on one hand, this section imparts unparalleled status on Egypt and Assyria, while on the other hand, it designates Israel as a catalyst for the transformation of these nations.

Despite the blessing for Egypt and Assyria and the focus on Egypt until this point of the oracle, it is clear that the main emphasis in this concluding section is on the future of Israel among the nations.[134] In particular, Israel's role as a blessing in the midst of the earth echoes the

---

[133] The LXX (εὐλογημένος ὁ λαός μου ὁ ἐν Αἰγύπτῳ καὶ ὁ ἐν Ἀσσυρίοις; "blessed be my people in Egypt and among Assyrians") and the Targum (בריך עמי דאפיקית ממצרים; "blessed be my people whom I have brought forth from Egypt") both reflect reactions to the difficulty of the implications posed by MT 19:25. For discussion of the LXX, see Wildberger, *Isaiah 13–27*, 263; van der Kooij, "The Old Greek of Isaiah 19:16–25," 150–56; idem, "'The Servant of the Lord,'" 391–2; Seeligmann, *The Septuagint Version of Isaiah*, 288; and for the Targum, see J. F. Stenning, *The Targum of Isaiah* (Oxford: Clarendon, 1949): 62–65; Bruce D. Chilton, *The Isaiah Targum* (ArBib 11; Edinburgh: T. & T. Clark, 1987), 39.

[134] For discussion, see André Feuillet, "Un sommet religieux de l'Ancient Testament: L'oracle d'Isaïe XIX (vv. 16–25) sur la conversion d'Égypte," *RSR* 39 (1951): 65–87; Josef Scharbert, "Fluchen und Segnen im Alten Testament," *Bib* 39 (1958): 25; Josef Schreiner, "Segen für die Völker in der Verheißung an die Väter," *BZ* 6 (1962): 20–26; J. Muilenburg, "Abraham and the Nations: Blessing and World History," *Int* 19 (1965): 396; Alfons Deissler, "Der Volk und Land überschreitende Gottesbund der Endzeit nach Jes 19,16–25," in *Zion: Ort der Begegnung: Festschrift für Laurentius Klein zur Vollendung des 65. Lebensjahres* (ed. Ferdinand Hahn, Frank-Lothar Hossfeld, Hans Jorissen, and Angelika Neuwirth; BBB 90; Bodenheim: Athenäum Hain Hanstein, 1993), 7–18; Matthias Köckert, "Die Erwählung Israels und das Ziel der Wege Gottes im Jesajabuch," in *"Wer ist wie du, Herr, unter den Göttern?" Studien zur Theologie und Religionsgeschichte Israels für Otto Kaiser zum 70. Geburtstag* (Göttingen: Vandenhoeck & Ruprecht, 1994), 277–300; Begg, "The Peoples and the Worship of Yahweh," 42; Franz Sedlmeier, "Israel—'Ein Segen inmitten der Erde': Das JHWH-Volk in der Spannung zwischen radikalem Dialog und Identitätsverlust nach Jes 19,16–25," in *Steht nicht geschrieben? Studien zur Bibel und ihrer Wirkungsgeschichte: Festschrift für Georg Schmuttermayr* (ed. Johannes Frühwald-König, Ferdinand R. Prostmeier, and Reinhold Zwick; Regensburg: Verlag Friedrich Pustet, 2001), 89–108; Keith N. Grüneberg, *Abraham, Blessing and the Nations: A Philological and Exegetical Study of Genesis 12:3 in its Narrative Context* (BZAW 332; Berlin: de Gruyter, 2003), 120.

Abrahamic promise of Gen 12:2–3 (cf. Gen 18:18; 22:18; 26:4; 28:14; Ps 47:10 [9]; Zech 2:15 [11]; 8:13).[135] That Israel is to be such a blessing places these verses in line with the promise to Abraham, and the choice of Egypt and Assyria to represent 'all the families of the earth' (Gen 12:3) may be based on their past reputation as Israel's greatest historical enemies. As Hans Walter Wolff remarks,

> In this reinterpretation the brutal empire, Assyria, together with the old oppressor, Egypt, is drawn into a triple alliance for the first time, with the people of blessing, Israel, in the middle.[136]

Since the depiction of Israel as a blessing for other nations seems to express a future hope, it is difficult to determine the precise circumstances under which 19:24–25 might have been composed. These final verses of Isa 19 are unique, not as much for their inclusion of foreign nations in the worship of Yhwh, as much as for their development of that theme beyond previous expressions. Several other passages in Isaiah seem to envision the conversion of foreign people (e.g., Isa 2:2–4; 45:20–23),[137] and many describe either the humiliation and subjection of foreign nations to Israel (cf. Isa 14:1–2; 45:14, 16–17; 49:22–23; 61:5–6) or the centrality of Jerusalem in attracting foreign nations (cf. Isa 2:2–3; 27:13; 56:6–8; 66:20).[138] Isaiah 19:24–25 seems to represent a reinterpretation of prior interest in foreign nations, such as that described in 60:21, in which Yhwh's people are also associated with 'the work of my hands' (cf. Isa 64:8).[139] By way of contrast with such other texts, however, in the course of the development toward 19:24–25, Jerusalem is assigned no role in the conversion of the nations, Israel is not given pride of place over foreign nations, and foreigners are no longer relegated to serving Israel.

---

[135] Duhm, *Jesaia*, 147; Gray, *Isaiah*, 341; A. S. Herbert, *The Book of the Prophet Isaiah 1–39* (CBC; Cambridge: Cambridge University Press, 1973), 124; Vogels, "L'Égypte mon peuple," 511; Monsengwo-Pasinya, "Isaïe XIX 16–25," 197; John D. W. Watts, *Isaiah 1–33* (rev. ed.; WBC 24; Nashville: Thomas Nelson, 2005), 317; Beuken, *Jesaja 13–27*, 199–203.

[136] Hans Walter Wolff, "The Kerygma of the Yahwist," *Int* 20 (1966): 156.

[137] Joseph Blenkinsopp ("Second Isaiah: Prophet of Universalism," *JSOT* 41 [1988]: 86) perceives Isa 44:3–5 as a reinterpretation of Gen 12:1–3 in a different direction.

[138] Kaiser, *Isaiah 13–39*, 110–12; Jacques Vermeylen, "L'Unité du livre d'Isaïe," in *The Book of Isaiah—Le livre de Isaïe: Les oracles et leurs relecture. Unité et complexité de l'ouvrage* (ed. Jacques Vermeylen; BETL 81; Leuven: Peeters, 1989), 51; Seitz, *Isaiah 1–39*, 151–2.

[139] Davies, "The Destiny of the Nations," 99.

11. Conclusion

The preceding survey has posited that the current shape of Isa 19 has been developed in a process spanning as many as five centuries. While concern for Egypt runs throughout, the most remarkable aspect may be the wide range of attitudes toward Egypt represented in this chapter. While the initial elements describe the downfall of Egypt, the latest additions speak of its salvation and refer to the nation as 'my people.' As we have seen, each contribution has served not only to bring new meaning to the oracle about Egypt, but also to reinterpret pre-existing material in response to changing circumstances.

Finally, a few comments should be made about the relationship of Isa 19 to the surrounding chapters. Our earlier discussion in Chapter 2 regarding the formation of the nations oracles in Isa 13–23 proposed that the original form of the Egypt oracle (19:1–4) was a component of the initial collection of four oracles. The survey of the formation of Isa 18–20 in Chapter 6, below, will show that the material in Isa 18 and 20 has been added around the centerpiece of the Egypt oracle, and that the first two expansions of this oracle (19:11–14 and 19:5–10, 15) are connected with the broader shaping of Isa 18–20. Thus, the remaining verses relating to Egypt, namely, the five 'in that day' sections in 19:16–25, have been added after the basic formation of the Cush/Egypt grouping in 18–20. In this light, however, we may note that none of these subsequent additions in 19:16–25 makes any mention of Cush. While additions within the Cush oracle (18:3, 7; see Chapter 3, above) demonstrate ongoing interest in Cush during the late- and post-exilic periods, the absence of any reference to Cush in the latter part of Isa 19 may be due to the interpretation of the oracle in reference to the Jewish communities living in Egypt. In this way, Egypt in the latter portions of Isa 19 no longer represents a foreign nation, but identifies members of the Jewish community who are geographically separated from Palestine.

CHAPTER FIVE

THE REDACTIONAL FORMATION OF ISAIAH 20

1. Introduction

The narrative about the prophet Isaiah in Isa 20 is unique within the collection of nations oracles in 13–23. Not only is it among the few passages in this section that lack a מַשָּׂא superscription (cf. 14:24–27; 17:12–14; 18:1–7), it is also the only narrative about Isaiah in this group, and as such, bears some initial resemblance to Isa 7; 36–39. At the same time, the thematic interest in both Cush and Egypt in Isa 20 would seem to indicate that its current placement in relation to the oracles about these nations in Isa 18–19 is deliberate.

The present chapter will consider the internal formation of Isa 20:1–6, while the subject of its location following the oracles about Cush and Egypt will be treated more fully in Chapter 6, below. This chapter will posit the development of Isa 20 in two stages, involving three main units of material. The first stage involves joining together a pre-existing narrative in verses 1–4 with the composition of verse 5, while verse 6 represents a second stage of expansion. In the following paragraphs, each of these literary pieces (verses 1–4, 5, 6) will be examined separately with particular interest in the influences that have led to their development.

2. Isaiah 20:1–4

In the narrative that occupies Isa 20:1–4, the prophet Isaiah walks naked and barefoot for three years to demonstrate his expectation of the manner in which Egypt and Cush would be led into captivity by the Assyrian army. Since it is explicitly set in the eighth century B.C.E., many commentators have assumed that except for a few possible glosses, the narrative originated either from Isaiah himself or possibly from a close disciple, given the third-person style.[1] Despite this

---

[1] Bernhard Duhm, *Das Buch Jesaia* (4th ed.; HKAT; Göttingen: Vandenhoeck

eighth-century setting, however, the language of the narrative is distinctive of the Deuteronomistic History (see below). This would suggest that neither Isaiah ben Amoz nor his immediate successors composed these verses, but that they stem from a period possibly more than a century after his lifetime.[2] After a brief survey of historical matters, we may then turn to this question of the literary characteristics of verses 1–4.

Isaiah 20:1 explicitly links the prophet's actions with the Ashdod rebellion against Assyria in 711 B.C.E., an event that has also been recorded from the Assyrian perspective.[3] In the years preceding 711,

---

& Ruprecht, 1922), 147–8; T. K. Cheyne, *Introduction to the Book of Isaiah* (London: Adam and Charles Black, 1895), 119–20; Karl Marti, *Das Buch Jesaja* (KHC 10; Tübingen: Mohr [Siebeck], 1900), 159–61; George Buchanan Gray, *The Book of Isaiah: I–XXVII* (ICC; Edinburgh: T. & T. Clark, 1912), 344; Otto Procksch, *Jesaia I* (KAT 9/1; Leipzig: Deichert, 1930), 255; Edward J. Kissane, *The Book of Isaiah* (2 vols.; rev. ed.; Dublin: Browne and Nolan, 1960), 1:214; Georg Fohrer, *Das Buch Jesaja* (3 vols.; ZBK; Zürich: Zwingli, 1960–64), 215–18; Herbert Donner, *Israel unter den Völkern: Die Stellung der klassischen Propheten des 8. Jahrhunderts v. Chr. zur Aussenpolitik der Könige von Israel und Juda* (VTSup 11; Leiden: Brill, 1964), 113–16; Seth Erlandsson, *The Burden of Babylon: A Study of Isaiah 13:2–14:23* (ConBOT 4; Lund: Gleerup, 1970), 80–1; Hans Werner Hoffmann, *Die Intention der Verkündigung Jesajas* (BZAW 136; Berlin: de Gruyter, 1974), 74–6; Friedrich Huber, *Jahwe, Juda und die anderen Völker beim Propheten Jesaja* (BZAW 137; Berlin: De Gruyter, 1976), 107–10; Jacques Vermeylen, *Du prophète Isaïe à l'apocalyptique: Isaïe, I–XXXV* (2 vols; EBib; Paris: Gabalda, 1977–78), 1:324; Hans Wildberger, *Isaiah 13–27* (trans. Thomas H. Trapp; Minneapolis: Fortress, 1997), 288–91; Ronald E. Clements, *Isaiah 1–39* (NCB; Grand Rapids: Eerdmans; London: Marshall, Morgan & Scott, 1980), 173–4; W. David Stacey, *Prophetic Drama in the Old Testament* (London: Epworth, 1990), 122–3; Christopher R. Seitz, *Isaiah 1–39* (IBC; Louisville: John Knox, 1993), 143; Alviero Niccacci, "Isaiah XVIII–XX from an Egyptological Perspective," *VT* 48 (1998): 224–5; Brevard S. Childs, *Isaiah* (OTL; Louisville: Westminster John Knox, 2001), 142–3. On the basis of the third-person narrative, Marvin A. Sweeney (*Isaiah 1–39* [FOTL 16; Grand Rapids: Eerdmans, 1996], 272) attributes Isa 20 to the Josianic redaction of the seventh century B.C.E.; see also Hermann Barth, *Die Jesaja-Worte in der Josiazeit: Israel und Assur als Thema einer Produktiven Neuinterpretation der Jesajaüberlieferung* (WMANT 48; Neukirchen-Vluyn: Neukirchener, 1977), 9 n. 18, 216–17.

[2] Alternatively, some argue for the secondary insertion of individual Deuteronomistic phrases; see Willem A. M. Beuken, *Jesaja 13–27* (HTKAT; Freiburg: Herder, 2007), 208–9; Matthijs J. de Jong, *Isaiah Among the Ancient Near Eastern Prophets: A Comparative Study of the Earliest Stages of the Isaiah Tradition and the Neo-Assyrian Prophecies* (VTSup 117; Leiden: Brill, 2007), 151. However, considering the wealth of Deuteronomistic expressions in these verses, very little would remain without them.

[3] "The Great 'Summary' Inscription," translated by K. Lawson Younger (*COS* 2.118E:296–7); "The Small 'Summary' Inscription," translated by K. Lawson Younger (*COS* 2.118F:297); Andreas Fuchs, *Die Annalen des Jahres 711 v. Chr. nach Prismenfragmenten aus Ninive und Assur* (SAAS 8; Helsinki: Neo-Assyrian Text Corpus Project, 1998), 44–6, 73–4, 124–31; Anthony Spalinger, "The Year 712 B.C. and Its Implications for Egyptian History," *JARCE* 10 (1973): 95–101; Zdzisław J. Kapera,

King Azuri of Ashdod sent letters to neighboring kings to gather support in a bid to overthrow the Assyrian occupation. Sargon claims that several vassal states were initially involved, including Philistia, Judah, Edom, Moab, and Egypt, but all of these apparently withdrew support at an early stage and avoided direct conflict with Assyria. In the end, Sargon swiftly defeated Ashdod and appointed an Assyrian governor over the city.

The narrative in Isa 20:1–4 gives clear evidence of familiarity with the basic historical circumstances of the Ashdod rebellion, particularly regarding the involvement of Egypt, Cush, and Judah as potential co-conspirators with Ashdod. In addition, verse 1 refers to the Assyrian commander as the תַּרְתָּן ('commander in chief'), a term borrowed from the Akkadian word ta/turtānu (also in 2 Kgs 18:17, but not its parallel, Isa 36:2), and the same verse contains the only mention of Sargon by name in the Hebrew Bible. The point of Isaiah's demonstration is that Judah must not align itself with Egypt and Cush because they are unable to withstand the Assyrian army and will be unreliable allies in the end (cf. Isa 18:1–2, 4–6; 30:1–5; 31:1–3; 36:6).

In addition to these historical elements, the central message against foreign alliances in Isa 20:1–4 resonates with other anti-Egypt material in Isaiah relating to the eighth century B.C.E. Isaiah 31:1, for example, declares, "Woe, those who go down to Egypt for help and rely on horses...but do not look to the Holy One of Israel." Or similarly, in 30:2, the prophet denounces those "who set out to go down to Egypt...taking refuge in the protection of Pharaoh, and seeking shelter in the shadow of Egypt." Both of these texts are widely thought to have originated from the eighth-century prophet, and both are usually understood to refer to the Assyrian king Sennacherib's campaign

---

"Was Ya-ma-ni a Cypriot?," *FO* 14 (1972–73): 207–18; idem, "The Ashdod Stele of Sargon II," *FO* 17 (1976): 87–99; idem, "The Oldest Account of Sargon II's Campaign against Ashdod," *FO* 24 (1987): 29–39; Nadav Na'aman, "Hezekiah and the Kings of Assyria," *TA* 21 (1994): 235–54; James K. Hoffmeier, "Egypt's Role in the Events of 701 B.C. in Jerusalem," in *Jerusalem in Bible and Archaeology: The First Temple Period* (ed. Andrew G. Vaughn and Ann E. Killebrew; SBLSymS 18; Atlanta: Society of Biblical Literature, 2003), 226–7; K. Lawson Younger, "Assyrian Involvement in the Southern Levant at the End of the Eighth Century B.C.E.," in *Jerusalem in Bible and Archaeology: The First Temple Period* (ed. Andrew G. Vaughn and Ann E. Killebrew; SBLSymS 18; Atlanta: Society of Biblical Literature, 2003), 240–2; J. J. M. Roberts, "Egypt, Assyria, Isaiah, and the Ashdod Affair: An Alternative Proposal," in *Jerusalem in Bible and Archaeology: The First Temple Period* (ed. Andrew G. Vaughn and Ann E. Killebrew; SBLSymS 18; Atlanta: Society of Biblical Literature, 2003), 272–82.

against Jerusalem in 701.[4] It is possible that the prophet's objections against a coalition with Egypt are rooted in his perception of Assyria as the chosen instrument of Yhwh's judgment against Judah (cf. 10:5–6), but the denunciations of Egyptian assistance in Isa 30; 31 are directly linked with Judah's failure to 'look to the Holy One of Israel,' with the implication that they are seeking foreign aid instead. In any event, the dramatic portrayal in Isa 20:1–4 of Egypt and Cush in captivity to Assyria aligns with eighth-century Isaianic sentiments about political affiliation with Egypt.

Despite these historical considerations, the literary characteristics of Isa 20:1–4 suggest Deuteronomistic composition. The notion of Deuteronomistic material in the book of Isaiah is not implausible, since the episodes about Isaiah and Hezekiah in Isa 36–39 are largely paralleled in 2 Kgs 18–20. Opinions about the origin of this material vary, but the abundance of Deuteronomistic characteristics suggests that it was not first developed in the book of Isaiah.[5] There is no need to resolve the issue here, since the present aim is simply to observe Deuteronomistic language in Isa 20, and few would deny the presence of similar features in Isa 36–39.

Joseph Blenkinsopp has identified several Deuteronomistic elements in Isa 20, to which a few additional points may be added.[6] First, the military campaign formula that introduces the narrative at 20:1 appears many times in the Deuteronomistic History (e.g., 1 Kgs 14:25–26; 2 Kgs 12:18; 15:29; 18:9, 13; 24:10; 25:1), but occurs

---

[4] Duhm, *Jesaia*, 215, 229; Marti, *Jesaja*, 218–20, 233; Donner, *Israel unter den Völkern*, 132–9; Joseph Blenkinsopp, *Isaiah 1–39* (AB 19; New York: Doubleday, 2000), 411–12, 427.

[5] The usual view is that Isa 36–39 has been borrowed from 2 Kings; see Francolino J. Gonçalves, *L'Expédition de Sennachérib en Palestine dans la littérature hébraïque ancienne* (EBib 7; Paris: Gabalda, 1986), 342–50. For recent defenses of the opposite perspective, see Klaas A. D. Smelik, "Distortion of Old Testament Prophecy: The Purpose of Isaiah xxxvi and xxxvii," in *Crises and Perspectives: Studies in Ancient Near Eastern Polytheism, Biblical Theology, Palestinian Archaeology and Intertestamental Literature* (OtSt 24; Leiden: Brill, 1986), 70–93; Christopher R. Seitz, *Zion's Final Destiny: The Development of the Book of Isaiah: A Reassessment of Isaiah 36–39* (Minneapolis: Fortress, 1991). For a survey and discussion of the issue, see H. G. M. Williamson, *The Book Called Isaiah: Deutero-Isaiah's Role in Composition and Redaction* (Oxford: Oxford University Press, 1994), 188–211.

[6] Blenkinsopp, *Isaiah 1–39*, 321–2; idem, "The Prophetic Biography of Isaiah," in *Mincha: Festgabe für Rolf Rendtorff zum 75. Geburtstag* (ed. Erhard Blum; Neukirchen-Vluyn: Neukirchener Verlag, 2000), 13–26.

elsewhere in Isaiah only at 36:1, which has a parallel in 2 Kgs 18:13.[7] Similarly, the phrase בָּעֵת הַהִיא ('at that time') at the beginning of Isa 20:2 is used several times in the Deuteronomistic History to introduce a past event (e.g., Josh 5:2; 1 Kgs 14:1; 2 Kgs 16:6; 18:6; 20:12; 24:10), but it can be found elsewhere in the book of Isaiah only at 18:7 and 39:1. Of these, the occurrence at 18:7 introduces a future event and may be excluded from consideration. Thus, aside from 20:2, the phrase introduces a past event in Isaiah only at 39:1, which is paralleled in the Deuteronomistic History (2 Kgs 20:12).[8] The frequency of the phrase in the Deuteronomistic History and its scarcity in Isaiah suggest that the use of this expression to introduce a past event in Isa 20:2 has been influenced by the Deuteronomists.

There are additional particularly Deuteronomistic expressions in the Isa 20 narrative. The idiom דִּבֶּר יְהוָה בְּיַד ('Yhwh spoke through the hand of…') from verse 2 very frequently introduces divine communication through a messenger of Yhwh in the Deuteronomistic History (e.g., 1 Sam 28:17; 1 Kgs 8:53, 56; 12:15; 14:18; 15:29; 16:7, 12, 34; 17:16; 2 Kgs 9:36; 10:10; 14:25; 17:23; 21:10; 24:2), but Isa 20:2 is the only such occurrence in Isaiah. Also, the designation 'my servant' is a common way to refer to prophets in the Deuteronomistic literature (e.g., 1 Kgs 15:29; 2 Kgs 9:36; 10:10; 14:25).[9] While various other figures are called 'my servant' in the book of Isaiah (e.g., Isa 22:20; 37:35; 41:8–9; 65:8–9), the designation is never explicitly applied to any prophet, much less to Isaiah himself, except at Isa 20:3. Finally, elsewhere in the book of Isaiah, the prophet is called 'Isaiah ben Amoz' (20:2) only in secondary superscriptions that contribute to the shaping of the book as a whole (viz., 1:1; 2:1; 13:1),[10] and in chapters 36–39 (Isa 37:2, 21; 38:1; cf. 2 Kgs 19:2, 20; 20:1).

---

[7] Isaiah 7:1 could represent another example of this formula in Isaiah, although it substitutes the verb לחם ('to wage war') for the more usual reference to 'taking' (לכד) the enemy as final element of the formula (cf. 2 Kgs 16:5).

[8] Simon J. De Vries (From Old Revelation to New: A Tradition-Historical and Redaction-Critical Study of Temporal Transitions in Prophetic Prediction [Grand Rapids: Eerdmans, 1995], 65) considers the occurrence in 39:1 to be a 'redactional transition' that introduces an editorial addition, but he makes no mention of Isa 20:2 in his study.

[9] See Curt Lindhagen, The Servant Motif in the Old Testament: A Preliminary Study to the 'Ebed-Yahweh Problem' in Deutero-Isaiah (Uppsala: Lundequistska, 1950), 277–80.

[10] H. G. M. Williamson, Isaiah 1–27 (3 vols.; ICC; London: T. & T. Clark, 2006), 1:16–17, 163–5.

Since several of these Deuteronomistic literary characteristics in Isa 20 are also shared with Isa 36–39, Blenkinsopp assumes that both texts are likely part of the same 'narrative complex,' but this designation is not entirely clear.[11] On one hand, since both passages are characteristic of the Deuteronomistic literature, they theoretically could have belonged to the same corpus of material at one time, even though only Isa 36–39 is paralleled in the present form of the Deuteronomistic History (2 Kgs 18–20). On the other hand, the common literary features cannot support any claim that both passages have been incorporated into the book by the same hand. The positive message of reassurance in Isa 36–39, including the miraculous deliverance of Jerusalem in 37:36–38, contrasts sharply with the warning presented in Isa 20:1–4. Even the prediction of Jerusalem's downfall in 39:5–8 is interpreted by Hezekiah as good news, while the prophetic condemnation of foreign dependency in 20:1–4 is unequivocal.

Similar remarks could be made about Isa 7, which is also a third-person narrative about Isaiah[12] and could be an expansion of the report in 2 Kgs 16:5. However, unlike Isa 20:1–4, the narrative in Isa 7 deliberately corresponds at a number of points with the material in 36–39.[13] Therefore, while all three passages show some level of influence from the Deuteronomistic literature, there is no basis to suppose that they represent the same layer of redactional activity in the book of Isaiah. Furthermore, we may also note that none of these passages is repeated precisely from the Deuteronomistic History. While Isa 36–39 largely parallels 2 Kgs 18–20, there are a few departures, including the

---

[11] Blenkinsopp, *Isaiah 1–39*, 321; cf. Kissane, *Isaiah*, 1:214; Bernard Gosse, "Isaïe 14,28–32 et les traditions sur Isaïe d'Isaïe 36–39 et Isaïe 20,1–6," *BZ* 35 (1991): 97–98.

[12] An obvious difficulty with the proposal of an Isaianic *Denkschrift* as set forth by Karl Budde (*Jesajas Erleben: Eine gemeinverständliche Auslegung der Denkschrift des Propheten [Kap. 6,1–9,6]* [Gotha: Leopold Klotz, 1928]) is that it requires emending 7:3, 13 to refer to Isaiah in the first person, so that they agree with the first-person accounts of the surrounding chapters. See, for example, Ronald E. Clements, "The Prophet as an Author: The Case of the Isaiah Memoir," in *Writings and Speech in Israelite and Ancient Near Eastern Prophecy* (ed. Ehud Ben Zvi and Michael H. Floyd; SBLSymS 10; Atlanta: Society of Biblical Literature, 2000), 98.

[13] For similarities between Isa 7 and 39 see Peter R. Ackroyd, "Isaiah 36–39: Structure and Function," in *Studies in the Religious Traditions of the Old Testament* (London: SCM, 1987), 116–19; Edgar Conrad, *Reading Isaiah* (OBT; Minneapolis: Fortress, 1991), 38–40. For discussion of the insertion of Isa 7 into the surrounding material, see H. G. M. Williamson, *Variations on a Theme: King, Messiah and Servant in the Book of Isaiah* (Carlisle: Paternoster, 1998), 73–112.

addition of Hezekiah's prayer in Isa 38:9–20. At the same time, the only point of correspondence with the narrative of Isa 7 is 2 Kgs 16:5, while no part of Isa 20 can be found in the Deuteronomistic History. In the case of Isa 20:1–4 at least, the fact that no trace of this narrative is found in the Deuteronomistic History despite its literary affinities suggests a Deuteronomistic literary source that differed somewhat from the current recension of the Deuteronomistic History.

In summary, the Deuteronomistic language of 20:1–4 speaks against Isaianic authorship, despite sound historical memory of eighth-century circumstances and themes that resonate with other anti-Egypt passages in the book. The account is ostensibly associated with the Ashdod revolt of 711 B.C.E., but after examining additional evidence, we will propose that the incorporation of this passage into the book of Isaiah relates specifically to the reign of Zedekiah in connection with the fall of Jerusalem (586 B.C.E.).[14]

As with the eighth-century King Hezekiah in the face of the Assyrian threat, Zedekiah was also inclined to turn to Egypt for help more than a century later, in rebellion against the Babylonian King Nebuchadnezzar.[15] As the following paragraphs show, several non-biblical texts describe conditions favoring the likelihood of a diplomatic agreement between Judah and Egypt, while prophetic literature in Jeremiah and Ezekiel speaks directly against foreign coalitions during the reign of Zedekiah. Following this discussion, we will consider how these data relate to the Isa 20 narrative.

Zedekiah was installed by King Nebuchadnezzar of Babylon around 597 B.C.E. to replace Jehoiachin as king over Judah, which had become a Babylonian vassal state. Although Zedekiah was under obligation of loyalty to Nebuchadnezzar,[16] the evidence suggests that he pursued a détente with Egypt in rebellion against the Babylonian king.[17] The ruling pharaoh over Egypt for most of Zedekiah's reign was

---

[14] Otto Kaiser (*Isaiah 13–39* [trans. R. A. Wilson; OTL; London: SCM, 1974], 118) briefly mentions this possibility without pursuing it further.

[15] For an overview of the historical circumstances of Zedekiah's reign, see Oded Lipschits, *The Fall and Rise of Jerusalem: Judah under Babylonian Rule* (Winona Lake, Ind.: Eisenbrauns, 2005), 62–72.

[16] See Matitiahu Tsevat, "The Neo-Assyrian and Neo-Babylonian Vassal Oaths and the Prophet Ezekiel," *JBL* 78 (1959): 199–204.

[17] Moshe Greenberg, "Ezekiel 17 and the Policy of Psammetichus II," *JBL* 76 (1957): 304–9. Josephus (*Ant.* 10.7.1) describes Zedekiah's treaty obligations to Nebuchadnezzar specifically in terms of showing no friendliness toward Egypt.

Psammetichus II (594–588 B.C.E.),[18] and one papyrus document from Egypt describes Psammetichus visiting 'the land of Kharu,'[19] an Egyptian expression for the region of Syria-Palestine.[20] The details of this event are not fully known, but the text refers to Psammetichus visiting cultic places in Kharu with priests bringing bouquets from the deities of Egypt.[21] Although the circumstances are explicitly religious, it would be difficult to maintain that an Egyptian royal visit to Babylonian vassal states would not have political implications.[22]

In addition, the *Letter of Aristeas* speaks about Jews being sent to Egypt to serve as mercenaries for Psammetichus in his fight against the Ethiopians (*Let. Aris.* 13). According to Herodotus, this particular battle between Egypt and Ethiopia took place in 590 B.C.E., which coincides with the reign of Zedekiah (*Hist.* 2.161).[23] Again, this is only a passing reference, but it could indicate reciprocal military arrangements between Egypt and Judah,[24] and at least, some degree of political affiliation between these countries.

Finally, in the third letter from Lachish, which is generally dated shortly before the fall of Jerusalem during Zedekiah's reign,[25] Hoshaʿyahu writes about a military commander named Konyahu going

---

[18] K. S. Freedy and D. B. Redford, "The Dates in Ezekiel in Relation to Biblical, Babylonian and Egyptian Sources," *JAOS* 90 (1970): 462–85, 474. Abraham Malamat dates Psammetichus II to 595–589 B.C.E., in "The Twilight of Judah in the Egyptian-Babylonian Maelstrom," in *History of Biblical Israel: Major Problems and Minor Issues* (CHANE 7; Leiden: Brill, 2001), 318 n. 40; repr. from VTSup 28 (1975): 123–45.

[19] Francis Llewellyn Griffith, *Catalogue of the Demotic Papyri in the John Rylands Library, Manchester* (3 vols.; Manchester: Manchester University Press; London: B. Quaritch, 1909), 3:92–6; Günther Vittmann, *Der demotische Papyrus Rylands 9* (2 vols.; ÄAT 38; Wiesbaden: Harrassowitz, 1998), 1:162–5, 2:502–7; Albrecht Alt, "Psammetich II. in Palästina und in Elephantine," *ZAW* 30 (1910): 288–97.

[20] Eugen Täubler, "Kharu, Horim, Dedanim," *HUCA* 1 (1924): 97–123.

[21] A stele from Beth Shean depicts a lotus being offered to a deity; see *ANEP*, no. 475. Cited in Malamat, "The Twilight of Judah," 318–19 n. 42.

[22] Greenberg, "Ezekiel 17," 306–7; Malamat, "The Twilight of Judah," 319.

[23] S. Sauneron and J. Yoyotte ("Sur la politique palestinienne des rois saïtes," *VT* 2 [1952]: 131–6) and Bezalel Porten ("Settlement of the Jews at Elephantine and the Arameans at Syene," in *Judah and the Judeans in the Neo-Babylonian Period* [ed. Oded Lipschits and Joseph Blenkinsopp; Winona Lake, Eisenbrauns, 2003], 459–61) attribute this reference to the reign of Psammetichus I, but this seems less likely. See the discussion in Freedy and Redford, "The Dates in Ezekiel," 476–7 n. 69.

[24] Greenberg, "Ezekiel 17," 307.

[25] Harry Torczyner, et al., *The Lachish Letters* (London: Oxford University Press, 1938), 68–9; "Lachish 3: Complaints and Information," translated by Dennis Pardee (*COS* 3.42B:79–80), 78.

down to Egypt.[26] This particular letter also includes a certain unnamed prophet extending a warning to be careful, but details concerning the background of the letter are unknown.[27] Nonetheless, this reference provides another witness to military and political relations with Egypt during the reign of Zedekiah in rebellion against his obligations as a vassal of Nebuchadnezzar. It also offers a glimpse of a prophetic figure playing some cautionary role in the exchange.[28]

Biblical texts refer more directly to Zedekiah's interest in Egyptian aid and offer several prophetic denunciations of rebellion against Babylon. Ezekiel 17, for example, relates a parable about two powerful eagles, which represent Babylon and Egypt, while Judah is a tender vine in the middle that spreads its branches toward each nation.[29] This text explicitly warns that the Egyptian army will not provide assistance to Judah when the Babylonians surround Jerusalem (Ezek 17:17).

Also, Jer 27 describes a coalition of envoys from neighboring states that had gathered in Jerusalem to meet with Zedekiah, presumably with the prospect of overthrowing Nebuchadnezzar. Egypt is not mentioned with Edom, Moab, Ammon, Tyre, and Sidon,[30] but these smaller states very likely sought to approach Egypt for military assistance, since they could not have entertained the possibility of defeating Babylon without Egypt's help.[31] In a sign-act of his own, Jeremiah fashions a yoke

---

[26] William F. Albright, "A Supplement to Jeremiah: The Lachish Ostraca," *BASOR* 61 (1936): 10–16; Freedy and Redford, "The Dates in Ezekiel," 481; see also Simon B. Parker, "The Lachish Letters and Official Reactions to Prophecies," in *Uncovering Ancient Stones: Essays in Memory of H. Neil Richardson* (ed. L. M. Hopfe; Winona Lake, Ind.: Eisenbrauns, 1994), 65–78.

[27] Torczyner, et al. (*The Lachish Letters*, 69) suggest this may refer to the prophet Uriah (cf. Jer 26:20–23); against this, see D. Winton Thomas, "Again 'The Prophet' in the Lachish Ostraca," in *Von Ugarit nach Qumran: Beiträge zur alttestamentlichen und altorientalischen Forschung Otto Eissfeldt zum 1. September dargebracht* (ed. Johannes Hempel and Leonhard Rost; BZAW 77; Berlin: Töpelmann, 1958), 244–9.

[28] Hans M. Barstad ("Lachish Ostracon III and Ancient Israelite Prophecy," *ErIsr* 24 [1993]: 8*–12*) posits linguistic connections between Lachish letter 3 and the book of Jeremiah, including the expression מאת הנבא לאמר ('from the prophet, saying,….'; cf. Lachish 3:20–21; Jer 23:15, 30; 49:14). See also the discussion of the distinctly Jeremian expression מֵאֵת יְהוָה ('from Yhwh') in Chapter 2, above.

[29] See especially, Moshe Greenberg, "Ezekiel 17," 304–9.

[30] Oracles against each of these member nations of the coalition can be found in Jer 48:1–49:16, with remnants of the Tyre and Sidon oracles supposedly embedded within the Philistia oracle in 47:1–7 (cf. 47:4), according to Rainer Albertz, *Israel in Exile: The History and Literature of the Sixth Century B.C.E.* (trans. David Green; StBL 3; Atlanta: Society of Biblical Literature, 2003), 185 n. 144.

[31] Lipschits, *The Fall and Rise of Jerusalem*, 64–5; Donald B. Redford, *Egypt, Canaan, and Israel in Ancient Times* (Princeton: Princeton University Press, 1992), 461–2.

and places it on himself to demonstrate that the only hope of survival would be through submission to Babylon (Jer 27:12).

Another example of Zedekiah's political affiliation with Egypt can be found in Jer 37, which relates to events toward the end of Zedekiah's reign. In the midst of the Babylonian siege of Jerusalem, Zedekiah sends two messengers to ask Jeremiah to pray. At that point, Egypt had advanced slightly, causing the Babylonians to withdraw temporarily, which may have offered some glimmer of hope in the Egyptian army. Nonetheless, Jeremiah's response to Zedekiah's messengers in 37:7–8 is unequivocal:

> Thus says Yhwh, God of Israel: This is what the two of you shall say to the king of Judah, who sent you to me to inquire of me: Pharaoh's army, which set out to help you, is going to return to its own land, to Egypt. And the Chaldeans shall return and fight against this city; they shall take it and burn it with fire. (Jer 37:7–8)

The Deuteronomistic History attributes the ultimate destruction of Jerusalem to Zedekiah's rebellion against Nebuchadnezzar (cf. 2 Kgs 24:20b; Jer 52:3b). The Babylonians broke through the city walls, burned down the houses, and forced Zedekiah to watch the slaughter of his sons and officers before gouging out his eyes and carrying him off to Babylon. Lamentations 4:17 offers a poignant reflection on the expectation of foreign assistance: "Our eyes failed, ever watching vainly for help; we were watching eagerly for a nation that could not save."

The narrative involving the prophet Isaiah in Isa 20:1–4 provides an apt complement to these prophetic denunciations of Zedekiah's rebellion against Babylon. Ashdod's eighth-century effort to recruit the assistance of Judah and Egypt in rebellion against Assyria resembles the sixth-century coalition described in Jer 27, and the prophetic reactions are particularly similar, since both involve sign-acts that address the matter of foreign dependency.[32] Moreover, in both Isa 20 and Jer 27

---

[32] For discussion of prophetic symbolic actions, see Georg Fohrer, "Die Gattung der Berichte über symbolische Handlungen der Propheten," in *Studien zur alttestamentlichen Prophetie (1949–1965)* (BZAW 99; Berlin: Töpelmann, 1967), 92–112; repr. from *ZAW* 64 (1952): 101–20; idem, *Die symbolischen Handlungen der Propheten* (2d ed.; ATANT 54; Zurich: Zwingli Verlag, 1968); Bernhard Lang, "Prophecy, Symbolic Acts, and Politics: A Review of Recent Studies," in *Monotheism and the Prophetic Minority: An Essay in Biblical History and Sociology* (SWBA 1; Sheffield: Almond Press, 1983), 83–91; Stacey, *Prophetic Drama*, 122–6.

the prophet engages himself in an act of submission: Isaiah walks naked and barefoot to depict the humiliation of Egypt and Ethiopia by the Assyrians, while Jeremiah illustrates the mandate for Judah to remain under the yoke of Nebuchadnezzar. The narrative of Isa 20:1–4 does not simply denounce Egyptians and Cushites, but rather, enacts their subjugation to emphasize the unreliability of these nations in a revolt against Assyria. This narrative is easily applicable to the historical context of the sixth-century Babylonian occupation, with the implication that Zedekiah should not participate in ill-advised alliances with Egypt against Babylon. This objection against Egyptian aid coincides with the prophetic conviction of Jer 27 that Jerusalem's survival can only be sustained by submission to Babylon.

If the account in Isa 20 has been incorporated into the book of Isaiah to address political circumstances relating to the fall of Jerusalem, the involvement of Isaiah ben Amoz in the narrative seems to serve as an implicit appeal to the eighth-century prophet. In this way, the prophetic protest against an Egyptian alliance is imbued with a demonstration by Isaiah himself, as if, more than a century after his death, the prophet were able to lend his own voice to the denunciation of Zedekiah's foreign policy. Of course, Isa 20 gives no explicit indication of who might have added this narrative to the book. However, the close similarities in theme and intent between the prophetic enactments in Isa 20 and Jer 27 would seem to suggest a common perspective. With regard to the idea that the message of Jeremiah may have drawn support from this story about Isaiah, it should be noted by way of comparison that Jer 26:18 similarly makes explicit reference to the eighth-century prophet Micah in support of the prophecy against Jerusalem and the temple (cf. Mic 3:12).[33]

3. ISAIAH 20:5

Most of the preceding observations about the literary characteristics of Isa 20 pertain only to the narrative in verses 1–4, whereas the ambiguous plural verbs of verse 5 suggest that it is a separate addition to the

---

[33] Mark H. McEntire, "A Prophetic Chorus of Others: Helping Jeremiah Survive in Jeremiah 26," *RevExp* 101 (2004): 304.

chapter.[34] Without naming a specific subject, the verse abruptly states, "They shall be dismayed and ashamed because of Cush their hope and Egypt their boast." Even if 'they' were to be understood as Ashdod on the basis of the preceding verses, this interpretation would nonetheless point to verse 5 as a secondary addition, since references to this city in verses 1–4 are always in the singular. Furthermore, Egypt and Cush are the objects of humiliation in verses 1–4, but the perspective in verse 5 shifts to the shame of those who have depended on these nations.

In addition to the likelihood of Isa 20:5 being an expansion of the previous verses, there are several close linguistic connections between this verse and the literature of Jeremiah.[35] In Isa 20:5, the unnamed subjects are dismayed and ashamed because of Ethiopia their hope and Egypt their boast. For 'hope' in verse 5, the MT has the noun מַבָּט, but 1QIsaᵃ has the more common noun מִבְטָח ('hope, trust'). Aside from Isa 20:5–6, the noun מַבָּט only occurs in Zech 9:5, but this has probably been influenced by Isa 20, since it names several Philistine cities, including Ashdod, in connection with the downfall of Tyre.[36] If מַבָּט is related to the verb נבט ('to look at, regard'), the term may suggest looking toward something for assistance, a meaning that is not very different from the idea expressed by מִבְטָח. However, the Qumran reading (מִבְטָח) is well suited to this context and it provides an apt parallel to תִּפְאֶרֶת ('glory, boast') within the same verse.

It is rather striking that מִבְטָח is used in a similar way also in Jer 2:36–37:

> How you are so worthless, changing your ways! You shall be put to shame by Egypt as you were put to shame by Assyria. From there also you will come away with your hands on your head, for Yhwh has rejected those in whom is your hope (מִבְטָח), and you will not prosper through them. (Jer 2:36–37)

---

[34] Marti, *Jesaja*, 160; Stacey, *Prophetic Drama*, 126; de Jong, *Isaiah*, 152. Marti assumes that 20:5 has been inserted to explain 20:6, but this is unlikely, since the initial subject and verb of 20:6 are actually singular in the Hebrew, and the precise identity of 'the inhabitant of this coastland' is never specified.

[35] The relationship between Isa 20:5 and Jeremiah is never mentioned in Ute Wendel, *Jesaja und Jeremia: Worte, Motive und Einsichten Jesajas in der Verkündigung Jeremias* (BibTS 25; Neukirchen-Vluyn: Neukirchener-Verlag, 1995).

[36] See F. Nötscher, "Entbehrliche Hapaxlegomena in Jesaia," *VT* 1 (1951): 301.

As with Isa 20:5, this text also connects hoping in Egypt with being put to shame (בוש). In addition to this, an earlier verse in the same chapter directly addresses the theme of Judah seeking aid from Egypt (Jer 2:18).[37]

Another notable occurrence of מִבְטָח can be found in Jer 48:13, which is part of an oracle directed against Moab: "Then Moab shall be ashamed of Chemosh, as the house of Israel was ashamed of Bethel, their hope (מִבְטָח)." Although the context involves Moab rather than Egypt, this verse is similar to Isa 20:5 in its juxtaposition of the themes of hope and shame (בוש). With one additional instance (Jer 17:7), these account for all occurrences of מִבְטָח in the book of Jeremiah.

The only occurrence of מִבְטָח in the book of Ezekiel is part of an oracle against Egypt, in 29:16: "The Egyptians shall never again be the hope (מִבְטָח) of the house of Israel; they will recall their iniquity, when they turned to them for aid. Then they shall know that I am the Lord GOD." As with Isa 20:5, this verse also uses מִבְטָח to refer to dependency on Egypt, and the shame of Egypt is clearly expressed in the preceding verse (Ezek 29:15): "It shall be the most lowly of the kingdoms, and never again exalt itself above the nations; and I will make them so small that they will never again rule over the nations."

Despite these common elements, this particular example in Ezek 29 is different from the other מִבְטָח passages we have surveyed. In the first place, Egypt is the object of humiliation, and instead of בוש, the adjective שָׁפָל ('low') is used in Ezek 29:15 as the antithesis of exaltation, which is expressed using a *hitpaʿel* form of the verb נשא ('to lift up'). The only other pairing of שָׁפָל and הִתְנַשֵּׂא in the Hebrew Bible is at Ezek 17:14, which, as we noted earlier, explains the parable of the eagles and the vine, in reference to Zedekiah's presumed alliance with Egypt. Ezekiel 29:13–16 is probably a subsequent development of Ezek 17, however, because the humiliation of Egypt in Ezek 29 reverses the sentiment from the earlier chapter. For this reason, despite the similarities with Isa 20:5, Ezek 29:13–16 probably relates to a later period, and is not directly relevant to our analysis of Isa 20:5. Nonetheless, we have observed that Jer 2:37 and 48:13 share three elements in common with Isa 20:5: (1) the use of the term מִבְטָח for 'hope'; (2) a description

---

[37] Abraham Malamat, "The Kingdom of Judah Between Egypt and Babylon: A Small State within a Great Power Confrontation," in *History of Biblical Israel: Major Problems and Minor Issues* (CHANE 7; Leiden: Brill, 2001), 325; repr. from *ST* 44 (1990): 55–65.

of shame (בוש); and (3) reference to Egypt, except in the oracle about
Moab at Jer 48.

Concerning the topic of shame, we may draw attention to the pair
of verbs at the beginning of Isa 20:5, וְחַתּוּ וָבֹשׁוּ ('they shall be dismayed
and ashamed'). Aside from 2 Kgs 19:26 and its parallel in Isa 37:27,[38]
these two verbs are never collocated elsewhere in the Hebrew Bible
except in the book of Jeremiah, where the pair recurs no less than nine
times (Jer 8:9; 14:3–4; 17:18 [twice]; 48:1, 20, 39; 50:2 [twice]). There is
no need to examine all of these, but it is noteworthy that three occurrences of the verb pair are concentrated within a single chapter at Jer
48, the oracle against Moab (48:1, 20, 39), which is linked with Isa 20:5
by the occurrence of מִבְטָח ('hope') in Jer 48:13.[39] At the very least, the
frequency and limitation of this verb pair within the book of Jeremiah
suggests that the occurrence in Isa 20:5 is probably influenced by the
same literary tradition.

Before moving on, some consideration may be given to the insertion
of 20:1–5 into its current location following the Egypt oracle, although
this matter will be addressed in greater detail in Chapter 6, below.
Since the narrative of verses 1–4 has been expanded by the addition
of verse 5, it would seem that this latter verse would offer insight into
the insertion of this material. This short verse uses ambiguous plural
verbs to refer to 'they' being dismayed and ashamed on account of
their misplaced hope in Egypt and Cush. The identity of the intended
subject is not immediately clear, since the previous references to Ashdod and also 'the inhabitant of this coastland' in verse 6 are expressed
in the singular. However, a comparison of related passages in the book
of Jeremiah suggests that Isa 20:5 presents a critique against the people
of Judah.

Jeremiah 8:8–9 also uses the rare verb pair חתת and בוש to declare
that those who are wise will be ashamed and dismayed because of
their rejection of the word of Yhwh. In a similar fashion, Isa 19:11–14
derides the purported wisdom of Pharaoh's sages in an objection against
Zedekiah's foreign relations with Egypt (see Chapter 4, above). These
verses are further linked with Jer 8:8 by their denunciation of claims
of wisdom using the rhetorical phrase, 'How can you say…?,' which is

---

[38] For the significance of these occurrences, see Chapter 6, below.
[39] At the same time, there is evidence that Jer 48 has borrowed from the oracle
about Moab in Isa 15–16; see Brian C. Jones, *Howling over Moab: Irony and Rhetoric
in Isaiah 15–16* (SBLDS 157; Atlanta: Scholars Press, 1996), 89–111.

otherwise unique to the book of Jeremiah (also Jer 2:23; 48:14). Since
Isa 19:11–14 contains literary and thematic connections with Jer 8:8–9,
it would seem that Isa 20:5 is also linked with these verses in Jer 8
by means of the common verbs חתת and בוש. If so, this reference to
being dismayed and ashamed would suggest that Isa 20:5 extends the
critique of the supposed wisdom of Judah's leaders from Jer 8:8–9 by
relating it to misguided dependency on the Egyptian military.

While a prophetic condemnation against influential Judeans who
claim to be wise corresponds with both the proposed historical context of the reign of Zedekiah and the intertextual connection between
Isa 19:11–14 and Jer 8:8–9, the text of Isa 20:5 never specifies which
people are dismayed and ashamed. The ambiguity of this verse may
indicate general concern for those who hold positions of influence in
the royal court of Jerusalem, rather than an interest in pinpointing any
particular group. The book of Jeremiah similarly condemns not only
the wise (Jer 4:22; 8:8–9; 10:7–8; 18:18), but also kings, officials, and
prophets (1:18; 2:26–27; 4:9; 8:1; 24:1–10; 25:18–19; 26:7–11, 16; 32:32;
34:18–19, 21; 37:14–15; 38:24–28; 52:10).

Finally, the addition of 20:5 provides an appropriate complement
for the narrative of verses 1–4, which depicts the defeat of Egypt and
Cush at the hands of the Assyrians. Whereas the initial verses relate a
past event involving the prophet Isaiah, the *waw*-consecutive perfect
verbs in verse 5 predict the future regret of those who have depended
on these fallen nations. The anticipatory perspective of this verse suggests that it serves as a warning to those who may be considering an
alliance with Egypt and Cush. If verse 5 has been composed to accompany the incorporation of the narrative, as the preceding discussion
has proposed, the predictive nature of this verse would seem to indicate that the downfall of those who depend on these nations is not yet
a *fait accompli*.

4. Isaiah 20:6

The final verse of Isa 20 is probably a subsequent expansion of the
preceding material.[40] In 20:5, the unspecified 'they' are dismayed and

[40] Wildberger, *Isaiah 13–27*, 297; Uwe Becker, *Jesaja: von der Botschaft zum
Buch* (FRLANT 178; Göttingen: Vandenhoeck & Ruprecht, 1997), 277–8; de Jong,
Isaiah, 152.

ashamed on account of their misplaced trust in Cush and Egypt. By contrast, verse 6 names a subject ('the inhabitant of this coastland') and refers more directly to the downfall of hoped-for saviors. In the course of its reinterpretation of the chapter, 20:6 reapplies מַבָּט/מִבְטָח from the previous verse as a means of identifying the people in question, but this and other elements from the chapter are reused in a more general way. Instead of 'Ashdod,' as in 20:1, this final verse of the chapter speaks ambiguously of 'the inhabitant of this coastland,' and the generic 'king of Assyria' is preferred over 'Sargon, king of Assyria.' Likewise, instead of specifying Egypt and Cush, verse 6 vaguely refers to 'our hope, to whom we fled for help and deliverance.' Moreover, whereas 20:5 is implicitly directed against Judah, 20:6 redirects the critique against a different subject. Thus, 20:6 extends the basic message against foreign dependency so that 'the inhabitant of this coastland' expresses despair at the destruction of former allies.

Besides Isa 20:6, inhabitants of the 'coastland' (singular) are mentioned in the Hebrew Bible only at Isa 23:2, 6, in reference to the people of Tyre in an oracle against that city.[41] While other passages make reference to the coastlands and their inhabitants (e.g., Isa 42:10; Ezek 27:35; 39:6), the singular form of the noun אִי, as in Isa 20:6; 23:2, 6, is unusual. 'The coastlands' (plural) is a common motif of Isa 40–55 (40:15; 41:1, 5; 42:4, 10, 12, 15; 49:1; 51:5; cf. 11:11; 59:18; 60:9; 66:19), but the only other occurrences of אִי in the singular are in Jer 25:22; 47:4, both of which are also associated with the city of Tyre.[42] Thus, the use of the rare phrase 'the inhabitant of this coastland' suggests a link between Isa 20:6 and 23:2, 6. All the same, if this phrase serves as a deliberate link between these texts, Isa 20:6 gives no explicit indication of how such an allusion to the people of Tyre might relate to Isa 20, which has been principally focused on Cush and Egypt until this point.[43] This development in Isa 20:6 can be elucidated by first survey-

---

[41] Some commentators interpret 'the inhabitant of this coastland' as a general reference to Philistia: Gray, *Isaiah*, 347; Procksch, *Jesaia I*, 258–9; Donner, *Israel unter den Völkern*, 115; Clements, *Isaiah 1–39*, 173. Others, however, would include Judah among these: Duhm, *Jesaia*, 149; Marti, *Jesaja*, 161; Huber, *Jahwe, Juda und die anderen Völker*, 110–12; Hoffmann, *Die Intention der Verkündigung Jesajas*, 74.

[42] Seitz (*Isaiah 1–39*, 144) and Childs (*Isaiah*, 143) attempt to link Isa 20:6 with Deutero-Isaiah on the basis of its reference to the coastland, but they observe no distinction in the rare singular use of אִי.

[43] C. F. Burney ("The Interpretation of Isa. xx 6," *JTS* 13 [1912]: 419–23) connects Yamani, the leader of the Ashdod rebellion, with the reference in 20:6 to 'this coastland,' which he identifies as Cyprus (cf. Gen 10:4; Joel 4:6 [3:6]), to conclude that

ing the historical background of the oracles about Tyre in Ezek 26–28, before turning to the Tyre oracle in Isa 23.

The current arrangement of Ezek 26–28 contains several oracles specifically directed against the Phoenician city of Tyre, most of which are dated close to the time of the fall of Jerusalem (e.g., Ezek 26:1–2). After defeating Jerusalem, Nebuchadnezzar moved to control the rest of Palestine, but because of its strategic island position, Tyre was able to resist the Babylonian army for thirteen years.[44] Despite Nebuchadnezzar's inability to capture Tyre, the oracles against Tyre in Ezek 26–28 expect that he will press on to gain control over Egypt.[45] This viewpoint is expressed no more explicitly than in Ezek 29:17–20, an oracle dated around 571 B.C.E., which coincides roughly with the end of the siege against Tyre. In this passage, the anticipated downfall of Egypt is portrayed as the compensation due to the Babylonians for their fruitless efforts against Tyre:

Yamani could be a Cypriot. See also Cheyne, *Isaiah*, 121; Kapera, "Was Ya-ma-ni a Cypriot?," 207–18.

[44] For discussion of Nebuchadnezzar's attack on Tyre, see H. Jacob Katzenstein, *A History of Tyre from the Beginning of the Second Millenium B.C.E. until the Fall of the Neo-Babylonian Empire in 538 B.C.E.* (Jerusalem: Schocken Institute for Jewish Research of the Jewish Theological Seminary of America, 1973), 318–39; idem, "Gaza in the Neo-Babylonian Period (626–539 B.C.E.)," *Transeu* 7 (1994): 35–49; Oded Lipschits, "Nebuchadrezzar's Policy in 'Ḫattu-land' and the Fate of the Kingdom of Judah," *UF* 30 (1998): 467–87. There is some difficulty with the dating according to Josephus (*Ant.* 10.11.1; *Ag. Ap.* 1.21), who places the siege during Nebuchadnezzar's seventh year (Albertz, *Israel in Exile*, 57). Since this date is more likely a reference to the reign of Ethbaal, king of Tyre (Katzenstein, *A History of Tyre*, 328), the thirteen-year Babylonian siege of Tyre probably took place during 586–573 B.C.E.; see J. Maxwell Miller and John H. Hayes, *A History of Ancient Israel and Judah* (London: SCM, 1999), 425.

[45] Probably on the basis of the oracles against Egypt in Ezekiel, Josephus claims that Nebuchadnezzar invaded Egypt, installed a new king, and deported Egyptian Jews to Babylon (*Ant.* 10.11.1). While it is true that Amasis replaced the Egyptian Pharaoh Apries around the same time, there is little support for Josephus' assertion that the Babylonians defeated Egypt. For the text describing a Babylonian invasion of Egypt during Nebuchadnezzar's thirty-seventh year, see Stephen Langdon, *Die neubabylonischen Königsinschriften* (VAB 4; Leipzig: Hinrichs, 1912), 206–7; Paul-Richard Berger, *Die neubabylonischen Königsinschriften: Königsinschriften des ausgehenden babylonischen Reiches (626–539 a.Chr.)* (AOAT 4/1; Neukirchen-Vluyn: Neukirchener Verlag, 1973), 68–9, 321. See also Elmar Edel, "Amasis und Nebukadrezar II.," *GM* 29 (1978): 13–20; Donald J. Wiseman, *Nebuchadrezzar and Babylon* (Schweich Lectures; Oxford: Oxford University Press, 1985), 39–41; Anthony Leahy, "The Earliest Dated Monument of Amasis and the End of the Reign of Apries," *JEA* 74 (1988): 183–99; Albertz, *Israel in Exile*, 56–7; Miller and Hayes, *A History of Ancient Israel and Judah*, 427–8; Israel Eph'al, "Nebuchadnezzar the Warrior: Remarks on His Military Achievements," *IEJ* 53 (2003): 186–8.

Therefore, thus says the Lord God: I am giving to King Nebuchadrezzar
of Babylon the land of Egypt, and he will carry off its wealth and plunder
its spoil. It will be the wages for his army. I have given him the land of
Egypt as payment for his service that he did for me, declares the Lord
God. (Ezek 29:20; cf. Jer 43:8–13; 46:13–26)

Since the oracles against Egypt in Ezek 29–32 follow immediately after
those about Tyre in 26–28 with only a small amount of intervening
material (28:20–24, 25–26), the present arrangement of the collection
reflects the anticipation of the fall of Egypt on the heels of the Babylonian attack on Tyre.[46] This suggests an underlying attitude that the
invasion of Tyre, even if unsuccessful, points to the more substantial
event of Egypt's downfall (cf. Jer 44:30).

   Isaiah 23 contains an oracle that names Tyre, but since Sidon is also
named, the literary and historical background is uncertain.[47] Because
either Tyre or Sidon was under attack on several occasions, proposals
for the date of the earliest form of the oracle vary widely, including
the end of the eighth century B.C.E.,[48] the reign of Esarhaddon during 681–669,[49] and the defeat of either Sidon in 343 by Artaxerxes III
Ochus,[50] or Tyre in 332 by Alexander the Great.[51] The present discus-

---

   [46] Lawrence Boadt, *Ezekiel's Oracles against Egypt: A Literary and Philological Study
of Ezekiel 29–32* (BibOr 37; Rome: Biblical Institute Press, 1980), 10. Along similar
lines, Freedy and Redford ("The Dates in Ezekiel," 485) observe that the chronological order of the oracles has been disrupted (cf. 26:1; 29:1) in order to arrange the
oracles in such a way that the judgment against Egypt is viewed in connection with the
Tyre collection; cf. Walther Zimmerli, *Ezekiel 2* (trans. by James D. Martin; Hermeneia; Philadelphia: Fortress, 1983), 3–4. Herculaas F. van Rooy ("Ezekiel's Prophecies
against Egypt and the Babylonian Exiles," in *Proceedings of the Tenth World Congress
of Jewish Studies, Division A* [Jerusalem: Magnes, 1990], 115–22) interprets the Ezekiel
oracles against Egypt as a message of salvation for Israel, but these oracles make no
mention of it, and as Isa 20 demonstrates, judgment against Egypt does not necessarily
imply salvation for Israel.
   [47] The מַשָּׂא heading at 23:1 names only Tyre (also 23:5, 8, 13, 15, 17), but Sidon is
also mentioned at 23:2, 4, 12. Because of this, Duhm (*Jesaia*, 166–72), Marti (*Jesaja*,
177), and Kaiser (*Isaiah 13–39*, 162) assume the original oracle concerned Sidon, and
explain all references to Tyre as either later additions or misreadings of the text.
   [48] Cheyne, *Isaiah*, 143–5; Kissane, *Isaiah*, 1:248; W. Rudolph, "Jesaja 23:1–14," in
Festschrift für Friedrich Baumgärtel zum 70. Geburtstag, 14. Januar 1958 (EF 10; Erlangen: Universitätsbund, 1959), 166–74; Erlandsson, *The Burden of Babylon*, 100–1.
   [49] Wildberger, *Isaiah 13–27*, 417–19; Vermeylen, *Du prophète Isaïe*, 1:343; Clements, *Isaiah 1–39*, 191–2.
   [50] Duhm, *Jesaia*, 166; Marti, *Jesaja*, 180–1; Kaiser, *Isaiah 13–39*, 162.
   [51] Procksch, *Jesaia I*, 295–301; Fohrer, *Jesaja*, 1:239–40; Johannes Lindblom, "Der
Ausspruch über Tyrus in Jes. 23," *ASTI* 4 (1965): 56–73; Thomas Fischer and Udo
Rütersworden, "Aufruf zur Volksklage in Kanaan (Jesaja 23)," *WO* 13 (1982): 36–49;
Blenkinsopp, *Isaiah 1–39*, 344–5.

sion does not require a precise date for the earliest Tyre/Sidon oracle, but Isa 23:13 appears to offer a retrospective view of the period of Assyrian domination.[52] If this verse is a secondary addition, as it seems to be, the oracle presumably would have originated sometime before the exilic period.[53]

Despite a pre-exilic date for much of the oracle, the description in Isa 23:5 of the Egyptians trembling (חיל) upon hearing of Tyre's downfall reflects an expectation that aligns with the Tyre/Egypt material in Ezekiel, shortly after the fall of Jerusalem. Many commentators have suspected that Isa 23:5 is a later insertion, usually on stylistic and metrical grounds.[54] In addition to these factors, a distinction between two different meanings of חיל in verses 4 and 5 of Isa 23 offers further support for the secondary character of 23:5. In 23:4 חיל clearly refers to a woman being in labor (in parallel with ילד, 'to give birth'), in much the same way that it appears elsewhere in Isaiah (13:8; 26:17–18; 45:10; 54:1; 66:7–8). Although the term is repeated in 23:5, no contextual reference to giving birth is supplied. Instead, the verse describes the Egyptians 'trembling,' as the term is used a number of times outside of the book of Isaiah (cf. Pss 55:5 [4]; 77:17 [16]; 97:4; 114:7; Jer 4:19; Ezek 30:16; Zech 9:5).[55] Of the ten times חיל is used in the book of Isaiah, only the occurrence at 23:5 makes no reference to being in labor. However, the occurrence at Isa 23:5 is very much like the appearance of the same verb at Ezek 30:16, which likewise refers to Egypt 'trembling' (not 'being in labor') in reaction to impending doom (see also the noun חַלְחָלָה, 'trembling,' in Ezek 30:4, 9). Thus, it is very likely that the addition of Isa 23:5 to the Tyre oracle in Isaiah has been carried out in connection with the Tyre/Egypt material in Ezekiel. This

---

[52] It is possible that 23:13 has been added in relation to Nebuchadnezzar's thirteen-year siege of Tyre, as we are proposing for 23:5 (see below); see Cheyne, *Isaiah*, 141; Vermeylen, *Du prophète Isaïe*, 1:344–5; Clements, *Isaiah 1–39*, 192. Elsewhere ("The Prophecies of Isaiah and the Fall of Jerusalem in 587 B.C.," *VT* 30 [1980]: 428–9), Clements links Isa 23:13 with the fall of Jerusalem in 587 B.C.E.

[53] To avoid a reference to Assyria in 23:13, Duhm (*Jesaia*, 170) and Vermeylen (*Du prophète Isaïe*, 1:344–5) emend 'Assyria' (אַשּׁוּר) to the relative pronoun (אֲשֶׁר).

[54] Duhm, *Jesaia*, 168; Cheyne, *Isaiah*, 138; Marti, *Jesaja*, 178; Gray, *Isaiah*, 389; Procksch, *Jesaia I*, 298; Fohrer, *Jesaja*, 240; Edward Lipiński, "The Elegy on the Fall of Sidon in Isaiah 23," *ErIsr* 14 (1978): 79*, 82*; Kaiser, *Isaiah 13–39*, 162; Vermeylen, *Du prophète Isaïe*, 1:344; Wildberger, *Isaiah 13–27*, 426–7; Blenkinsopp, *Isaiah 1–39*, 342–3.

[55] *HALOT* ("חיל I," 1:310) cites both occurrences in Isa 23:4, 5 as 'to be in labour,' but offers no support for this sense in 23:5.

portrayal of Egypt's reaction to the news about Tyre in Isa 23:5 is very much in line with the sentiment of the oracles in Ezekiel, which portray the Babylonian siege of Tyre as an overture to the destruction of Egypt.

Returning to Isa 20:6, we previously observed that the unique reference to 'the inhabitant of this coastland' is otherwise reserved for the people of Tyre (cf. Isa 23:2, 6). Since they are never mentioned specifically in Isa 20, the question remains, What is the connection between this chapter and the people of Tyre? Against the background of the Tyre and Egypt oracles in the book of Ezekiel, the allusion in Isa 20:6 to the anticipated downfall of Tyre projects the focus of the verse forward to the destruction of Egypt. In this light, this verse is not as much concerned with the wellbeing of the coastal dwellers, nor even with identifying them, as much as it seeks to emphasize the destruction of Egypt as their source of dependency. Since this verse implies that the destruction has yet to take place in the future, it alludes to the plight of Tyre in order to give voice to the expectation of Egypt's downfall within the literary context of the preceding narrative about Egypt.

In summary, the rare use of 'the inhabitant of this coastland' in Isa 20:6 provides a link with the oracles about Tyre and Egypt in Ezek 26–32. This is supported by the observation that the insertion of Isa 23:5 into the Tyre oracle has likewise been influenced by the Egypt oracle in Ezek 30:1–19. Thus, both insertions at Isa 20:6 and 23:5 reflect the expectation that Egypt would be defeated by Nebuchadnezzar following the Babylonian attack on Tyre, as described explicitly in Ezek 29:17–20. The prospect of Egypt's imminent downfall in Isa 20:6 represents a culmination of the preceding material. Whereas 20:1–5 depicts Egypt in chains, the expansion in verse 6 anticipates a Babylonian conquest as the realization of prior expectations.

5. Conclusion

The previous discussion has proposed that the current form of Isa 20 has been produced in two main stages of redactional activity. The first of these involves the incorporation of the narrative of verses 1–4 and the addition of verse 5 in their current setting. Since the narrative seems to reflect strong familiarity with eighth-century events and its literary characteristics indicate Deuteronomistic composition, it would seem that it has been borrowed from a Deuteronomistic source that has not survived in the present recension of the Deuteronomistic History. By contrast, verse 5 has been composed to accompany the narrative on the occasion of its incorporation into the current location after the Egypt oracle, and reflects close literary and thematic ties with material in the book of Jeremiah.

We have concluded that Isa 20:1–5 has been supplied in response to Zedekiah's interest in Egyptian assistance prior to the fall of Jerusalem. Although these verses do not make explicit reference to the matter, the books of Jeremiah and Ezekiel unequivocally condemn Zedekiah's rebellion against Nebuchadnezzar, and a few non-biblical texts support the likelihood of diplomatic relations between Judah and Egypt during this time. Viewed against this background, the account of Isaiah's demonstration serves as a sixth-century prophetic warning against dependency on these nations.

Isaiah 20:6 is also concerned with the destruction of Egypt and Cush, but from a different perspective. The viewpoint of this verse aligns with that of the oracles about Tyre and Egypt in Ezek 26–32, especially 29:17–20. Although Nebuchadnezzar failed to defeat Tyre after a thirteen-year attempt shortly after the fall of Jerusalem, this material anticipates that Egypt will fall into Babylonian hands. Since we have already posited that Isa 19:5–10, 15 has also been added in conjunction with the same circumstances (see Chapter 4, above), the addition of 20:6 seems to be part of a broader redactional effort.

The remaining question concerns impulses that have led to the incorporation of the pieces that constitute Isa 20. The chapter that follows will discuss the incorporation of both 20:1–5 and 20:6 as part of the larger formation of the group of material about Cush and Egypt in Isa 18–20.

CHAPTER SIX

THE REDACTIONAL FORMATION OF ISAIAH 18–20

1. Introduction

The discussion of the preceding chapters found evidence for internal redactional development within each of the chapters of Isa 18–20. At the same time, it is clear that the texts have been brought together deliberately to form a coherent unit of material about Cush and Egypt. Since the chapters of Isa 18–20 have already been analyzed individually, it is now necessary to examine the formation of these chapters as a group. There are two main layers of redaction that relate to the development of these chapters around the general theme of Cush and Egypt.

As proposed in Chapter 2, above, the initial collection of nations oracles in Isa 13–23 consisted of the four oracles that address Philistia (14:28–32), Moab (15–16), Damascus (17), and Egypt (19). The last of these served as the central axis around which other material has been added to form the current group about Cush and Egypt in 18–20. This includes the addition of the Cush oracle at 18 and the narrative about Cush and Egypt at 20. In addition, the initial Egypt oracle of 19:1–4 has been expanded over several stages by the Egypt-related texts in 19:5–25.

The discussion of the formation of Isa 20 in the previous chapter provides the basis for consideration of the formation of Isa 18–20 as a whole, since the basic framework of these chapters corresponds with the two main layers of development in Isa 20. It was shown that the first phase of editing in Isa 20 involves the addition of the core narrative in 20:1–4 and the composition of 20:5 in response to Zedekiah's rebellious pursuit of aid against the Babylonian occupation during the years preceding the fall of Jerusalem. However, this stratum of literary activity extends beyond the incorporation of 20:1–5 to include the insertion of 18:1–2, 4–6 and 19:11–14. The second phase, based on the addition of 20:6, also involves the incorporation of 19:5–10, 15. These two layers of redaction will be considered in greater detail in the following paragraphs, while the remaining elements in Isa 18–20 (*viz.*, 18:3, 7; 19:16–25) will only be summarized briefly since they have already been examined as disparate additions to their respective chapters.

2. First Redaction

In Chapter 3, above, the discussion of the Cush oracle at Isa 18 observed that on one hand, this הוֹי ('woe') oracle is rare among nations oracles that mainly begin with מַשָּׂא ('oracle'), while on the other hand, it might be better suited alongside the similar הוֹי oracles about Egypt that begin Isa 30; 31. In the book of Isaiah, הוֹי oracles are generally collected with others of the same type (e.g., Isa 5; 28–31). This would seem to suggest that the Cush oracle has been transferred to its present location at Isa 18 from an earlier provenance among the הוֹי oracles that comprise the collection in Isa 28–31.

At the same time, it should be noted that while the narrative about Egypt and Cush in Isa 20 contains an obvious thematic connection with the Egypt oracle that precedes it, the Egypt oracle alone only partially complements 20:1–4. For one thing, the narrative in Isa 20 involves both Egypt and Cush, but the Egypt oracle in Isa 19 makes no mention of Cush. In addition, no specific reference is made in 19:1–4 to the matter of foreign alliances, which is a central issue in the narrative of 20:1–4. These factors suggest that the Cush oracle of Isa 18 would serve to provide an essential balance to the Egypt oracle in coordination with the addition of the narrative in 20.

In fact, the addition of Isa 18 conveniently supplies both of these essential components of the narrative that the Egypt oracle lacks. Whereas the Egypt oracle makes no mention of Cush, the narrative about both nations is now situated so that it follows oracles about each of these nations. Moreover, the explicit rejection of the Cushite delegation in Isa 18 corresponds with the denunciation of foreign assistance in Isa 20. Although the Egypt oracle does not specifically address the topic of foreign dependency, 19:1–4 can be reinterpreted in such a way that aligns with the assertion about Egypt's military inadequacy in 20:1–4. The depiction of the internal collapse of Egypt in 19:2, for example, demonstrates its incapacity as a political ally. These factors suggest that the insertion of the Cush oracle into its present location preceding the Egypt oracle corresponds with the addition of the narrative about both nations at Isa 20.

The literary features of Isa 18 provide additional support for the plausibility of this oracle as a secondary insertion preceding the Egypt oracle. The Cush oracle lacks the usual מַשָּׂא title that characterizes most of the nations oracles in Isa 13–23, and is one of only two הוֹי oracles within the collection (also 17:12–14). At the same time, the discussion in Chapter 3, above, showed that the original Cush oracle (18:1–2, 4–6) is similar in both form and content to the group of הוֹי oracles in Isa 28–31, especially those that condemn political relations with Egypt in 30:1–5; 31:1–3. The fact that multiple הוֹי oracles are often grouped together in Isaiah further suggests that the Cush oracle was previously situated elsewhere in the book. Given the thematic correspondence that we have already observed between Isa 20 and the preceding oracles about Cush and Egypt, we may conclude that the addition of the narrative has played the governing role for the insertion of the Cush oracle, with the effect of producing the basic framework for the small collection about Cush and Egypt in Isa 18–20.

One additional detail links the insertion of the Cush oracle in Isa 18 with the composition of 20:5, which has been added in conjunction with the insertion of 20:1–4. In the narrative of 20:1–4, the two nations are paired together with Egypt consistently named first ('Egypt and Cush'). It might initially appear odd, therefore, to discover that 20:5 goes against the precedent by mentioning 'Cush and Egypt,' in that order. This disruption of the pattern is more comprehensible in light of the current proposal that 20:5 has been composed to accompany the insertion of the Cush oracle at Isa 18 and the narrative at 20:1–4. Thus, the reversed mention of these two nations in 20:5 coincides with present order of the oracles about Cush and Egypt, in Isa 18 and 19, respectively.

The discussion of Isa 19 and 20 in the preceding chapters has argued that the composition and incorporation of 19:11–14 and 20:5 relate to the reign of Zedekiah and that both texts exhibit strong literary affinity with the book of Jeremiah. In the case of Isa 20:5, this brief verse refers to hope (מִבְטָח) in Cush and Egypt (cf. Jer 2:37; 48:13), and uses the verbs חתת and בושׁ, which are collocated almost exclusively in the book of Jeremiah (Jer 8:8–9; 14:4; 17:18; 48:1, 20, 39; 50:2; also 2 Kgs 19:26//Isa 37:27).

Isaiah 19:11–14 also corresponds with Zedekiah's interest in Egyptian support against Babylonian occupation of Judah using expressions that resonate with the language of the book of Jeremiah. For example, Isa 19:11–14 refers to the foolishness of the Egyptian leaders and describes Egypt staggering in vomit like a drunkard (cf. Jer 25:15–27; 51:57). Similarly, the deception (נשׁא) of the officials of Memphis in Isa 19:13 echoes Zedekiah's own delusion (נשׁא) in Jer 37:9, when Egypt advanced against Babylon prior to the fall of Jerusalem. In addition, the portrayal of the advice of Pharaoh's counselors as 'foolish' in Isa 19:11 uses a sense of בער that appears most frequently in Jeremiah (Jer 10:8, 14, 21; 51:17; also Ps 94:8; Ezek 21:36 [31]), and reference to 'the wisest of the counselors of Pharaoh' (חַכְמֵי יֹעֲצֵי פַרְעֹה) in Isa 19:11 is syntactically identical to 'the wisest of the nations' (חַכְמֵי הַגּוֹיִם) in Jer 10:7.

Since both Isa 19:11–14 and 20:5 contain several close linguistic similarities with passages in Jeremiah and both seem to address the same circumstances, we may conclude that these texts have been composed and added to the book of Isaiah as part of the same redactional effort. This can be further supported by comparing both passages with Jer 8:8–9. Isaiah 19:11–14 and Jer 8:8–9 both describe the foolishness of those who claim to be wise, using the rhetorical question 'How can you say…?,' which is especially characteristic of the book of Jeremiah (cf. Jer 2:23; 48:14). At the same time, Jer 8:8–9 and Isa 20:5 are linked together by the common use of the rare verb pair חתת and בושׁ to refer to being dismayed and ashamed. Whereas Jer 8:8–9 speaks of the purported wisdom of Judah's leaders, Isa 19:11–14 reapplies the theme to denounce Egypt's famed wisdom (cf. Gen 41:8, 33, 39; Exod 7:11; 1 Kgs 5:10 [4:30]; Ps 105:22; Isa 31:2). In the case of Isa 20:5, the ambiguous 'they' are dismayed and ashamed because of their dependency on Cush and Egypt. In light of the influence of Jer 8:8–9 on this verse, the reference to 'they' in Isa 20:5 would seem to refer to the despair of Judeans who have misplaced their hope in foreign military aid.

In summary, this layer of redaction has produced the basic shape of the collection about Cush and Egypt in Isa 18–20. This has been brought about by the concurrent addition of the original Cush oracle of Isa 18 (verses 1–2, 4–6) and the narrative of 20:1–4 to surround the core oracle about Egypt in 19:1–4. At the same time, the Egypt oracle itself has been expanded by the composition of 19:11–14, and 20:5 has also been written to round out the newly formed group about these nations.

Given the book of Jeremiah's portrayal of King Zedekiah's interest in Egyptian aid (see Chapter 5, above), it may come as little surprise to discover major reworking of the oracle about Egypt in Isaiah against the backdrop of these circumstances. Others have observed the possibility of redactional activity relating to Zedekiah elsewhere in Isaiah[1] and especially in the book of Jeremiah,[2] but this particular connection in Isa 18–20 has not been previously suggested. Although explorations of literary influence between Jeremiah and Isaiah in relation to Zedekiah tend to gravitate toward the narratives about Hezekiah in Isa 36–39 (//2 Kgs 18–20),[3] we have proposed similar influence from Jeremiah in the grouping of literary material about Cush and Egypt.

What factors would motivate such a re-working in the book of Isaiah in light of the reign of Hezekiah? A few clues seem to emerge from the relevant texts themselves. An obvious element is the concern about Judah's involvement with Egypt. Texts like Jer 27 and Ezek 17 witness to the prophetic conviction that Zedekiah's interest in Egyptian aid was misguided. We have argued that the material that constitutes this layer of redaction in Isa 18–20 is in line with the same sentiment. Therefore, it would appear that this updating of the book of Isaiah serves to substantiate the prophetic denunciation of alliances with Egypt by appealing to history. As the examination of Isa 20 showed, the narrative at 20:1–4 seems to have ties to actual historical events. These verses refer explicitly to Ashdod's rebellion against Assyria around 711 B.C.E., and they contain the only reference to Sargon by name in the Hebrew Bible. The incorporation of this narrative in response to Zedekiah's foreign policy illustrates that just as Yhwh condemned Egyptian aid in the late eighth century, Zedekiah's sixth-century attempts would also be doomed to failure.

---

[1] Ronald E. Clements, "The Prophecies of Isaiah and the Fall of Jerusalem in 587 B.C.," *VT* 30 (1980): 421–36.

[2] Christopher R. Seitz, *Theology in Conflict: Reactions to the Exile in the Book of Jeremiah* (BZAW 176; Berlin: de Gruyter, 1989); A. R. Pete Diamond, "Portraying Prophecy: Of Doublets, Variants and Analogies in the Narrative Representation of Jeremiah's Oracles—Reconstructing the Hermeneutics of Prophecy," *JSOT* 57 (1993): 99–119; Hermann-Josef Stipp, "Zedekiah in the Book of Jeremiah: On the Formation of a Biblical Character," *CBQ* 58 (1996): 627–48; John Applegate, "The Fate of Zedekiah: Redactional Debate in the Book of Jeremiah," *VT* 48 (1998): 137–60, 301–8; Mark Roncace, *Jeremiah, Zedekiah, and the Fall of Jerusalem* (LHBOTS 423; London: T. & T. Clark, 2005).

[3] See especially Christof Hardmeier (*Prophetie im Streit vor dem Untergang Judas: Erzählkommunikative Studien zur Entstehungssituation der Jesaja- und Jeremiaerzählungen in II Reg 18–20 und Jer 37–40* [BZAW 187; Berlin: de Gruyter, 1990]), who proposes that the Hezekiah narratives were composed shortly after the fall of Jerusalem in reaction against the policy of submission to Babylon as described in such passages as Jer 37.

More significantly, this redactional activity serves to substantiate the critique against Zedekiah by appealing to the message of the prophet Isaiah. Since we have observed that the message is similar to that of the book of Jeremiah and that it uses some of the same expressions, one might just as well expect the substance of the message to be contained within the book of Jeremiah. However, the fact that this literary activity is found in the book of Isaiah suggests that this prophet plays a central role in affirming the message, well over a century after his lifetime. That is to say, the formation of this group of literary material about Cush and Egypt is deliberately set in the literary context of the book of Isaiah in order to garner further support for the critique against Zedekiah. The incorporation of the narrative especially allows a later redactor to invoke the eighth-century prophet's 'voice' in support of the prophetic message that Judean kings cannot hope to prevail by aligning themselves with Egypt. This practice is not entirely unlike that described in Jer 26:18, in which the eighth-century prophet Micah provides a basis of support for the word of judgment against Jerusalem and the temple (cf. Mic 3:12).

3. Second Redaction

In much the same way that Isa 20:1–5 serves as a vantage point for the initial movement toward the formation of Isa 18–20, the addition of 20:6 indicates another stage of major reworking within the group. The preceding discussion of 20:6 (see Chapter 5, above) showed that the unusual phrase 'the inhabitant of this coastland,' which only recurs in the Hebrew Bible in reference to Tyre (Isa 23:2, 6), suggests an underlying association between Tyre and Egypt in 20:6. The association between these nations can also be observed in the arrangement of a group of oracles about Tyre and Egypt in Ezek 26–32. It also explicitly serves as the basis for Ezek 29:17–20, dated to 571 B.C.E., which anticipates the destruction of Egypt as compensation due to Nebuchadnezzar for his unsuccessful bid to defeat Tyre. It was also noted that the insertion of the comment about Egypt into the Tyre oracle at Isa 23:5 provides another example of the influence of the Tyre and Egypt oracles from the book of Ezekiel on the nations oracles of Isaiah. This increases the likelihood that the allusion to Tyre in Isa 20:6 also reflects the belief that the Babylonian attack on Tyre is a harbinger of Egypt's impending downfall.

In this way, the insertion of both Isa 20:6 and 23:5 in connection with the oracles about Tyre and Egypt in Ezek 26–32 points to a common layer of redactional activity among the nations oracles of Isaiah. Additional evidence reveals the same perspective in the insertion of Isa 19:5–10, 15. These latter verses echo the general themes of desolation of Egyptian waterways (cf. Ezek 29:3–5, 9–10; 30:7, 12) and fishing (cf. Ezek 29:4–5) from Ezek 29–32, and several particularly close ties can be identified between Isa 19:5–10 and the oracle about Egypt in Ezek 30:1–19. For example, the expression 'the streams of Egypt will dry up' (וְחָרְבוּ יְאֹרֵי מָצוֹר) in Isa 19:6 is very similar to 'I will make the streams dry' (וְנָתַתִּי יְאֹרִים חָרָבָה) in Ezek 30:12. Also, the insertion of the ecological destruction in Isa 19:5–10 to illustrate the results of the deliverance of the Egyptians into 'the hand of a hard master' (cf. Isa 19:4) corresponds with the defeat of the Egyptians by 'the hand of Nebuchadrezzar' in Ezek 30:10, which is followed by a similar description of ensuing devastation of the land and desiccation of the streams (see also Ezek 29:18–20).

Although not directly relevant to the formation of Isa 18–20, we would include the inserted poem at 2 Kgs 19:21–28 (//Isa 37:22–29) as part of the same level of development as Isa 19:5–10, 15; Ezek 30:1–19. As with the latter texts, this poem similarly portrays the ruination of the land of Egypt as a direct result of an attack by a powerful ruler. In this case, the Assyrian king Sennacherib boasts of devastation that he brought upon Egypt, using expressions that are strikingly similar to Isa 19:5–10. For example, וְשָׁתִיתִי מַיִם ('I drank waters') in 2 Kgs 19:24 (//Isa 37:25) sounds like וְנִשְּׁתוּ־מַיִם ('the waters are dried up') in Isa 19:5, while both Isa 19:6 and 2 Kgs 19:24 (//Isa 37:25) refer to 'drying up' (חרב) the 'streams of Egypt' (יְאֹרֵי מָצוֹר). The unusual phrase יְאֹרֵי מָצוֹר provides a particularly strong literary link between these texts, since Egypt is called מָצוֹר elsewhere in the Hebrew Bible only at Mic 7:12.[4] In this way, both passages also recall the motif of Egypt's streams drying up in Ezek 30:12. Other links between 2 Kgs 19:21–28 (//Isa 37:22–29) and the Egypt oracles of Ezekiel include Sennacherib's reference to felling tall cedars (2 Kgs 19:23//Isa 37:24; cf. Ezek 31:18) and the use of the 'hook' (חָח) as a tool of oppression (2 Kgs 19:28//Isa 37:29; cf. Ezek 29:4). Furthermore, both 2 Kgs 19:21–28 (//Isa 37:22–29) and Ezek 30:1–19 emphasize that although the destruction of Egypt is

---

[4] For מָצוֹר, LXX Mic 7:12 has ἀπὸ Τύρου ('from Tyre' = מִצֹּר).

carried out at the hands of the enemy king, the ultimate power over these events belongs to Yhwh.

The rare verb pair חתת ('to be dismayed') and בוש ('to be ashamed'), which occurs in Isa 20:5 and 2 Kgs 19:26 (//Isa 37:27), provides a particularly close link between Isa 20 and the poem about Sennacherib in 2 Kgs 19 (//Isa 37), since these are the only occurrences of this verb pair outside of the book of Jeremiah. Despite this close linguistic connection, however, the two non-Jeremianic occurrences cannot be attributed to the same hand.[5] On the contrary, Isa 20:5 refers to the dismay and shame of those who depend on Cush and Egypt, while 2 Kgs 19:26 (//Isa 37:27) applies the terms to the destruction of Egypt itself. Since close literary connections between 2 Kgs 19:21–28 (//Isa 37:22–29) and Isa 19:5–10 have already been noted, and since the use of חתת and בוש is related in some way to Egypt in both 2 Kgs 19:26 (//Isa 37:27) and Isa 20:5, it is likely that the occurrence of the rare verb pair in 2 Kgs 19:26 (//Isa 37:27) reflects a subsequent development from the influence of Isa 20:5.

While the joint occurrence of חתת and בוש in 2 Kgs 19:26 (//Isa 37:27) seems to have been influenced by Isa 20:5, the perspective of the poem in 2 Kgs 19:21–28 (//Isa 37:22–29) aligns more closely with Isa 20:6. In the case of Isa 20:6, the portrayal of the dismay and shame of those who had depended on Cush and Egypt from verse 5 is extended specifically to 'the inhabitant of this coastland,' who expresses disappointment in the tragedy that befell former sources of dependency. This resonates with the reference to certain inhabitants in 2 Kgs 19:26 (//Isa 37:27) who are similarly dismayed and ashamed at destruction in Egypt. On this basis, we may conclude that the expansion in Isa 20:6 corresponds not only with the insertion of Isa 19:5–10, 15, but also with the insertion of the poem in 2 Kgs 19:21–28 (//Isa 37:22–29).

In summary, it would appear that 2 Kgs 19:21–28 (//Isa 37:22–29); Isa 19:5–10; Ezek 30:1–19 have all been provided by the same hand. All speak of the devastation of the land of Egypt as the direct consequence of an overpowering ruler, and Isa 20:6, which should be included as part of the same layer of redaction, also refers to the destruction of Egypt. More particularly, each of the texts in the former group specifi-

---

[5] *Contra* Erich Bosshard-Nepustil, *Rezeptionen von Jesaia 1–39 im Zwölfprophetenbuch: Untersuchungen zur literarischen Verbindung von Prophetenbüchern in babylonischer und persischer Zeit* (OBO 154; Freiburg: Universitätsverlag Freiburg Schweiz; Göttingen: Vandenhoeck & Ruprecht, 1997), 35–6.

cally describes Egypt's streams (יְאֹר) drying up (חרב), using terms that are not brought together elsewhere in the Hebrew Bible.[6]

The literary connections with Ezek 30:1–19 can help determine the date of composition for the other related texts, and consequently, the second redaction of Isa 18–20. Ezekiel 30 appears within the literary context of a group of oracles about Tyre (Ezek 26–28) followed by another group about Egypt (Ezek 29–32). Most of the oracles in Ezek 26–32 are dated around the time of the fall of Jerusalem in 587 B.C.E., but the date assigned to the oracle at 29:17–20 is much later (571). Thus, this oracle constitutes the latest dated material in the book of Ezekiel. Located near the division between the Tyre and Egypt oracles, Ezek 29:17–20 reflects on the unfruitful Babylonian siege against Tyre and anticipates the fall of Egypt as compensation for Nebuchadnezzar's failed effort. Although Ezek 30:1–19 is among the few undated texts in the Tyre-Egypt collection, this passage corresponds closely with 29:17–20, since it also identifies Nebuchadnezzar specifically as the agent of Yhwh's judgment and it borrows several themes from the other Egypt oracles that are dated to earlier periods.[7] Furthermore, this oracle follows immediately after Ezek 29:17–20, with only a brief intervening 'in that day' statement, which may be a later addition.[8] Although Nebuchadnezzar campaigned against Egypt in 568 B.C.E., there is no evidence that he successfully conquered that nation.[9]

---

[6] Zechariah 10:11 uses יבשׁ to speak of drying up the Nile (יְאֹר).

[7] For a summary, see Herculaas F. van Rooy, "Ezekiel's Prophecies against Egypt and the Babylonian Exiles," in *Proceedings of the Tenth World Congress of Jewish Studies, Div. A* (Jerusalem: Magnes, 1990), 118.

[8] Walther Zimmerli, *Ezekiel 2* (trans. by James D. Martin; Hermeneia; Philadelphia: Fortress, 1983), 120–1.

[9] The fragmented Babylonian text describes an invasion of Egypt in Nebuchadnezzar's thirty-seventh year, but gives no indication of any conquest, despite the claims made by Josephus (*Ant.* 10.11.1), who seems to depend primarily on the biblical record. For the text and discussion, see Stephen Langdon, *Die neubabylonischen Königsinschriften* (VAB 4; Leipzig: Hinrichs, 1912), 206–7; Paul-Richard Berger, *Die neubabylonischen Königsinschriften: Königsinschriften des ausgehenden babylonischen Reiches (626–539 a.Chr.)* (AOAT 4/1; Neukirchen-Vluyn: Neukirchener Verlag, 1973), 68–9, 321; Donald J. Wiseman, *Nebuchadrezzar and Babylon* (Schweich Lectures; Oxford: Oxford University Press, 1985), 39–41; Israel Eph'al, "Nebuchadnezzar the Warrior: Remarks on His Military Achievements," *IEJ* 53 (2003): 186–8. While there was a change in the monarchy of Egypt around this time, Rainer Albertz (*Israel in Exile: The History and Literature of the Sixth Century B.C.E.* [trans. David Green; StBL 3; Atlanta: Society of Biblical Literature, 2003], 56–7) suggests that this was more likely caused by civil war in Egypt than by Babylonian influence. Moreover, Herodotus describes the usurpation of the Egyptian throne without mentioning any Babylonian

However, since these passages clearly anticipate the destruction of Egypt, we may conclude that they antedate the actual invasion, which would suggest a date sometime between the end of the siege of Tyre (ca. 573) and the invasion of Egypt (568). Of course, this period corresponds suitably with the date of 571 that is given for Ezek 29:17–20.

Whereas the initial stage in the redaction of Isa 18–20 was undertaken as an objection against Zedekiah's pursuit of Egyptian aid, the material in the second redaction does not reflect this same concern. A proposal by van Rooy suggests that because earlier prophetic declarations of Egypt's destruction had not yet been fulfilled, Babylonian exiles may have come to doubt the power of Yhwh.[10] Thus, the anti-Egypt passages that postdate the unsuccessful Babylonian siege of Tyre (*viz.*, Ezek 29:17–20; 30:1–19) seek to reaffirm Yhwh's sovereignty by portraying Nebuchadnezzar as Yhwh's instrument of judgment against Egypt. In one sense, van Rooy is undoubtedly correct in supposing that these texts are concerned with the sovereignty of Yhwh. On the basis of Ezek 29:17–20, it may be possible to assert further that the central concern is with the problem of the apparent failure of prophecy. These verses are forthright in acknowledging that the Babylonians failed to defeat Tyre, despite the oracles against Tyre in Ezekiel that expect its downfall. Undaunted by this historical development, Ezek 29:17–20 updates the material to declare that Nebuchadnezzar would nevertheless go on to a successful siege against Egypt. As we have argued, Ezek 30:1–19 explicitly reflects this later anticipation of Nebuchadnezzar's defeat of Egypt.

Indeed, all of the texts relating to this layer of redaction in one way or another assert the divine impetus for the attack on Egypt. In Ezek 30:10, for example, Yhwh declares his direct involvement in the end of Egypt, using the hand of Nebuchadnezzar. In 30:12, Yhwh explicitly states that he will dry up the waterways of Egypt. In Isa 19, the insertion of verses 5–10 extend Yhwh's intent to deliver the Egyptians into the hand of a hard master, resulting in similar environmental devastation. Similarly, the inserted poem of 2 Kgs 19 (//Isa 37) makes a point of saying that despite Sennacherib's boastful claims to have

---

involvement (*Hist.* 2.161–169). Piers Crocker ("Egypt in Biblical Prophecy," *BurH* 34 [1998]: 105–10) provides no support for his view of the defeat of Egypt by Nebuchadnezzar. See also the discussion in Chapter 5, above.

[10] Van Rooy, "Ezekiel's Prophecies," 120.

dried up Egypt's waterways, he is only carrying out that which Yhwh had planned long ago.[11]

It would appear, therefore, that the editorial additions that constitute this layer of redaction (Isa 19:5–10, 15; 20:6; 23:5; 2 Kgs 19:21–28 [//Isa 37:22–29]; Ezek 30:1–19) have been supplied to provide support for the reorientation of prophetic expectations, as exemplified in Ezek 29:17–20. This text itself implies an interest in defending the legitimacy of earlier prophecies that predicted the downfall of Tyre. If this is the case, it is reasonable to suppose that the related additions to the book of Isaiah function primarily for the same purpose. Thus, while the initial oracle at Isa 19:1–4 predicts that Yhwh will deliver Egypt into the hand of a hard master, the insertion of verses 5–10 confirms this by portraying the resultant environmental fallout. Similarly, Isa 20:1–5 anticipates the disappointment of those who have depended on Egypt, while the addition of verse 6 provides an expression of their dismay and emphasizes the inevitability of Egypt's downfall.

As proposed earlier, the initial redaction of Isa 18–20 in connection with the reign of Zedekiah was deliberately interested in the formation of a Cush-Egypt group of literary material to coincide with the addition of the narrative that occupies the first part of Isa 20. By contrast, the second major stage does not exhibit the same level of interest in the formation of a bloc of literary material. Rather, these additions (19:5–10, 15; 20:6) are primarily concerned with updating earlier material in the book of Isaiah in such a way that demonstrates the divine impetus in the downfall of Egypt. Since the related material in Ezekiel particularly stresses that Yhwh will instigate the fall of Egypt despite Babylon's failure to defeat Tyre, it is likely that the same motive underlies the additions in Isaiah. Specifically, it seems that the association of relevant material with the eighth-century prophet provides an additional measure of support for the updated prophecies about Egypt in the book of Ezekiel. In this regard, it is worth noting

---

[11] Peter R. Ackroyd, "An Interpretation of the Babylonian Exile: A Study of II Kings 20 and Isaiah 38–39," in *Studies in the Religious Tradition of the Old Testament* (London: SCM, 1987), 168–9. Ronald E. Clements ("The Prophecies of Isaiah to Hezekiah Concerning Sennacherib 2 Kings 19.21–34//Isa 37.22–35," in *Prophetie und geschichtliche Wirklichkeit im alten Israel: Festschrift für Siegfried Herrmann zum 65. Geburtstag* [ed. Rüdiger Liwak and Siegfried Wagner; Stuttgart: Kohlhammer, 1991], 73–4) also views 2 Kgs 19:21–28 (//Isa 37:22–29) as a redactional insertion in the wake of the fall of Jerusalem, but he interprets this passage as a reaffirmation of Jerusalem's inviolability (cf. 2 Kgs 19:21//Isa 37:22).

that the appeal to Isaiah to legitimate later prophecy also seems to be an important motive in the first stage of the formation of Isa 18–20.

4. CONCLUSION

The preceding discussion has posited two redactional movements contributing to the formation of Isa 18–20. The first of these consists of the insertion of the Cush oracle (Isa 18:1–2, 4–6) and the Isaiah narrative (20:1–4) to enclose the Egypt oracle (19:1–4), as well as the composition of 19:11–14; 20:5. This editorial work has been undertaken in response to Zedekiah's rebellion against Nebuchadnezzar around the time of the fall of Jerusalem. The second stage consists of the addition of 19:5–10, 15 and 20:6, which were most likely composed for their insertion. These verses anticipate the defeat of Egypt by Nebuchadnezzar around 571–568 B.C.E. in terms of devastation in Egypt and the disappointment of those who depended on that nation.

The remaining textual material in Isa 18–20 is comprised of subsequent, independent additions in chapters 18 and 19. These have already been discussed in the individual studies of these chapters, but their incorporation into the book may be briefly summarized here. Isaiah 18:7, which combines a reiteration of 18:2 with language similar to the Zion psalms to describe Cushites bringing tribute to Zion, has probably been added during the late exilic period. The composition and insertion of 18:3 has been directly influenced by Isa 13:2 and Jer 51:27, while its universalistic outlook is similar to the material found in Isa 24–27. Thus, a date of composition for 18:3 shortly after the end of the exile would be plausible.

The only remaining material in Isa 18–20 is a series of five 'in that day' phrases in 19:16–25 (verses 16–17, 18, 19–22, 23, 24–25). These are probably separate additions, since the perspective toward Egypt is not uniform throughout. To the contrary, each seems to reinterpret preceding material. The first of these (19:16–17) may plausibly correlate with Cambyses' invasion of Egypt in 525 B.C.E., while the viewpoint toward Egypt grows increasingly more positive in subsequent additions (see Chapter 4, above). This culminates in a remarkable portrayal of harmony between Israel, Egypt, and Assyria in 19:23, 24–25, which would seem to express hope for peaceful relations during the Hellenistic period. If so, these verses could be among the latest elements in the book of Isaiah, which would be appropriate for such an extraordinary expectation.

CHAPTER SEVEN

SUMMARY AND CONCLUSION

1. Summary

The present study has been primarily concerned with the formation of Isa 18–20 as a collection of literary material dealing with the nations of Cush and Egypt. It has attempted to trace the shaping of the material as a group, as well as the internal development of the oracle about Cush (Isa 18), the oracle about Egypt (19), and the narrative about both nations (20).

The development of Isa 18–20 is closely related to the formation of the larger collection of nations oracles in Isa 13–23. In the case of Isa 13–23, most of the literary units are introduced by a 'מַשָּׂא GN' superscription, but other texts within these chapters have different headings or none at all. Moreover, these chapters mainly consist of oracles about foreign nations, but they also contain some narrative material. The task of retracing the formation of these chapters is further complicated by the observation that the dating of individual oracles does not seem to be tied to literary categories within the collection. That is to say, some of the מַשָּׂא oracles can be plausibly dated to the eighth century B.C.E., while others almost certainly relate to the end of the exilic period or later. At the same time, many of the non-מַשָּׂא texts have been widely attributed to Isaiah ben Amoz, while some of this material arguably reflects a different compositional background. As the first two chapters of this study have shown, these factors present considerable challenges to the usual proposals for the formation of Isa 13–23.

As the discussion in the preceding chapters has shown, Isa 18–20 plays an important role in determining the formation of Isa 13–23, since the smaller group reflects much of the same literary diversity as the larger collection in which it is situated. Thus, Isa 18 contains one of only two הוֹי ('woe') oracles in Isa 13–23 (also 17:12–14), Isa 19 is introduced by the 'מַשָּׂא GN' title, and Isa 20 contains a narrative involving Cush and Egypt. This diversity in Isa 18–20 demonstrates that the primary factor in the organization of these chapters is not their literary form, but their thematic interest in Cush and Egypt. Thus, these chapters serve as a microcosm of the redactional activity leading to the formation of the larger collection of 13–23.

The usual tendency among scholars has been to approach the formation of Isa 13–23 from the perspective of the types of literary material contained within these chapters. Since most of the oracles begin with a 'מַשָּׂא GN' title, it is widely assumed that the addition of these oracles as a collection constitutes a major stage in the formation of Isa 13–23. Thus, the major point of disagreement is usually whether this collection of מַשָּׂא oracles was added before or after the remaining material. However, this assumption is challenged by the recognition that material in both מַשָּׂא and non-מַשָּׂא oracles can be plausibly dated either to the eighth century B.C.E. or to periods well after the lifetime of Isaiah ben Amoz. Moreover, it was shown that in at least some cases, the מַשָּׂא titles are secondary additions to the oracles. Since it is entirely possible that the titles could have been attached sometime after the oracles were incorporated into the book, even on an individual basis, this further weakens the prevailing notion of the addition of a collection of 'מַשָּׂא oracles.'

These factors invite a new proposal for the formation of Isa 13–23. Rather than taking as a starting point the distinction between מַשָּׂא and non-מַשָּׂא texts, this proposal begins by distinguishing two different patterns in the application of the מַשָּׂא superscriptions. In the case of the introductory elements of the מַשָּׂא oracles concerning Moab (15:1), Damascus (17:1), and Egypt (19:1), the reference to the geographical name as part of the מַשָּׂא title (e.g., מַשָּׂא מוֹאָב; 'oracle concerning Moab') is redundant, since the name is already mentioned immediately after the title, within the initial part of the body of the oracle. This would suggest that the 'מַשָּׂא GN' title has been added secondarily, to provide a unifying element to bring coherence to the group. The present study has posited that the oracle concerning Philistia, beginning at 14:28, initially stood at the head of this small collection of oracles against foreign entities. The Philistia oracle also has מַשָּׂא as an introductory element, but unlike all others, it is part of an introductory statement: "In the year of the death of King Ahaz, this oracle (הַמַּשָּׂא) came." Thus, the appearance of מַשָּׂא at 14:28 is dissimilar not because it has poorly imitated the others, but because it serves as the prototype for the headings of the oracles that follow. Therefore, the oracles about Moab, Damascus, and Egypt were assigned 'מַשָּׂא GN' titles as an extension of the initial oracle beginning at 14:28, and as an element of continuity among the four oracles of this initial collection. Further support for this proposal is raised by the recognition that the introduction at 14:28 parallels 6:1, which also introduces a distinct literary unit in the book of Isaiah.

In one or more stages, several more oracles were added to the small collection and similar 'מַשָּׂא GN' titles were added to assimilate them into the group. These מַשָּׂא oracles are distinguished from those of the early group (beginning at 15:1; 17:1; 19:1) by the recognition that the addressee is not reiterated immediately following the title. The most conspicuous of these oracles is the one against Babylon (13:1–14:23), since it has been placed in front of the Philistia oracle, which previously headed the group. Thus, the Babylon oracle now introduces the entire collection of oracles (13–23), and the heading at 13:1 coincides with the introductory material at 2:1. If 6:1 and 14:28 contain parallel introductions of major literary units of an earlier stage in the development of the book of Isaiah, the parallel headings at 2:1 and 13:1 represent a subsequent stage of expansion by means of the addition of new introductory material.

The non-מַשָּׂא texts that remain in Isa 13–23 may represent material that was added in various stages in the formation of the book. In any event, the absence of the מַשָּׂא titles suggests little regard for maintaining the continuity of the מַשָּׂא titles. This is the case for the הוֹי oracle about Cush (Isa 18) and the narrative about Cush and Egypt (Isa 20). Since the מַשָּׂא oracle about Egypt (Isa 19) was part of the initial group, it has been proposed that the Cush oracle and the narrative have been deliberately situated to surround the Egypt oracle, thereby creating a group of literary material with Cush and Egypt as its primary focus. While these insertions show clear thematic continuity, it is equally evident that no effort has been made to present these added texts (18; 20) as constituents of the מַשָּׂא group. The redactional development within each of these chapters (18–20) and the processes leading to the formation of this group as a whole occupy the remainder of the present study.

Against this framework of a basic proposal for the formation of Isa 13–23, it is possible to consider how the literary material about Cush and Egypt in Isa 18–20 came to be brought together, despite formal diversity in these chapters. Since each of these chapters shows evidence of editorial expansion, this study has also sought to retrace the internal development. In the case of Isa 18, the oracle about Cush initially contained only what is now located at 18:1–2, 4–6. This הוֹי oracle can be plausibly attributed to the eighth-century prophet Isaiah ben Amoz, but similarities of both form and content suggest that it was initially situated among the collection of other הוֹי oracles at Isa 28–31. Thus, it has since been relocated to its present literary context by virtue of its relationship with the Egypt oracle that follows. The original oracle has been expanded twice. Verse 7, which may have been added around the end of the exilic period, reiterates much of 18:2 to envision people from 'beyond the rivers of Cush' bringing tribute to Zion. It seems to be dependent also on the Psalter (cf. 68:30 [29]), and reflects an outlook similar to Isa 2:2–4. The insertion of 18:3 adds a much more universalistic perspective to the oracle, alerting the entire world to Yhwh's activity. This verse has some affinities with Isa 24–27, and could have been influenced by that material.

According to the prevailing view that a single collection of מַשָּׂא oracles has been added to the book of Isaiah, the latest מַשָּׂא material serves as the *terminus a quo* for the entire collection. Since some of the מַשָּׂא oracles in Isa 13–23 seem to describe the fall of Babylon (Isa 13:1–14:23; 21:1–10), it is usually assumed that the מַשָּׂא oracles have been added around the late exilic period, at the earliest. Accordingly, individual oracles must be dated no earlier than this same period.

Against this view, the present study has argued that the earliest form of the מַשָּׂא oracle about Egypt at Isa 19 was included with the initial group of oracles that were collocated and assigned 'מַשָּׂא GN' titles. Since the מַשָּׂא title is secondary, there is no need to date the contents of Isa 19 on the basis of other מַשָּׂא oracles. Without this restriction, it is possible to consider seriously the plausibility of eighth-century roots for the original form of this oracle, namely 19:1–4. These verses anticipate the downfall of Egypt due to internecine conflict, in way that is similar to the description of Jerusalem in 3:1–7.

The earliest expansion of the Egypt oracle can be found in 19:11–14, which were added in condemnation of the Judean king Zedekiah's pursuit of a coalition with Egypt. The language and themes of these verses are closely connected with various texts from the book of Jeremiah, which explicitly denounce Zedekiah's rebellion against the Babylonian occupation of Judah.

In a subsequent re-working of Isa 19, verses 5–10, 15 were added in anticipation of a Babylonian conquest of Egypt. These verses share several close ties with the oracles against Egypt in Ezek 29–32. As Ezek 29:17–20 makes clear, this material anticipates that Egypt will fall to Nebuchadnezzar, despite his failure to conquer Tyre after a thirteen-year siege (586–573 B.C.E.). These verses of Isa 19 also resonate with 2 Kgs 19:21–28 (//Isa 37:22–29), in which the Assyrian king Sennacherib boasts of causing ecological devastation in Egypt by drying up its waterways.

Isaiah 19:16–25 contains a series of five 'in that day' passages, which paint an increasingly positive picture of Egypt and the worship of Yhwh in that land. Because of considerable variance in the outlook toward Egypt, it is most likely that these have been added in increments. As proposed in Chapter 4, above, the first addition (19:16–17) may plausibly relate to the invasion of Egypt by Cambyses in 525 B.C.E., while the final expansion at 19:24–25 seems to refer to the divided Ptolemaic and Seleucid empires. By way of comparison, it is possible that these accretions in 19:16–25 all post-date the latest material in either Isa 18 or 20.

At the core of Isa 20 is a narrative (20:1–4) involving Isaiah ben Amoz, who enacts his anticipation of Assyria's captivity of Egypt and Cush. Despite the involvement of the prophet and an explicit historical setting in the eighth century B.C.E., the linguistic characteristics of the narrative are similar to the Deuteronomistic literature, which would suggest that the narrative is a later composition. Assuming that the narrative may have circulated previously within a corpus of Deuteronomistic material, it has been inserted into its present position to address Zedekiah's foreign relations with Egypt in the period leading up to the fall of Jerusalem.

Isaiah 20:5 has been composed to accompany the insertion of the narrative of verses 1–4 into the book. A few uncommon expressions reveal particularly close affinities with the book of Jeremiah, which also contains the most explicit condemnations of Zedekiah's rebellion against Nebuchadnezzar (cf. Jer 27; 37).

In a subsequent expansion, Isa 20:6 has been added in light of the Tyre and Egypt oracles in Ezek 26–32. As previously observed concerning Isa 19:5–10, 15, the addition of 20:6 reflects the viewpoint that Nebuchadnezzar's attack against Tyre heralds the impending destruction of Egypt. From the perspective of the mid-sixth century, Isa 20:6 portrays the regret of those who depended on Egypt to express the underlying belief that Egypt would finally face destruction.

The survey of redactional activity in the individual chapters relating to Cush and Egypt (Isa 18–20) reveals that some elements are interrelated and have contributed toward the overall shaping of a literary unit that is held together primarily by its interest in these two nations.

Thus, this study proposes that the first layer of redactional activity is primarily concerned with developing the initial Egypt oracle (19:1–4) into a broader group of literary material about Cush and Egypt. This was accomplished by enveloping the Egypt oracle with the Cush oracle (18:1–2, 4–6) and the Cush-Egypt narrative (20:1–4). Indeed, the narrative provides a schematic for the simultaneous addition of the Cush oracle. The involvement of both Cush and Egypt in the narrative requires the incorporation of a Cush oracle to accompany the Egypt oracle. This redactional layer also includes the composition of 19:11–14 and 20:5. Both texts echo themes and language from the book of Jeremiah, and reflect the historical circumstances of the final years of Zedekiah's reign prior to the fall of Jerusalem.

A second stage in the formation of Isa 18–20 reflects the literary and historical background of Nebuchadnezzar's unsuccessful thirteen-year siege against Tyre. As Ezek 29:17–20 illustrates best, this development anticipates that the Babylonians will move on to destroy Egypt in compensation for their unfruitful effort against Tyre. A major feature of the Egypt material in Ezekiel (especially 30:1–19) and the insertion of Isa 19:5–10, 15, is the conviction that a harsh ruler (cf. Isa 19:4) will wreak ecological havoc on the land of Egypt (cf. 2 Kgs 19:21–28//Isa 37:22–29). Along with this, the addition of Isa 20:6 expresses the regret of those who had depended on Egypt, referring to 'the inhabitant of this coastland,' a phrase that is otherwise used only to describe Tyrians (Isa 23:2, 6). The insertion of Isa 23:5 (cf. Ezek 30:16) provides a supplementary example of redactional activity among the nations oracles of Isaiah in response to the anticipated destruction of Egypt. There is no evidence, however, of any redactional activity within the Cush oracle of Isa 18 in connection with the same circumstances.

These two redactional strata account for much of the present shape of Isa 18–20, specifically, 18:1–2, 4–6; 19:1–15; 20:1–6). The remaining additions within these chapters are limited to individual expansions of the oracles about Cush and Egypt (18:3, 7; 19:16–25). The earliest of these could be the portrayal of Cushites streaming to Zion in 18:7, while 19:24–25 could be among the latest additions to the book of Isaiah.

2. Conclusion

Although this project has been primarily concerned with Isa 18–20, the results of this study may have some bearing on related matters. The following discussion articulates several contributions to the broader field of study that the present work has made, while also indicating future directions that may be taken in light of the foregoing proposals concerning the formation of Isa 18–20.

1. *The מַשָּׂא Titles*

Although most of the nations oracles in Isa 13–23 are introduced by the מַשָּׂא superscription, we have cast some doubt on whether the titles serve to identify any particular compositional genre of literature. Rather, we have proposed that the titles function primarily to link the oracles together as a unified collection. Aside from the superscription, there is no common literary form among the so-called מַשָּׂא oracles, and in at least some of the occurrences, the title has been added secondarily to the body of the oracle.

At the same time, it would appear that some of the oracles in Isa 13–23 can be considered among the earliest instances of the use of מַשָּׂא as an oracular title in the Hebrew Bible. Specifically, the first occasions of the application of the title in the book of Isaiah are at 15:1; 17:1; 19:1, which are linked with 14:28 to form the initial collection of nations oracles. Other מַשָּׂא titles in the Hebrew Bible, such as the introduction at Hab 1:1 (cf. Isa 13:1), are probably influenced by the occurrences in Isaiah. If this is the case, the innovation of using this title to introduce oracles can be plausibly attributed to the earliest development of the nations oracles in the book of Isaiah.

2. *The Formation of Isaiah 13–23*

Whereas a key element of most proposals for the formation of Isa 13–23 is the assumption that a corpus of מַשָּׂא oracles has been added to the book either before or after the non-מַשָּׂא material, the present study has posited that the oracles have been assembled incrementally within the literary context of the growth of the book of Isaiah. Because the מַשָּׂא titles in Isa 13–23 are secondary additions, questions concerning the date of the oracles cannot be addressed on the basis of other מַשָּׂא oracles. Thus, some of the מַשָּׂא oracles may plausibly originate in the eighth century B.C.E., while others are probably later compositions.

With regard to non-מַשָּׂא material in Isa 13–23, even if a text seems to relate to the eighth century B.C.E., it does not necessarily follow that it was initially contained within the collection of nations oracles. On the contrary, we have proposed that the initial collection was formed by the assembly of four oracles that now have מַשָּׂא headings of some type, rather than by any non-מַשָּׂא texts. It would seem, therefore, that various other explanations must be sought for the incorporation of each non-מַשָּׂא text into the collection. For example, close similarities between Isa 10 and 14:24–27 suggest that the latter verses may have been displaced from their original association with Isa 10 as intervening material was added.[1] Although the present study has been mainly concerned with the insertion of chapters 18 and 20, further study may yield explanations for the addition of other non-מַשָּׂא texts in light of the present proposal for the formation of Isa 13–23.

3. *Exilic-Period Redactional Activity in Isaiah*

This study has argued for the bulk of the formation of Isa 18–20 as the result of two main stages of redactional activity, probably during the early part of the exilic period. The material produced as a result of the first stage (Isa 18:1–2, 4–6; 19:11–14; 20:1–5) corresponds with the end of the reign of Zedekiah, in the years prior to the fall of Jerusalem. The second stage (19:5–10, 15; 20:6) has been prompted by the failed Babylonian attack against Tyre, and the anticipation of the defeat of Egypt. In addition to the material in Isa 18–20, it was observed that Isa 23:5 also seems to have been inserted in connection with the Tyre and Egypt oracles of Ezekiel. If so, this raises the possibility of further editorial activity elsewhere in Isa 13–23 in connection with one or both of these redactional stages.

At the same time, we may note that as far as Isa 18–20 is concerned, the earliest redactional activity was not undertaken until the period around the beginning of the exile. While some scholars have argued for a large-scale redaction of Isaiah in connection with the reign of Josiah during the seventh century B.C.E.,[2] we have found no evidence for any such work in Isa 18–20 during this period.

[1] Jacques Vermeylen, *Du prophète Isaïe à l'apocalyptique: Isaïe, I–XXXV* (2 vols; *EBib*; Paris: Gabalda, 1977–78), 1:253–4; H. G. M. Williamson, *The Book Called Isaiah: Deutero-Isaiah's Role in Composition and Redaction* (Oxford: Oxford University Press, 1994), 162–4.

[2] See especially, Hermann Barth, *Die Jesaja-Worte in der Josiazeit: Israel und Assur als Thema einer Produktiven Neuinterpretation der Jesajaüberlieferung* (WMANT 48; Neukirchen-Vluyn: Neukirchener Verlag, 1977); Vermeylen, *Du prophète Isaïe*; Ronald E. Clements, *Isaiah 1–39* (NCB; Grand Rapids: Eerdmans; London: Marshall,

4. *Isaiah and the Deuteronomistic History*

The present study may also have implications for the relationship between the book of Isaiah and the Deuteronomistic History. Specifically, several close literary and thematic connections were observed between the insertions of Isa 19:5–10 and the poem about Sennacherib in 2 Kgs 19:21–28 (//Isa 37:22–29). In addition to the linguistic links, both insertions serve the same redactional purpose of depicting ecological destruction in Egypt as the outcome of an oppressive regime. As argued above, these factors suggest that the same hand is responsible for the composition and insertion of both passages.

With regard to 2 Kgs 19:21–28 (//Isa 37:22–29), these verses occur within the literary context of a group of narratives about Isaiah and Hezekiah that is paralleled in 2 Kgs 18–20 and Isa 36–39. While some have argued for the priority of the Isaiah material,[3] the more common view is that these particular chapters first appeared in Kings, from which they were largely copied into the book of Isaiah. The latter option can be supported by linguistic characteristics of these chapters that are closely aligned with the Deuteronomistic History. Alternatively, it is possible that both 2 Kgs 18–20 and Isa 36–39 have drawn from a different literary source that has no longer survived.

In any case, the literary connections between the insertions at 2 Kgs 19:21–28 and Isa 19:5–10 present an instance in which the Deuteronomistic material has been shaped in conversation with the book of Isaiah. Whether the poem of 2 Kgs 19:21–28 was inserted directly into the book of 2 Kings or into its source, its link with the insertion of Isa 19:5–10 indicates some degree of reshaping of Deuteronomistic material in connection with Isaiah.[4] Moreover, this would seem to have some bearing on the date of the addition of Isa 36–39 to the book of

---

Morgan & Scott, 1980); Marvin A. Sweeney, *King Josiah of Judah: The Lost Messiah of Israel* (Oxford: Oxford University Press, 2001), 234–55.

[3] See Klaas A. D. Smelik, "Distortion of Old Testament Prophecy: The Purpose of Isaiah xxxvi and xxxvii," *OtSt* 24 (1989): 70–93; Christopher Seitz, *Zion's Final Destiny: The Development of the Book of Isaiah: A Reassessment of Isaiah 36–39* (Minneapolis: Fortress, 1991); Jacques Vermeylen, "Hypothèses sur l'origine d'Isaïe 36–39," in *Studies in the Book of Isaiah: Festschrift Willem A. M. Beuken* (ed. Jacques van Ruiten and Marc Vervenne; BETL 132; Leuven: Leuven University Press, 1997), 95–118.

[4] This point is also raised by Ronald E. Clements, "The Prophecies of Isaiah to Hezekiah Concerning Sennacherib 2 Kings 19.21–34//Isa 37.22–35," in *Prophetie und geschichtliche Wirklichkeit im alten Israel: Festschrift für Siegfried Herrmann zum 65. Geburtstag* (ed. Rüdiger Liwak and Siegfried Wagner; Stuttgart: Kohlhammer, 1991), 76.

Isaiah. If we have correctly drawn the conclusion that 2 Kgs 19:21–28 has been inserted around 571–568 B.C.E. in connection with the anticipated Babylonian invasion of Egypt, the fact that the poem occurs in both 2 Kgs 19 and Isa 37 suggests that the Hezekiah narratives had not yet been incorporated into the book of Isaiah at that time.

5. *The Theme of Egypt in the Book of Isaiah*

Although this thesis has made no attempt to offer a comprehensive study of Egypt's role in Isaiah, the group of chapters about Cush and Egypt contains the highest concentration of material about Egypt in the book of Isaiah. At the same time, the present redactional study of the oracle about Egypt in Isa 19 posits that this chapter contains some of the earliest and latest material about Egypt in the book, and that it has been redeveloped many times over the course of several centuries. For this reason, the current form of Isa 19 offers an extensive diachronic display of perspectives toward Egypt in the book of Isaiah. For example, while earlier redactional contributions consistently speak negatively of Egypt (19:5–17), later stages of editing recast Egypt in an increasingly positive light (19:18–25). There may also be some heuristic value in observing certain themes that are raised at different points. For example, Egypt's famed wisdom plays a central role in the addition of 19:11–14, while the ecological impact of the Nile is brought to the forefront of the later insertion of 19:5–10, 15. Similarly, we have observed that the exodus motif has played no role in the oracle about Egypt until the addition of 19:19–22. Since Egypt is frequently mentioned in Isaiah, this study of the redactional formation of 18–20 may offer insight into the development of themes relating to Egypt elsewhere in the book.

6. *Methodology*

Finally, a few comments can be made concerning the methodological approach taken in the present study. First, it remains to be seen whether the present approach taken toward determining the formation of the collection of nations oracles in Isa 13–23 might also be applicable in some way to similar collections in other prophetic books. Since we have already observed some elements of literary influence from Jeremiah and Ezekiel, it would seem possible that some of the redactional activity observed in Isa 13–23 might have been undertaken on a broader scale. To be sure, Jeremiah and Ezekiel would not have such a long history of development as the book of Isaiah, which begins in the late eighth century B.C.E. Still, there may be evidence of similar editorial measures taken toward the formation of other collections of nations oracles. We may observe, for example, that the oracles against Moab, Ammon, Edom, and others (Jer 47–49) seem to reflect such texts as Jer 25:15–31; 27:1–5, both of which resonate with some of the material in Isa 18–20. As another example, we have already argued that oracles against Tyre and Egypt in Ezek 26–32 have been arranged to correspond with the anticipated defeat of Egypt as depicted in Ezek 29:17–20, which has also been considerably influential in the formation of Isa 18–20. These examples suggest the possibility of broad-scale redactional activity across prophetic books in light of changing circumstances in Judah's history during and after the exilic period.

Additionally, a few observations can be made regarding the methodological approach to redaction criticism that this study has taken. A central question of diachronic approaches to texts is the dating of literary material, to which the current work has been no exception. However, the present study has generally found it more beneficial to posit a tentative date for texts on the basis of certain literary characteristics, rather than other factors that may be more commonly considered. For example, many commentators have dated the earliest form of the מַשָּׂא oracle about Egypt (beginning at Isa 19:1) on the basis of other מַשָּׂא material, in particular the oracles describing the fall of Babylon (13:1–14:23; 21:1–10). Since the מַשָּׂא oracles about Babylon could not have been written before the final days of the exile, it is often assumed that the same must be true about the Egypt oracle. To the contrary, I have argued that the מַשָּׂא title has been added secondarily to the Egypt oracle, in which case an earlier date of composition cannot be ruled out. As another example of a different nature, the narrative about Cush and Egypt at 20:1–4 is often thought to originate in the eighth century, since it involves the prophet Isaiah himself. Despite the recognition that the story may very well be set against actual historical circumstances, the use of characteristically Deuteronomistic language suggests that the account itself did not originate with Isaiah ben Amoz.

Another element in the current approach concerns the question of a מַשָּׂא genre. The matter has not been treated substantially here, since it is worth a sustained examination. Instead, this study has simply sought to raise the question whether the texts in Isa 13–23 that are introduced by מַשָּׂא can be viewed as constitutive of a unique genre of literature. The initial conclusion that has been drawn from the present work is that considering the fact that these texts have relatively little in common with each other except for the title, it is difficult to assert that this single characteristic is sufficient to define the genre.

Finally, it should be noted that the present study may bear some relevance on questions concerning the formation of the book of Isaiah. Of course, this has not been the primary focus, but there has been some concern to be conscious about aligning the proposed redactional stages of Isa 18–20, and to a greater degree, Isa 13–23, within the framework of the formation of the book. For example, it has been observed that the proposed initial beginning of the nations oracles at 14:28 corresponds with the material beginning at Isa 6:1, while a secondary introduction at 13:1 corresponds closely with the introduction at 2:1. Thus, the two main stages of development in the collection of nations oracles at 13–23 seem to correspond with broad movements involving the formation of the entire book of Isaiah. It remains to be seen, however, whether additional elements in Isa 18–20 may also relate to other aspects of the formation of the book.

BIBLIOGRAPHY

Ackerman, Susan. *Under Every Green Tree: Popular Religion in Sixth-Century Judah.* Harvard Semitic Monographs 46. Winona Lake, Ind.: Eisenbrauns, 2001.

Ackroyd, Peter R. "An Interpretation of the Babylonian Exile: A Study of II Kings 20 and Isaiah 38–39." Pages 152–71 in *Studies in the Religious Tradition of the Old Testament.* London: SCM, 1987. Repr. from *Scottish Journal of Theology* 27 (1974): 329–52.

———. "Isaiah 36–39: Structure and Function." Pages 105–20 in *Studies in the Religious Traditions of the Old Testament.* London: SCM, 1987.

———. "Note on Isaiah 2:1." *Zeitschrift für die alttestamentliche Wissenschaft* 75 (1963): 320–1.

Adamo, David Tuesday. "The Images of Cush in the Old Testament: Reflections on African Hermeneutics." Pages 65–74 in *Interpreting the Old Testament in Africa: Papers from the International Symposium on Africa and the Old Testament in Nairobi, October 1999.* Edited by Mary Getui, Knut Holter, and Victor Zinkuratire. Bible and Theology in Africa 2. New York: Peter Lang, 2001.

Africa, Thomas W. "Herodotus and Diodorus on Egypt." *Journal of Near Eastern Studies* 22 (1963): 254–8.

Ahituv, Shmuel. "Egypt that Isaiah Knew." Pages 3–7 in *Jerusalem Studies in Egyptology.* Edited by Irene Shirun-Grumach. Ägypten und Altes Testament 40. Wiesbaden: Harrassowitz, 1998.

Aitken, K. T. "Hearing and Seeing: Metamorphoses of a Motif in Isaiah 1–39." Pages 12–41 in *Among the Prophets: Language, Image and Structure in the Prophetic Writings.* Edited by Philip R. Davies and David J. A. Clines. Journal for the Study of the Old Testament: Supplement Series 144. Sheffield: JSOT Press, 1993.

Albertz, Rainer. *Israel in Exile: The History and Literature of the Sixth Century B.C.E.* Translated by David Green. Studies in Biblical Literature 3. Atlanta: Society of Biblical Literature, 2003.

Albright, William F. "A Catalogue of Early Hebrew Lyric Poems (Psalm LXVIII)." *Hebrew Union College Annual* 23 (1950–51): 1–40.

———. "The Elimination of King 'So'." *Bulletin for the American Schools of Oriental Research* 171 (1963): 66.

———. "A Supplement to Jeremiah: The Lachish Ostraca." *Bulletin of the American Schools of Oriental Research* 61 (1936): 10–16.

Allegro, John M. "Uses of the Semitic Demonstrative Element Z in Hebrew." *Vetus Testamentum* 5 (1955): 309–12.

Alt, Albrecht. "Psammetich II. in Palästina und in Elephantine." *Zeitschrift für die alttestamentliche Wissenschaft* 30 (1910): 288–97.

Alter, Robert. *The Art of Biblical Poetry.* Edinburgh: T. & T. Clark, 1990.

Andersen, Francis I. *Habakkuk.* Anchor Bible 25. New York: Doubleday, 2001.

Anderson, Bernhard W. "Exodus and Covenant in Second Isaiah and Prophetic Tradition." Pages 339–60 in *Magnalia Dei, The Mighty Acts of God: Essays on the Bible and Archaeology in Memory of G. Ernest Wright.* Edited by F. M. Cross, W. E. Lemke, and P. D. Miller. Garden City, N.Y.: Doubleday, 1976.

———. "Exodus Typology in Second Isaiah." Pages 177–95 in *Israel's Prophetic Heritage: Essays in Honor of James Muilenburg.* Edited by Bernhard W. Anderson and Walter Harrelson. London: SCM, 1962.

Anderson, Robert W. Jr. "Zephaniah ben Cushi and Cush of Benjamin: Traces of Cushite Presence in Syria-Palestine." Pages 45–70 in *The Pitcher Is Broken: Memorial Essays for Gösta W. Ahlström*. Edited by Steven W. Holloway and Lowell K. Handy. Journal for the Study of the Old Testament: Supplement Series 190. Sheffield: Sheffield Academic Press, 1995.

Applegate, John. "The Fate of Zedekiah: Redactional Debate in the Book of Jeremiah: Part I." *Vetus Testamentum* 48 (1998): 137–60.

——. "The Fate of Zedekiah: Redactional Debate in the Book of Jeremiah: Part II." *Vetus Testamentum* 48 (1998): 301–8.

Armayor, Kimball. "Did Herodotus Ever Go to Egypt?" *Journal of the American Research Center in Egypt* 15 (1978): 59–73.

Asheri, David, Alan B. Lloyd, and Aldo Corcella. *A Commentary on Herodotus Books I–IV*. Oxford: Oxford University Press, 2007.

Assis, Elie. "The Position and Function of Jos 22 in the Book of Joshua." *Zeitschrift für die alttestamentliche Wissenschaft* 116 (2004): 528–41.

Badè, William F. "The Seal of Jaazaniah." *Zeitschrift für die alttestamentliche Wissenschaft* 51 (1933): 150–6.

Barstad, Hans M. "Lachish Ostracon III and Ancient Israelite Prophecy." *Eretz-Israel* 24 (1993): 8*–12*.

Barth, Hermann. *Die Jesaja-Worte in der Josiazeit: Israel und Assur als Thema einer produktiven Neuinterpretation der Jesajaüberlieferung*. Wissenschaftliche Monographien zum Alten und Neuen Testament 48. Neukirchen-Vluyn: Neukirchener Verlag, 1977.

Barthélemy, Dominique, ed. *Critique textuelle de l'Ancien Testament*. 3 vols. Orbis biblicus et orientalis 50. Göttingen: Vandenhoeck & Ruprecht, 1982–1986.

Barton, John. *Amos's Oracles Against the Nations: A Study of Amos 1.3–2.5*. Society for Old Testament Studies Monograph Series 6. Cambridge: Cambridge University Press, 1980.

Becker, Joachim. *Isaias: Der Prophet und sein Buch*. Stuttgarter Bibelstudien 30. Stuttgart: Katholisches Bibelwerk, 1968.

Becker, Uwe. *Jesaja: Von der Botschaft zum Buch*. Forschungen zur Religion und Literatur des Alten und Neuen Testaments 178. Göttingen: Vandenhoeck & Ruprecht, 1997.

Begg, Christopher T. "The Peoples and the Worship of Yahweh in the Book of Isaiah." Pages 35–55 in *Worship and the Hebrew Bible: Essays in Honour of John T. Willis*. Edited by M. Patrick Graham, Rick R. Marrs, and Steven L. McKenzie. Journal for the Study of the Old Testament: Supplement Series 284. Sheffield: Sheffield Academic Press, 1999.

Begrich, Joachim. "Jesaja 14,28–32: Ein Beitrag zur Chronologie der israelitisch-judäischen Königszeit." *Zeitschrift der deutschen morgenländischen Gesellschaft* 86 (1932): 66–79.

Benardete, Seth. *Herodotean Inquiries*. The Hague: Martinus Nijhoff, 1969.

Berger, Paul-Richard. *Die neubabylonischen Königsinschriften: Königsinschriften des ausgehenden babylonischen Reiches (626–539 a.Chr.)*. Alter Orient und Altes Testament 4/1. Neukirchen-Vluyn: Neukirchener Verlag, 1973.

Berges, Ulrich. *Das Buch Jesaja: Komposition und Endgestalt*. Herders biblische Studien 16. Freiburg: Herder, 1998.

Bergmann, Claudia. "We Have Seen the Enemy, and He is Only a 'She': The Portrayal of Warriors as Women." *Catholic Biblical Quarterly* 69 (2007): 651–72.

Beuken, Willem A. M. "Isaiah Chapters LXV–LXVI: Trito-Isaiah and the Closure of the Book of Isaiah." Pages 204–21 in *Congress Volume: Leuven, 1989*. Edited by J. A. Emerton. Vetus Testamentum Supplements 43. Leiden: Brill, 1991.

——. *Jesaja 13–27*. Herders theologischer Kommentar zum Alten Testament. Freiburg: Herder, 2007.

Bewer, Julius A. "Critical Notes on Old Testament Passages." Pages 205–26 in vol. 2 of *Old Testament and Semitic Studies in Memory of William Rainey Harper*. Edited by Robert Francis Harper, Francis Brown, and George Foot Moore. 2 vols. Chicago: University of Chicago Press, 1908.

———. "The Date in Isa. 14:28." *American Journal of Semitic Languages and Literature* 54 (1937): 62.

———. "Textkritische Bemerkungen zum alten Testament." Pages 65–76 in *Festschrift Alfred Bertholet zum 80. Geburtstag*. Edited by Walter Baumgartner, Otto Eissfeldt, Karl Elliger, and Leonhard Rost. Tübingen: Mohr (Siebeck), 1950.

Birnbaum, Solomon A. "The Dates of the Cave Scrolls." *Bulletin of the American Schools of Oriental Research* 115 (1949): 20–22.

Blenkinsopp, Joseph. "Bethel in the Neo-Babylonian Period." Pages 93–107 in *Judah and the Judeans in the Neo-Babylonian Period*. Edited by Oded Lipschits and Joseph Blenkinsopp. Winona Lake, Ind.: Eisenbrauns, 2003.

———. *Isaiah 1–39*. Anchor Bible 19. New York: Doubleday, 2000.

———. "The Judaean Priesthood during the Neo-Babylonian and Achaemenid Periods: A Hypothetical Reconstruction." *Catholic Biblical Quarterly* 60 (1998): 25–43.

———. "The Mission of Udjahorresnet and Those of Ezra and Nehemiah." *Journal of Biblical Literature* 106 (1987): 409–21.

———. "The Prophetic Biography of Isaiah." Pages 13–26 in *Mincha: Festgabe für Rolf Rendtorff zum 75. Geburtstag*. Edited by Erhard Blum. Neukirchen-Vluyn: Neukirchener Verlag, 2000.

———. "Second Isaiah: Prophet of Universalism." *Journal for the Study of the Old Testament* 41 (1988): 83–103.

Boadt, Lawrence. *Ezekiel's Oracles against Egypt: A Literary and Philological Study of Ezekiel 29–32*. Biblica et orientalia 37. Rome: Biblical Institute Press, 1980.

Boda, Mark J. "Freeing the Burden of Prophecy: *Maśśāʾ* and the Legitimacy of Prophecy in Zech 9–14." *Biblica* 87 (2006): 338–57.

Boer, P. A. H. de. "An Inquiry into the Meaning of the Term משא." *Oudtestamentische Studiën* 5 (1948): 197–214.

Bohak, Gideon. "CPJ III, 520: The Egyptian Reaction to Onias' Temple." *Journal for the Study of Judaism* 26 (1995): 32–41.

Boling, Robert G. *Joshua*. Anchor Bible 6. Garden City, N.Y.: Doubleday, 1982.

Bosshard-Nepustil, Erich. *Rezeptionen von Jesaia 1–39 im Zwölfprophetenbuch: Untersuchungen zur literarischen Verbindung von Prophetenbüchern in babylonischer und persischer Zeit*. Orbis biblicus et orientalis 154. Freiburg: Universitätsverlag Freiburg Schweiz; Göttingen: Vandenhoeck & Ruprecht, 1997.

Botterweck, G. Johannes, Helmer Ringgren, and Heinz-Josef Fabry, eds. *Theological Dictionary of the Old Testament*. Translated by Geoffrey W. Bromiley, John T. Willis, David E. Green, and Douglas W. Stott. 15 vols. Grand Rapids: Eerdmans, 1974–.

Box, G. H. *The Book of Isaiah*. London: Pitman and Sons, 1908.

Bresciani, Edda. "Oracles d'Égypte et prophéties bibliques." *Le Monde de la Bible* 45 (1986): 44–45.

———. "La sixième satrapie: L'Égypte perse et ses sémites." Pages 87–99 in *Le livre de traverse: De l'exégèse biblique à l'anthropologie*. Edited by Olivier Abel and Françoise Smyth. Paris: Cerf, 2002.

Brewer, Douglas J., and Renée F. Friedman. *Fish and Fishing in Ancient Egypt*. Natural History of Egypt 2. Warminster: Aris & Phillips, 1989.

Brewer, Douglas J., and Emily Teeter. *Egypt and the Egyptians*. 2d ed. Cambridge: Cambridge University Press, 2007.

Brown, Truesdell S. "Herodotus' Portrait of Cambyses." *Historia* 31 (1982): 387–403.

Budde, Karl. *Jesajas Erleben: Eine gemeinverständliche Auslegung der Denkschrift des Propheten (Kap. 6,1–9,6)*. Gotha: Leopold Klotz, 1928.

——. "The Poem in 2 Kings xix 21–28 (Isaiah xxxvii 22–29)." *Journal of Theological Studies* 35 (1934): 307–13.

Burney, C. F. "The Interpretation of Isa. xx 6." *Journal of Theological Studies* 13 (1912): 419–23.

Calderone, P. J. "The Rivers of 'Maṣor.'" *Biblica* 42 (1961): 423–32.

Cathcart, Kevin J. "Treaty-Curses and the Book of Nahum." *Catholic Biblical Quarterly* 35 (1973): 179–87.

Cazelles, Henri. "Problèmes de la guerre Syro-Ephraimite." *Eretz-Israel* 14 (H. L. Ginsberg Volume, 1978): 70*–78*.

Chapman, Cynthia R. *The Gendered Language of Warfare in the Israelite-Assyrian Encounter*. Harvard Semitic Monographs 62. Winona Lake, Ind.: Eisenbrauns, 2004.

Cheyne, T. K. *Introduction to the Book of Isaiah*. London: Adam and Charles Black, 1895.

Childs, Brevard S. *Isaiah*. Old Testament Library. Louisville: Westminster John Knox, 2001.

——. *Isaiah and the Assyrian Crisis*. Studies in Biblical Theology 2/3. London: SCM, 1967.

Chilton, Bruce D. *The Isaiah Targum*. The Aramaic Bible 11. Edinburgh: T. & T. Clark, 1987.

Christensen, Duane L. "The Identity of 'King So' in Egypt (2 Kings XVII 4)." *Vetus Testamentum* 39 (1989): 140–53.

——. *Prophecy and War in Ancient Israel: Studies in the Oracles against the Nations in Old Testament Prophecy*. Berkeley: BIBAL, 1989.

Clements, Ronald E. "Beyond Tradition History: Deutero-Isaianic Development of First Isaiah's Themes." *Journal for the Study of the Old Testament* 31 (1985): 95–113.

——. *Isaiah 1–39*. New Century Bible. Grand Rapids: Eerdmans; London: Marshall, Morgan & Scott, 1980.

——. "A Light to the Nations: A Central Theme of the Book of Isaiah." Pages 57–69 in *Forming Prophetic Literature: Essays on Isaiah and the Twelve in Honor of John D. W. Watts*. Edited by James W. Watts and Paul R. House. Journal for the Study of the Old Testament: Supplement Series 235. Sheffield: Sheffield Academic Press, 1996.

——. "Patterns in the Prophetic Canon: Healing the Blind and the Lame." Pages 189–200 in *Canon, Theology, and Old Testament Interpretation: Essays in Honor of Brevard S. Childs*. Edited by Gene M. Tucker, David L. Petersen, and Robert R. Wilson. Philadelphia: Fortress, 1988.

——. "The Prophecies of Isaiah and the Fall of Jerusalem in 587 B.C." *Vetus Testamentum* 30 (1980): 421–36.

——. "The Prophecies of Isaiah to Hezekiah Concerning Sennacherib 2 Kings 19.21–34//Isa 37.22–35." Pages 65–78 in *Prophetie und geschichtliche Wirklichkeit im alten Israel: Festschrift für Siegfried Herrmann zum 65. Geburtstag*. Stuttgart: Kohlhammer, 1991.

——. "The Prophet as an Author: The Case of the Isaiah Memoir." Pages 89–101 in *Writings and Speech in Israelite and Ancient Near Eastern Prophecy*. Edited by Ehud Ben Zvi and Michael H. Floyd. Society of Biblical Literature Symposium Series 10. Atlanta: Society of Biblical Literature, 2000.

——. "Psalm 72 and Isaiah 40–66: A Study in Tradition." *Perspectives in Religious Studies* 28 (2001): 333–41.

——. "The Unity of the Book of Isaiah." *Interpretation* 36 (1982): 117–29.

Clifford, Richard J. "The Use of *hôy* in the Prophets." *Catholic Biblical Quarterly* 28 (1966): 458–64.

Clines, David J. A. *Job 1–20*. Word Biblical Commentary 17. Dallas: Word, 1998.

Cobb, William Henry. "Isaiah xxi. 1–10 Reëxamined." *Journal of Biblical Literature* 17 (1898): 40–61.

Cogan, Mordechai, and Hayim Tadmor. *II Kings*. Anchor Bible 11. New York: Doubleday, 1988.

Conrad, Edgar W. *Reading Isaiah*. Overtures to Biblical Theology. Minneapolis: Fortress, 1991.

Crocker, Piers T. "Cush and the Bible." *Buried History* 22 (1986): 27–38.

———. "Egypt in Biblical Prophecy." *Buried History* 34 (1998): 105–10.

Cross, Frank Moore. *The Ancient Library of Qumran*. 3d ed. Sheffield: Sheffield Academic Press, 1995.

———. "The Development of the Jewish Scripts." Pages 133–202 in *The Bible and the Ancient Near East: Essays in Honor of William Foxwell Albright*. Edited by G. Ernest Wright. London: Routledge & Kegan Paul, 1961.

Croughs, Mirjam. "Intertextuality in the Septuagint: The Case of Isaiah 19." *Bulletin of the International Organization for Septuagint and Cognate Studies* 34 (2001): 81–94.

Dahood, Mitchell J. "Hebrew-Ugaritic Lexicography XI." *Biblica* 54 (1973): 351–66.

Dalley, Stephanie. "Recent Evidence from Assyrian Sources for Judaean History from Uzziah to Manasseh." *Journal for the Study of the Old Testament* 28 (2004): 387–401.

Davies, Graham I. "The Destiny of the Nations in the Book of Isaiah." Pages 93–120 in *The Book of Isaiah—Le Livre de Isaïe: Les oracles et leurs relecture. Unité et complexité de l'ouvrage*. Edited by Jacques Vermeylen. Bibliotheca ephemeridum theologicarum lovaniensium 81. Leuven: Peeters, 1989.

Davies, W. D., and Louis Finkelstein, eds. *The Cambridge History of Judaism*. 4 vols. Cambridge: Cambridge University Press, 1984–2006.

Day, John. *God's Conflict with the Dragon and the Sea: Echoes of a Canaanite Myth in the Old Testament*. Cambridge Oriental Publications 35. Cambridge: Cambridge University Press, 1985.

———. "The Problem of 'So, King of Egypt' in 2 Kings XVII 4." *Vetus Testamentum* 42 (1992): 289–301.

———. *Yahweh and the Gods and Goddesses of Canaan*. Journal for the Study of the Old Testament: Supplement Series 265. Sheffield: Sheffield Academic Press, 2000.

De Vries, Simon J. *From Old Revelation to New: A Tradition-Historical and Redaction-Critical Study of Temporal Transitions in Prophetic Prediction*. Grand Rapids: Eerdmans, 1995.

Deissler, Alfons. "Der Volk und Land überschreitende Gottesbund der Endzeit nach Jes 19,16–25." Pages 7–18 in *Zion: Ort der Begegnung: Festschrift für Laurentius Klein zur Vollendung des 65. Lebensjahres*. Edited by Ferdinand Hahn, Frank-Lothar Hossfeld, Hans Jorissen, and Angelika Neuwirth. Bonner biblische Beiträge 90. Bodenheim: Athenäum Hain Hanstein, 1993.

Delcor, M. "Le temple d'Onias en Egypte." *Revue biblique* 75 (1968): 188–205.

Dhorme, Edouard-Paul. "Le désert de la mer (Isaïe, XXI)." *Revue biblique* 31 (1922): 403–6.

Diamond, A. R. Pete. "Portraying Prophecy: Of Doublets, Variants and Analogies in the Narrative Representation of Jeremiah's Oracles—Reconstructing the Hermeneutics of Prophecy." *Journal for the Study of the Old Testament* 57 (1993): 99–119.

Dillmann, August. *Der Prophet Jesaia*. Leipzig: Hirzel, 1890.

Dixon, D. M. "The Origin of the Kingdom of Kush (Napata-Meroë)." *Journal of Egyptian Archaeology* 50 (1964): 121–32.

Donner, Herbert. *Israel unter den Völkern: Die Stellung der klassischen Propheten des 8. Jahrhunderts v. Chr. zur Aussenpolitik der Könige von Israel und Juda*. Vetus Testamentum Supplements 11. Leiden: Brill, 1964.

Driver, G. R. "Isaiah I–XXXIX: Textual and Linguistic Problems." *Journal of Semitic Studies* 13 (1968): 36–57.

Duhm, Bernhard. *Das Buch Jesaia*. 4th ed. Handkommentar zum Alten Testament. Göttingen: Vandenhoeck & Ruprecht, 1922.

Dus, Jan. "Der Brauch der Ladewanderung im alten Israel." *Theologische Zeitschrift* 17 (1961): 1–16.

———. "Die Lösung des Rätsels von Jos. 22." *Archiv Orientální* 32 (1964): 529–46.

Dussaud, René. "Sur le chemin de Suse et de Babylone." *Annuaire de l'institut de philologie et de l'histoire orientales et slaves* 4 (1936): 143–50.

Edel, Elmar. "Amasis und Nebukadrezar II." *Göttinger Miszellen* 29 (1978): 13–20.

Edelman, Diana V. *The Origins of the "Second" Temple: Persian Imperial Policy and the Rebuilding of Jerusalem*. BibleWorld. London: Equinox, 2005.

Eichrodt, Walther. *Der Herr der Geschichte: Jesaja 13–23 und 28–39*. Die Botschaft des Alten Testaments 17/2. Stuttgart: Calwer Verlag, 1967.

Eide, Tormod, Tomas Hägg, and Richard Holton Pierce. *Fontes Historiae Nubiorum: Textual Sources for the History of the Middle Nile Region between the Eighth Century BC and the Sixth Century AD*. 4 vols. Bergen: University of Bergen, 1994–2000.

Eissfeldt, Otto. *Hexateuch-Synopse: Die Erzählung der fünf Bücher Mose und des Buches Josua mit dem Anfange des Richterbuches*. Leipzig: Hinrichs, 1922.

Eitan, Israel. "An Egyptian Loan Word in Is. 19." *Jewish Quarterly Review* 15 (1925): 419–20.

Ellenbogen, Maximilian. *Foreign Words in the Old Testament: Their Origin and Etymology*. London: Luzac, 1962.

Eph'al, Israel. "Nebuchadnezzar the Warrior: Remarks on His Military Achievements." *Israel Exploration Journal* 53 (2003): 178–91.

Erlandsson, Seth. *The Burden of Babylon: A Study of Isaiah 13:2–14:23*. Coniectanea biblica: Old Testament Series 4. Lund: Gleerup, 1970.

Evans, Craig A. *To See and Not Perceive: Isaiah 6.9–10 in Early Jewish and Christian Interpretation*. Journal for the Study of the Old Testament: Supplement Series 64. Sheffield: JSOT Press, 1989.

Ewald, Georg Heinrich August von. *Commentary on the Prophets of the Old Testament*. Translated by J. Frederick Smith. 5 vols. London: Williams and Norgate, 1875–1881.

Feuillet, André. "Un sommet religieux de l'Ancien Testament: L'oracle d'Isa 19:19–25 sur la conversion de l'Egypte." *Recherches de science religiuse* 39 (1951): 65–87.

Fichtner, Johannes. "Jahves Plan in der Botschaft des Jesaja." *Zeitschrift für die alttestamentliche Wissenschaft* 63 (1951): 16–33.

Fischer, Thomas, and Udo Rüterswörden. "Aufruf zur Volksklage in Kanaan (Jesaja 23)." *Die Welt des Orients* 13 (1982): 36–49.

Fishbane, Michael. "Torah and Tradition." Pages 275–300 in *Tradition and Theology in the Old Testament*. Edited by D. A. Knight. 2d ed. The Biblical Seminar. Sheffield: JSOT Press, 1990.

Floyd, Michael H. "The מַשָּׂא (*maśśā'*) as a Type of Prophetic Book." *Journal of Biblical Literature* 121 (2002): 401–22.

Fohrer, Georg. *Das Buch Jesaja*. 3 vols. Zürcher Bibelkommentare. Zürich: Zwingli Verlag, 1960–64.

———. "Entstehung, Komposition und Überlieferung von Jesaja 1–39." Pages 113–47 in *Studien zur alttestamentlichen Prophetie (1949–1965)*. Beihefte zur Zeitschrift für die alttestamentliche Wissenschaft 99. Berlin: Töpelmann, 1967.

———. "Die Gattung der Berichte über symbolische Handlungen der Propheten." Pages 92–112 in *Studien zur alttestamentlichen Prophetie (1949–1965)*. Beihefte zur Zeitschrift für die alttestamentliche Wissenschaft 99. Berlin: Töpelmann, 1967. Repr. from *Zeitschrift für die alttestamentliche Wissenschaft* 64 (1952): 101–20.

———. "Jesaja 1 als Zusammenfassung der Verkündigung Jesajas." *Zeitschrift für die alttestamentliche Wissenschaft* 74 (1962): 251–68.

——. "The Origin, Tradition and Composition of Isaiah I–XXXIX." *Annual of Leeds University Oriental Society* 3 (1961–62): 3–38.

——. *Die symbolischen Handlungen der Propheten.* 2d ed. Abhandlungen zur Theologie des Alten und Neuen Testaments 54. Zurich: Zwingli Verlag, 1968.

Frame, Grant. "The Inscription of Sargon II at Tang-i Var." *Orientalia* 68 (1999): 31–57, plates i–xviii.

Freedman, David Noel. "Headings in the Books of the Eighth-Century Prophets." *Andrews University Seminary Studies* 25 (1987): 9–26.

——, ed. *Anchor Bible Dictionary.* 6 vols. New York: Doubleday, 1992.

Freedy, K. S. and D. B. Redford. "The Dates in Ezekiel in Relation to Biblical, Babylonian and Egyptian Sources." *Journal of the American Oriental Society* 90 (1970): 462–85.

Frey, Jörg. "Temple and Rival Temple: The Cases of Elephantine, Mt. Gerizim, and Leontopolis." Pages 171–203 in *Gemeinde ohne Tempel = Community without Temple: Zur Substituierung und Transformation des Jerusalemer Tempels und seines Kults im Alten Testament, antiken Judentum und frühen Christentum.* Edited by Beate Ego, Armin Lange, and Peter Pilhofer, with Kathrin Ehlers. Wissenschaftliche Untersuchungen zum Neuen Testament 118. Tübingen: Mohr Siebeck, 1999.

Fuchs, Andreas. *Die Annalen des Jahres 711 v. Chr. nach Prismenfragmenten aus Ninive und Assur.* State Archives of Assyria Studies 8. Helsinki: Neo-Assyrian Text Corpus Project, 1998.

——. *Die Inschriften Sargons II. aus Khorsabad.* Göttingen: Cuvillier, 1994.

Fullerton, Kemper. "Isaiah 14:28–32." *American Journal of Semitic Languages and Literature* 42 (1926): 86–109.

Gallagher, William R. *Sennacherib's Campaign to Judah: New Studies.* Studies in the History and Culture of the Ancient Near East 18. Leiden: Brill, 1999.

Galpaz-Feller, Pnina. "Is That So? (2 Kings XVII 4)." *Revue biblique* 107 (2000): 338–47.

Gehman, Henry S. "The 'Burden' of the Prophets." *Jewish Quarterly Review* 31 (1940): 107–21.

Gerstenberger, Erhard. "The Woe-Oracles of the Prophets." *Journal of Biblical Literature* 81 (1962): 249–63.

Geyer, John B. "Another Look at the Oracles about the Nations in the Hebrew Bible: A Response to A. C. Hagedorn." *Vetus Testamentum* 59 (2009): 80–87.

——. "Blood and the Nations in Ritual and Myth." *Vetus Testamentum* 57 (2007): 1–20.

——. "Desolation and Cosmos." *Vetus Testamentum* 49 (1999): 49–64.

——. "Mythology and Culture in the Oracles against the Nations." *Vetus Testamentum* 36 (1986): 129–45.

——. *Mythology and Lament: Studies in the Oracles about the Nations.* Aldershot: Ashgate, 2004.

Ginsberg, H. L. "Reflexes of Sargon in Isaiah after 715 B.C.E." *Journal of the American Oriental Society* 88 (1968): 47–53.

Goedicke, Hans. "The End of 'So, King of Egypt.'" *Bulletin of the American Schools of Oriental Research* 171 (1963): 64–66.

——. *Pi(ankh)y in Egypt: A Study of the Pi(ankh)y Stela.* Baltimore: Halgo, 1998.

Goldingay, John. *Isaiah.* New International Biblical Commentary on the Old Testament. Peabody, Mass.: Hendrickson, 2001.

——. "Isaiah I 1 and II 1." *Vetus Testamentum* 48 (1998): 326–32.

Gonçalves, Francolino J. *L'Expédition de Sennachérib en Palestine dans la littérature hébraïque ancienne.* Études bibliques 7. Paris: Gabalda; Leuven: Peeters, 1986.

Gosse, Bernard. "Isaïe VI et la tradition isaïenne." *Vetus Testamentum* 42 (1992): 340–9.

——. "Isaïe 14,28–32 et les traditions sur Isaïe d'Isaïe 36–39 et Isaïe 20,1–6." *Biblische Zeitschrift* 35 (1991): 97–98.

Gottwald, Norman K. *All the Kingdoms of the Earth: Israelite Prophecy and International Relations in the Ancient Near East.* New York: Harper & Row, 1964.

Grabbe, Lester L. "What Was Ezra's Mission?" Pages 295–7 in *Second Temple Studies.* Vol. 2 of *Temple and Community in the Persian Period.* Edited by Tamara C. Eskenazi and Kent H. Richards. Journal for the Study of the Old Testament: Supplement Series 175. Sheffield: JSOT Press, 1994.

——. *Yehud: A History of the Persian Province of Judah.* Vol. 1 of *A History of the Jews and Judaism in the Second Temple Period.* Library of Second Temple Studies 47. London: T. & T. Clark, 2004.

Graf, Karl Heinrich. *Der Prophet Jeremia.* Leipzig: Weigel, 1862.

Gray, George Buchanan. *The Book of Isaiah: I–XXVII.* International Critical Commentary. Edinburgh: T. & T. Clark, 1912.

Green, Alberto R. W. "The Identity of King So of Egypt—An Alternative Interpretation." *Journal of Near Eastern Studies* 52 (1993): 99–108.

Greenberg, Moshe. "Ezekiel 17 and the Policy of Psammetichus II." *Journal of Biblical Literature* 76 (1957): 304–9.

Griffith, Francis Llewellyn. *Catalogue of the Demotic Papyri in the John Rylands Library, Manchester.* 3 vols. Manchester: Manchester University Press; London: B. Quaritch, 1909.

Grimal, Nicolas C. *A History of Ancient Egypt.* Translated by Ian Shaw. Oxford: Blackwell, 1992.

——. *La stèle triomphale de Pi(ʿankh)y au Musée du Caire.* Cairo: Institut Français d'Archéologie Orientale du Caire, 1981.

Gruen, Erich S. *Heritage and Hellenism: The Reinvention of Jewish Tradition.* Hellenistic Culture and Society 30. Berkeley: University of California Press, 1998.

——. "The Origins and Objectives of Onias' Temple." *Scripta Classica Israelica* 16 (1997): 47–70.

Grüneberg, Keith N. *Abraham, Blessing and the Nations: A Philological and Exegetical Study of Genesis 12:3 in its Narrative Context.* Beihefte zur Zeitschrift für die alttestamentliche Wissenschaft 332. Berlin: de Gruyter, 2003.

Gunkel, Hermann. *Die Psalmen.* 2d ed. Handkommentar zum Alten Testament. Göttingen: Vandenhoek & Ruprecht, 1926.

Haag, Ernst. "'Gesegnet sei mein Volk Ägypten' (Jes 19:25): Ein Zeugnis alttestamentlicher Eschatologie." Pages 139–47 in *Aspekte spät-ägyptischer Kultur: Festschrift für Erich Winter zum 65. Geburtstag.* Edited by Martina Minas and Jürgen Zeidler. Aegyptiaca Treverensia 7. Mainz: von Zabern, 1994.

Haak, Robert D. "'Cush' in Zephaniah." Pages 238–51 in *The Pitcher Is Broken: Memorial Essays for Gösta W. Ahlström.* Edited by Steven W. Holloway and Lowell K. Handy. Journal for the Study of the Old Testament: Supplement Series 190. Sheffield: Sheffield Academic Press, 1995.

Hackmann, Heinrich Friedrich. *Die Zukunftserwartung des Jesaia.* Göttingen: Vandenhoeck & Ruprecht, 1893.

Hagelia, Hallvard. Coram Deo: *Spirituality in the Book of Isaiah, with Particular Attention to Faith in Yahweh.* Coniectanea biblica: Old Testament Series 49. Stockholm: Almqvist & Wiksell, 2001.

——. "A Crescendo of Universalism: An Exegesis of Isa 19:16–25." *Svensk exegetisk årsbok* 70 (2005): 73–88.

Hallo, William W. "Jerusalem under Hezekiah: An Assyriological Perspective." Pages 36–50 in *Jerusalem: Its Sanctity and Centrality to Judaism, Christianity, and Islam.* Edited by Lee I. Levine. New York: Continuum, 1999.

——, ed. *The Context of Scripture.* 3 vols. Leiden: Brill, 1997–2002.

Hardmeier, Christof. *Prophetie im Streit vor dem Untergang Judas: Erzählkommunikative Studien zur Entstehungssituation der Jesaja- und Jeremiaerzählungen in II Reg 18-20 und Jer 37-40.* Beihefte zur Zeitschrift für die alttestamentliche Wissenschaft 137. Berlin: de Gruyter, 1976.

Hayes, John H. "The Usage of Oracles against Foreign Nations in Ancient Israel." *Journal of Biblical Literature* 87 (1968): 81–92.

Hayes, John H., and Stuart A. Irvine. *Isaiah, the Eighth-Century Prophet: His Times and His Preaching.* Nashville: Abingdon, 1987.

Hays, J. Daniel. "The Cushites: A Black Nation in Ancient History." *Bibliotheca sacra* 153 (1996): 270–80.

———. "The Cushites: A Black Nation in the Bible." *Bibliotheca sacra* 153 (1996): 396–409.

Hayward, Robert. "The Jewish Temple at Leontopolis: A Reconsideration." *Journal of Jewish Studies* 33 (1982): 429–43.

Heidorn, Lisa A. "The Horses of Kush." *Journal of Near Eastern Studies* 56 (1997): 105–14.

Hendel, Ronald S. "The Exodus in Biblical Memory." *Journal of Biblical Literature* 120 (2001): 601–22.

Herbert, A. S. *The Book of the Prophet Isaiah, Chapters 1–39.* Cambridge Bible Commentary. Cambridge University Press, 1973.

Herz, N. "Isaiah 19,7." *Orientalistische Literaturzeitung* 15 (1912): 496–7.

Hess, Richard S. "Hezekiah and Sennacherib in 2 Kings 18–20." Pages 23–41 in *Zion, City of Our God.* Edited by Richard S. Hess and Gordon J. Wenham. Grand Rapids: Eerdmans, 1999.

Hibbard, J. Todd. *Intertextuality in Isaiah 24–27: The Reuse and Evocation of Earlier Texts and Traditions.* Forschungen zum Alten Testament 2/16. Tübingen: Mohr Siebeck, 2006.

Hillel, Daniel. *The Natural History of the Bible: An Environmental Exploration of the Hebrew Scriptures.* New York: Columbia University Press, 2006.

Hillers, Delbert R. "*Hôy* and *Hôy*-Oracles: A Neglected Syntactic Aspect." Pages 185–8 in *The Word of the Lord Shall Go Forth: Essays in Honor of David Noel Freedman.* Edited by Carol L. Meyers and M. O'Connor. Winona Lake, Ind.: Eisenbrauns, 1983.

Hobson, Russell. "Jeremiah 41 and the Ammonite Alliance." *Journal of Hebrew Scriptures* 10 (2010): 1–15.

Hoffmann, Hans Werner. *Die Intention der Verkündigung Jesajas.* Beihefte zur Zeitschrift für die alttestamentliche Wissenschaft 136. Berlin: de Gruyter, 1974.

Hoffmeier, James K. "Egypt's Role in the Events of 701 B.C. in Jerusalem." Pages 219–43 in *Jerusalem in Bible and Archaeology: The First Temple Period.* Edited by Andrew G. Vaughn and Ann E. Killebrew. Society of Biblical Literature Symposium Series 18. Atlanta: Society of Biblical Literature, 2003.

———. "Egypt's Role in the Events of 701 B.C.: A Rejoinder to J. J. M. Roberts." Pages 285–9 in *Jerusalem in Bible and Archaeology: The First Temple Period.* Edited by Andrew G. Vaughn and Ann E. Killebrew. Society of Biblical Literature Symposium Series 18. Atlanta: Society of Biblical Literature, 2003.

Høgenhaven, Jesper. *Gott und Volk bei Jesaja: Eine Untersuchung zur biblischen Theologie.* Acta theologica danica 24. Leiden: Brill, 1988.

———. "Prophecy and Propaganda: Aspects of Political and Religious Reasoning in Israel and the Ancient Near East." *Scandinavian Journal of the Old Testament* 3 (1989): 125–41.

Hoonacker, A. van. "Deux passages obscurs dans le chapitre XIX d'Isaïe (versets 11, 18)." *Revue bénédictine* 36 (1924): 297–306.

Huber, Friedrich. *Jahwe, Juda und die anderen Völker beim Propheten Jesaja.* Beihefte zur Zeitschrift für die alttestamentliche Wissenschaft 137. Berlin: de Gruyter, 1976.

Irwin, W. A. "The Exposition of Isaiah 14:28–32." *American Journal of Semitic Languages and Literature* 44 (1928): 73–87.

Irwin, William H. "Syntax and Style in Isaiah 26." *Catholic Biblical Quarterly* 41 (1979): 240–61.

Israelit-Groll, Sarah. "The Egyptian Background to Isaiah 19.18." Pages 300–3 in *Boundaries of the Ancient Near Eastern World: A Tribute to Cyrus H. Gordon.* Edited by Meir Lubetski, Claire Gottlieb, and Sharon Keller. Journal for the Study of the Old Testament: Supplement Series 273. Sheffield: Sheffield Academic Press, 1998.

Janzen, David. "The 'Mission' of Ezra and the Persian-Period Temple Community." *Journal of Biblical Literature* 119 (2000): 619–43.

Janzen, Waldemar. *Mourning Cry and Woe Oracle.* Beihefte zur Zeitschrift für die alttestamentliche Wissenschaft 125. Berlin: de Gruyter, 1972.

Jenkins, Allan K. "The Development of the Isaiah Tradition in Is 13–23." Pages 237–51 in *The Book of Isaiah—Le Livre de Isaïe: Les oracles et leurs relecture. Unité et complexité de l'ouvrage.* Edited by Jacques Vermeylen. Bibliotheca ephemeridum theologicarum lovaniensium 81. Leuven: Peeters, 1989.

Jenner, Konrad D. "The Big Shofar (Isaiah 27:13): A *Hapax Legomenon* to be Understood Merely as a Metaphor or as a *Crux Interpretum* for the Interpretation of Eschatological Expectation?" Pages 157–82 in *Studies in Isaiah 24–27.* Edited by Hendrik Jan Bosman, Harm van Grol, et al. *Oudtestamentische Studiën* 43. Leiden: Brill, 2000.

Jensen, Joseph. "Yahweh's Plan in Isaiah and in the Rest of the Old Testament." *Catholic Biblical Quarterly* 48 (1986): 443–55.

Jeppesen, Knud. "The *maśśāʾ Bābel* in Isaiah 13–14." Proceedings of the Irish Biblical Association 9 (1985): 63–80.

Jones, Brian C. *Howling over Moab: Irony and Rhetoric in Isaiah 15–16.* Society of Biblical Literature Dissertation Series 157. Atlanta: Scholars Press, 1996.

Jong, Matthijs J. de. *Isaiah Among the Ancient Near Eastern Prophets: A Comparative Study of the Earliest Stages of the Isaiah Tradition and the Neo-Assyrian Prophecies.* Vetus Testamentum Supplements 117. Leiden: Brill, 2007.

Kahn, Danʾel. "The Inscription of Sargon II at Tang-i Var and the Chronology of Dynasty 25." *Orientalia* 70 (2001): 1–18.

Kaiser, Otto. "Der geknickte Rohrstab: Zum geschichtlichen Hintergrund der Überlieferung und Weiterbildung der prophetischen Ägyptensprüche im 5. Jahrhundert." Pages 99–106 in *Wort und Geschichte: Festschrift für Karl Elliger zum 70. Geburtstag.* Edited by Hartmut Gese and Hans Peter Rüger. Alter Orient und Altes Testament 18. Neukirchen-Vluyn: Neukirchener Verlag, 1973.

——. *Isaiah 1–12.* Translated by John Bowden. 2d ed. Old Testament Library. London: SCM, 1983.

——. *Isaiah 13–39.* Translated by R. A. Wilson. Old Testament Library. Philadelphia: Westminster; London: SCM, 1974.

Kaminsky, Joel S., and Anne Stewart. "God of All the World: Universalism and Developing Monotheism in Isaiah 40–66." *Harvard Theological Review* 99 (2006): 139–63.

Kang, Seung Il. "A Philological Approach to the Problem of King So (2 Kgs 17:4)." *Vetus Testamentum* 60 (2010): 241–8.

Kapera, Zdzislaw J. "The Ashdod Stele of Sargon II." *Folia orientalia* 17 (1976): 87–99.

——. "The Oldest Account of Sargon II's Campaign against Ashdod." *Folia orientalia* 24 (1987): 29–39.

——. "Was Ya-ma-ni a Cypriot?" *Folia orientalia* 14 (1972–73): 207–18.

Katzenstein, H. Jacob. "Gaza in the Neo-Babylonian Period (626–539 B.C.E.)." *Transeuphratène* 7 (1994): 35–49.

——. *The History of Tyre: From the Beginning of the Second Millenium B.C.E. until the Fall of the Neo-Babylonian Empire in 538 B.C.E.* Jerusalem: Schocken Institute, 1973.

Kiesow, Anna. "Schwarz, stark, schon: Schwarze Menschen in alttestamentlichen Texten." Pages 144–52 in *Körperkonzepte im Ersten Testament: Aspekte einer feministischen Anthropologie.* Edited by Ulrike Bail, Gerlinde Baumann, and Isa Breitmaier. Stuttgart: Kohlhammer, 2003.

Kissane, Edward J. *The Book of Isaiah.* 2 vols. Rev. ed. Dublin: Browne and Nolan, 1960.

Kitchen, Kenneth A. "Egypt, the Levant and Assyria in 701 B.C." Pages 243–53 in *Fontes Atque Pontes: Eine Festgabe für Hellmut Brunner.* Edited by Manfred Görg. Ägypten und Altes Testament 5. Wiesbaden: Harrassowitz, 1983.

——. "Regnal and Geneological Data of Ancient Egypt (Absolute Chronology I): The Historical Chronology of Ancient Egypt, A Current Assessment." Pages 39–52 in *The Synchronisation of Civilisations in the Eastern Mediterranean in the Second Millennium B.C.: Proceedings of an International Symposium at Schloß Haindorf, 15th–17th of November 1996 and at the Austrian Academy, Vienna, 11th–12th of May 1998.* Edited by Manfred Bietak. Vienna: Österreichischen Akademie der Wissenschaften, 2000.

——. *The Third Intermediate Period in Egypt (1100–650 B.C.).* 2d ed. with supplement. Warminster: Aris & Phillips, 1986.

Kittel, Rudolf. *Geschichte des Volkes Israel.* 2 vols. 3d ed. Gotha: Perthes, 1917.

Kloppenborg, John S. "Joshua 22: The Priestly Editing of an Ancient Tradition." *Biblica* 62 (1981): 347–71.

Köckert, Matthias. "Die Erwählung Israels und das Ziel der Wege Gottes im Jesajabuch." Pages 277–300 in *"Wer ist wie du, Herr, unter den Göttern?" Studien zur Theologie und Religionsgeschichte Israels für Otto Kaiser zum 70. Geburtstag.* Göttingen: Vandenhoeck & Ruprecht, 1994.

Koehler, L., W. Baumgartner, and J. J. Stamm. *The Hebrew and Aramaic Lexicon of the Old Testament.* Translated and edited under the supervision of M. E. J. Richardson. 5 vols. Leiden: Brill, 1994–2000.

Kooij, Arie van der. *Die alten Textzeugen des Jesajabuches.* Orbis biblicus et orientalis 35. Freiburg: Universitätsverlag, 1981.

——. "The Old Greek of Isaiah 19:16–25: Translation and Interpretation." Pages 127–66 in *VI Congress of the International Organization for Septuagint and Cognate Studies, Jerusalem 1986.* Edited by C. E. Cox. Society of Biblical Literature Septuagint and Cognate Series 23. Atlanta: Scholars Press, 1987.

——. " 'The Servant of the Lord': A Particular Group of Jews in Egypt According to the Old Greek of Isaiah—Some Comments on LXX Isa 49,1–6 and Related Passages." Pages 383–96 in *Studies in the Book of Isaiah: Festschrift Willem A. M. Beuken.* Edited by Jacques van Ruiten and Marc Vervenne. Bibliotheca ephemeridum theologicarum lovaniensium 132. Leuven: Leuven University Press; Peeters, 1997.

——. "The Story of Hezekiah and Sennacherib (2 Kings 18–19): A Sample of Ancient Historiography." Pages 107–19 in *Past, Present, Future: The Deuteronomistic History and the Prophets.* Edited by Johannes C. de Moor and Harry F. van Rooy. *Oudtestamentische Studiën* 44. Leiden: Brill, 2000.

Kőszeghy, Miklós. *Der Streit um Babel in den Büchern Jesaja und Jeremia.* Beiträge zur Wissenschaft vom Alten und Neuen Testament 13. Stuttgart: Kolhammer, 2007.

Kottsieper, Ingo. " 'And They Did Not Care to Speak Yehudit': On Linguistic Change in Judah during the Late Persian Era." Pages 95–124 in *Judah and the Judeans in the Fourth Century B.C.E.* Edited by Oded Lipschits, Gary N. Knoppers, and Rainer Albertz. Winona Lake, Ind.: Eisenbrauns, 2007.

Krašovec, Jože. "Healing of Egypt Through Judgement and the Creation of a Universal Chosen People (Isaiah 19:16–25)." Pages 295–305 in *Jerusalem Studies in Egyptology.* Edited by Irene Shirun-Grumach. Ägypten und Altes Testament 40. Wiesbaden: Harrassowitz, 1998.

Kratz, Reinhard G. "The Second Temple of Jeb and of Jerusalem." Pages 247–64 in *Judah and the Judeans in the Persian Period*. Edited by Oded Lipschits and Manfred Oeming. Winona Lake, Ind.: Eisenbrauns, 2006. Repr. from Reinhard G. Kratz, *Judentum im Zeitalter des Zweiten Tempels* (FAT 42; Tübingen: Mohr-Siebeck, 2004), 60–78.

Kustár, Zoltán. *"Durch seine Wunden sind wir geheilt": Eine Untersuchung zur Metaphorik von Israels Krankheit und Heilung im Jesajabuch*. Beiträge zur Wissenschaft vom Alten und Neuen Testament 154. Stuttgart: Kohlhammer, 2002.

Kutscher, Eduard Yechezkel. *A History of the Hebrew Language*. Jerusalem: Magnes, 1982.

Laato, Antti. "Hezekiah and the Assyrian Crisis in 701 B.C." *Scandinavian Journal of the Old Testament* 2 (1987): 49–68.

Lambdin, Thomas O. "Egyptian Loan Words in the Old Testament." *Journal of the American Oriental Society* 73 (1953): 145–55.

Lang, Bernhard. "Prophecy, Symbolic Acts, and Politics: A Review of Recent Studies." Pages 83–91 in *Monotheism and the Prophetic Minority: An Essay in Biblical History and Sociology*. Social World of Biblical Antiquity 1. Sheffield: Almond Press, 1983.

Langdon, Stephen. *Die neubabylonischen Königsinschriften*. Vorderasiatische Bibliothek 4. Leipzig: Hinrichs, 1912.

Lavik, Marta Høyland. *A People Tall and Smooth-Skinned: The Rhetoric of Isaiah 18*. Vetus Testamentum Supplements 112. Leiden: Brill, 2006.

Leahy, Anthony. "The Earliest Dated Monument of Amasis and the End of the Reign of Apries." *Journal of Egyptian Archaeology* 74 (1988): 183–99.

Lemaire, André. "Ashdodien et judéen à l'époque perse: Ne 13:24," Pages 153–63 in *Immigration and Emigration within the Ancient Near East: Festschrift E. Lipiński*. Edited by K. van Lerberghe and A. Schoors. Orientalia lovaniensia analecta 65. Leuven: Peeters, 1995.

——. *Collections Moussaïeff, Jeselsohn, Welch et divers*. Vol. 2 of *Nouvelles inscriptions araméennes d'Idumée*. Supplément à *Transeuphratène* 9. Paris: Gabalda, 2002.

——. "New Aramaic Ostraca from Idumea and Their Historical Interpretation." Pages 413–56 in *Judah and the Judeans in the Persian Period*. Edited by Oded Lipschits and Manfred Oeming. Winona Lake, Ind.: Eisenbrauns, 2006.

Lichtheim, Miriam. *Ancient Egyptian Literature*. Berkeley and Los Angeles: University of California Press, 2006.

Liebreich, Leon J. "The Compilation of the Book of Isaiah." *Jewish Quarterly Review* 46 (1956): 259–77.

——. "The Compilation of the Book of Isaiah." *Jewish Quarterly Review* 47 (1956): 114–38.

Lindblom, Johannes. "Der Ausspruch über Tyrus in Jes. 23." *Annual of the Swedish Theological Institute* 4 (1965): 56–73.

Lindhagen, Curt. *The Servant Motif in the Old Testament: A Preliminary Study to the "Ebed-Yahweh Problem" in Deutero-Isaiah*. Uppsala: Lundequistska, 1950.

Lipiński, Edward. "The Elegy on the Fall of Sidon in Isaiah 23." *Eretz-Israel* 14 (1978): 79*–88*.

——. "Géographique linguistique de la Transeuphratène à l'époque achéménide." *Transeuphratène* 3 (1990): 95–107.

Lipschits, Oded. *The Fall and Rise of Jerusalem: Judah under Babylonian Rule*. Winona Lake, Ind.: Eisenbrauns, 2005.

——. "Nebuchadrezzar's Policy in 'Ḥattu-land' and the Fate of the Kingdom of Judah." *Ugarit-Forschungen* 30 (1998): 467–87.

Lloyd, Alan B. "Herodotus on Cambyses: Some Thoughts on Recent Work." Pages 55–66 in *Achaemenid History III: Method and History*. Edited by Amélie Kuhrt and Heleen Sancisi-Weerdenburg. Leiden: Nederlands Instituut voor het Nabije Oosten, 1988.

——. "The Inscription of Udjaḥorresnet: A Collaborator's Testament." *Journal of Egyptian Archaeology* 68 (1982): 166–80.

Lohfink, Norbert. "Gab es eine deuteronomistische Bewegung?" Pages 313–82 in *Jeremia und die "Deuteronomistische Bewegung."* Edited by Walter Groß. Bonner biblische Beiträge 98. Weinheim: Beltz Athenäum, 1995.

Loretz, Oswald. "Der ugaritische Topos *bʿl rkb* und die 'Sprache Kanaans' in Jes 19:1–25." *Ugarit-Forschungen* 19 (1987): 101–12.

Lubetski, Meir. "Beetlemania of Bygone Times." *Journal for the Study of the Old Testament* 91 (2000): 3–26.

Lubetski, Meir, and Claire Gottlieb. "Isaiah 18: The Egyptian Nexus." Pages 364–84 in *Boundaries of the Ancient Near Eastern World: A Tribute to Cyrus H. Gordon*. Edited by Meir Lubetski, Claire Gottlieb, and Sharon Keller. Journal for the Study of the Old Testament: Supplement Series 273. Sheffield: Sheffield Academic Press, 1998.

Lüddeckens, Erich. "Herodot und Ägypten." *Zeitschrift der deutschen morgenländischen Gesellschaft* 104 (1954): 330–46.

Lynch, Matthew J. "Zion's Warrior and the Nations: Isaiah 59:15b–63:6 in Isaiah's Zion Traditions." *Catholic Biblical Quarterly* 70 (2008): 244–63.

Macintosh, A. A. *Isaiah XXI: A Palimpsest*. Cambridge: Cambridge University Press, 1980.

MacLaurin, E. C. B. "Date of the Foundation of the Jewish Colony at Elephantine." *Journal of Near Eastern Studies* 27 (1968): 89–96.

Magen, Yitzhak. "The Dating of the First Phase of the Samaritan Temple on Mount Gerizim in Light of the Archaeological Evidence." Pages 157–211 in *Judah and the Judeans in the Fourth Century B.C.E.* Edited by Oded Lipschits, Gary N. Knoppers, and Rainer Albertz. Winona Lake, Ind.: Eisenbrauns, 2007.

Malamat, Abraham. "The Kingdom of Judah Between Egypt and Babylon: A Small State within a Great Power Confrontation." Pages 322–37 in *History of Biblical Israel: Major Problems and Minor Issues*. Culture and History of the Ancient Near East 7. Leiden: Brill, 2001. Repr. from *Studia theologica* 44 (1990): 55–65.

——. "The Twilight of Judah: In the Egyptian-Babylonian Maelstrom." Pages 299–321 in *History of Biblical Israel: Major Problems and Minor Issues*. Culture and History of the Ancient Near East 7. Leiden: Brill, 2001. Repr. from Supplements to Vetus Testamentum 28 (1975): 123–45.

Margulis, Barry B. "Studies in the Oracles against the Nations." Ph.D. diss., Brandeis University, 1967.

Marlow, Hilary. "The Lament over the River Nile—Isaiah xix 5–10 in Its Wider Context." *Vetus Testamentum* 57 (2007): 229–42.

Marti, Karl. *Das Buch Jesaja*. Kurzer Hand-Commentar zum Alten Testament 10. Tübingen: Mohr (Siebeck), 1900.

Mayes, A. D. H. *Deuteronomy*. New Century Bible. London: Marshall, Morgan & Scott; Grand Rapids: Eerdmans, 1981.

McEntire, Mark H. "A Prophetic Chorus of Others: Helping Jeremiah Survive in Jeremiah 26." *Review and Expositor* 101 (2004): 301–11.

McKane, William. *Jeremiah*. International Critical Commentary. 2 vols. Edinburgh: T. & T. Clark, 1986–96.

——. "משא in Jeremiah 23:33–40." Pages 35–54 in *Prophecy: Essays Presented to Georg Fohrer on His Sixty-fifth Birthday*. Edited by J. A. Emerton. Beihefte zur Zeitschrift für die alttestamentliche Wissenschaft 150. Berlin: de Gruyter, 1980.

——. *Prophets and Wise Men*. Studies in Biblical Theology 44. London: SCM, 1965.

——. "Worship of the Queen of Heaven (Jer 44)." Pages 318–24 in *"Wer ist wie du, Herr, unter den Göttern?" Studien zur Theologie und Religionsgeschichte Israels für Otto Kaiser zum 70. Geburtstag*. Göttingen: Vandenhoeck & Ruprecht, 1994.

McKenzie, Stephen L. *The Trouble with Kings: The Composition of the Book of Kings in the Deuteronomistic History*. Vetus Testamentum Supplements 42. Leiden: Brill, 1991.

Menes, A. "Tempel und Synagoge." *Zeitschrift für die alttestamentliche Wissenschaft* 50 (1932): 268–76.

Mettinger, Tryggve N. D. *The Dethronement of Sabaoth: Studies in the Shem and Kabod Theologies.* Translated by Frederick H. Cryer. Coniectanea biblica: Old Testament Series 18. Lund: Gleerup, 1982.

———. *No Graven Image?: Israelite Aniconism in Its Ancient Near Eastern Context.* Coniectanea biblica: Old Testament Series 42. Stockholm: Almqvist & Wiksell, 1995.

Meyer, Eduard. *Geschichte des alten Ägyptens.* 2 vols. Berlin: Grote, 1887.

Michaelis, Johannis D. *Observationes philologicae et criticae in Jeremiae Vaticinia et Threnos.* Edited by Johannes Fridericus Schleusner. Göttingen: Vandenhoeck & Ruprecht, 1793.

Middlemas, Jill. *The Templeless Age: An Introduction to the History, Literature, and Theology of the Exile.* Louisville: Westminster John Knox, 2007.

Miller, J. Maxwell, and John H. Hayes. *A History of Ancient Israel and Judah.* London: SCM, 1986.

Modrzejewski, Joseph M. *The Jews of Egypt: From Rameses II to Emperor Hadrian.* Translated by Robert Cornman. Edinburgh: T. & T. Clark, 1995.

Möhlenbrink, Kurt. "Die Landnahmesagen des Buches Josua." *Zeitschrift für die alttestamentliche Wissenschaft* 56 (1938): 238–68.

Monsengwo-Pasinya, L. "Isaïe XIX 16–25 et universalisme dans la LXX." Pages 192–207 in *Congress Volume: Salamanca, 1983.* Edited by J. A. Emerton. Vetus Testamentum Supplements 36. Leiden: Brill, 1985.

Moorey, Peter R. S. *Idols of the People: Miniature Images of Clay in the Ancient Near East.* Schweich Lectures. Oxford: Oxford University Press, 2003.

Morkot, Robert G. *The Black Pharaohs: Egypt's Nubian Rulers.* London: Rubicon Press, 2000.

Mowinckel, Sigmund. "Die Komposition des Jesajabuches Kap. 1–39." *Acta orientalia* 11 (1933): 267–92.

Muchiki, Yoshiyuki. *Egyptian Proper Names and Loanwords in North-West Semitic.* Society of Biblical Literature Dissertation Series 173. Atlanta: Society of Biblical Literature, 1999.

Muilenburg, J. "Abraham and the Nations: Blessing and World History." *Interpretation* 19 (1965): 387–98.

Naʾaman, Nadav. "The Brook of Egypt and Assyrian Policy on the Border of Egypt." *Tel Aviv* 6 (1979): 68–90.

———. "Hezekiah and the Kings of Assyria." *Tel Aviv* 21 (1994): 235–54.

———. "The Historical Background of the Conquest of Samaria." *Biblica* 71 (1990): 207–25.

———. "Sennacherib's 'Letter to God' on his Campaign to Judah." *Bulletin of the American Schools of Oriental Research* 214 (1974): 25–39.

Naudé, J. A. "*Maśśāʾ* in the OT with Special Reference to the Prophets." *Ou-Testamentiese Werkgemeenskap in Suid-Afrika* 12 (1969): 91–100.

Naveh, Joseph. "Hebrew Texts in Aramaic Script in the Persian Period?" *Bulletin of the American Schools of Oriental Research* 203 (1971): 27–32.

Neumann, Peter K. D. "Das Wort, das geschehen ist…: Zum Problem der Wortempfangsterminologie in Jer. I–XXV." *Vetus Testamentum* 23 (1973): 171–217.

Niccacci, Alviero. "Isaiah XVIII–XX from an Egyptological Perspective." *Vetus Testamentum* 48 (1998): 214–38.

Nicholson, Ernest W. *Preaching to the Exiles: A Study of the Prose Tradition in the Book of Jeremiah.* Oxford: Blackwell, 1970.

Noth, Martin. *Das Buch Josua.* Handbuch zum Alten Testament 7. Tübingen: Mohr (Siebeck), 1938.

Nötscher, F. "Entbehrliche Hapaxlegomena in Jesaia." *Vetus Testamentum* 1 (1951): 299–302.

Obermann, Julian. "Yahweh's Victory over the Babylonian Pantheon: The Archetype of Is. 21:1–10." *Journal of Biblical Literature* 48 (1929): 307–28.

O'Connor, David. *Ancient Nubia: Egypt's Rival in Africa.* Philadelphia: University Museum, University of Pennsylvania, 1993.

Oswalt, John N. *The Book of Isaiah, Chapters 1–39.* New International Commentary on the Old Testament. Grand Rapids: Eerdmans, 1986.

Otto, Eberhard. *Die biographischen Inschriften der Ägyptischen Spätzeit: Ihre geistesgeschichtliche un literarische Bedeutung.* Leiden: Brill, 1954.

Parker, Simon B. "The Lachish Letters and Official Reactions to Prophecies." Pages 65–78 in *Uncovering Ancient Stones: Essays in Memory of H. Neil Richardson.* Edited by Lewis M. Hopfe. Winona Lake, Ind.: Eisenbrauns, 1994.

Polaski, Donald C. *Authorizing an End: The Isaiah Apocalypse and Intertextuality.* Biblical Interpretation Series 50. Leiden: Brill, 2001.

Porten, Bezalel. *Archives from Elephantine: The Life of an Ancient Jewish Military Colony.* Berkeley: University of California Press, 1968.

——. "Settlement of the Jews at Elephantine and the Arameans at Syene." Pages 451–70 in *Judah and the Judeans in the Neo-Babylonian Period.* Edited by Oded Lipschits and Joseph Blenkinsopp. Winona Lake, Ind.: Eisenbrauns, 2003.

Porten, Bezalel, and Ada Yardeni, eds. *Textbook of Aramaic Documents from Ancient Egypt.* 4 vols. Jerusalem: Hebrew University Department of the History of the Jewish People, 1986–1999.

Posener, Georges. *La première domination perse en Égypt.* Bibliothèque d'Étude 11. Cairo: Imprimerie de l'Institut Français d'Archéologie Orientale, 1936.

Pritchard, James B., ed. *The Ancient Near East in Pictures Relating to the Old Testament.* 2d ed. Princeton: Princeton University Press, 1969.

——. *Ancient Near Eastern Texts Relating to the Old Testament.* 3d ed. Princeton: Princeton University Press, 1969.

Procksch, Otto. *Jesaja I.* Kommentar zum Alten Testament 9/1. Leipzig: Deichert, 1930.

Redford, Donald B. *Egypt, Canaan, and Israel in Ancient Times.* Princeton, N.J: Princeton University Press, 1992.

——. "A Note on the Chronology of Dynasty 25 and the Inscription of Sargon II at Tang-i Var." *Orientalia* 68 (1999): 58–60.

——. "A Note on II Kings, 17, 4." *Journal of the Society for the Study of Egyptian Antiquities* 11 (1981): 75–6.

——. "Sais and the Kushite Invasions of the Eighth Century B.C." *Journal of the American Research Center in Egypt* 22 (1985): 5–15.

Reider, Joseph. "Etymological Studies in Biblical Hebrew." *Vetus Testamentum* 2 (1952): 113–30.

Reimer, David J. *The Oracles against Babylon in Jeremiah 50–51: A Horror among the Nations.* San Francisco: Mellen Research University Press, 1993.

Rendtorff, Rolf. "Isaiah 6 in the Framework of the Composition of the Book." Pages 170–80 in *Canon and Theology: Overtures to an Old Testament Theology.* Translated and edited by Margaret Kohl. Edinburgh: T. & T. Clark, 1994. Repr. from "Jesaja 6 im Rahmen der Komposition des Jesajabuches," in *The Book of Isaiah—Le Livre de Isaïe: Les oracles et leurs relecture. Unité et complexité de l'ouvrage* (ed. Jacques Vermeylen; BETL 81; Leuven: Peeters, 1989), 73–82.

Richter, Sandra L. *The Deuteronomistic History and the Name Theology.* Beihefte zur Zeitschrift für die alttestamentliche Wissenschaft 318. Berlin: de Gruyter, 2002.

Roberts, J. J. M. "Egypt, Assyria, Isaiah, and the Ashdod Affair: An Alternative Proposal." Pages 265–83 in *Jerusalem in Bible and Archaeology: The First Temple Period.* Edited by Andrew G. Vaughn and Ann E. Killebrew. Society of Biblical Literature Symposium Series 18. Atlanta: Society of Biblical Literature, 2003.

——. "Isaiah's Egyptian and Nubian Oracles." Pages 201–9 in *Israel's Prophets and Israel's Past: Essays on the Relationship of Prophetic Texts and Israelite History in*

Honor of John H. Hayes. Edited by Brad E. Kelle and Megan Bishop Moore. Library of Hebrew Bible/Old Testament Studies 446. London: T. & T. Clark, 2006.

———. "Zion in the Theology of the Davidic-Solomonic Empire." Pages 331–47 in *The Bible and the Ancient Near East: Collected Essays*. Winona Lake, Ind.: Eisenbrauns, 2002. Repr. from *Studies in the Period of David and Solomon and Other Essays*. Edited by T. Ishida; Winona Lake, Ind.: Eisenbrauns, 1982.

Robinson, Geoffrey D. "The Motif of Deafness and Blindness in Isaiah 6:9–10: A Contextual, Literary, and Theological Analysis." *Bulletin for Biblical Research* 8 (1998): 167–86.

Roncace, Mark. *Jeremiah, Zedekiah, and the Fall of Jerusalem*. Library of Hebrew Bible/Old Testament Studies 423. London: T. & T. Clark, 2005.

Rooy, Herculaas F. van. "Ezekiel's Prophecies against Egypt and the Babylonian Exiles." Pages 115–22 in *Proceedings of the 10th World Congress of Jewish Studies, Division A*. Jerusalem: Magnes Press, 1990.

Rudolph, W. "Jesaja 23:1–14." Pages 166–74 in *Festschrift für Friedrich Baumgärtel zum 70. Geburtstag, 14. Januar 1958*. Erlanger Forschungen 10. Erlangen: Universitätsbund, 1959.

Sadler, Rodney Steven Jr. *Can a Cushite Change His Skin? An Examination of Race, Ethnicity, and Othering in the Hebrew Bible*. Library of Hebrew Bible/Old Testament Studies 425. London: T. & T. Clark, 2005.

Saebø, Magne. *Sacharja 9–14: Untersuchungen von Text und Form*. Wissenschaftliche Monographien zum Alten und Neuen Testament 34; Neukirchen-Vluyn: Neukirchener Verlag, 1969.

Sáenz-Badillos, Angel. *A History of the Hebrew Language*. Translated by John Elwolde. Cambridge: Cambridge University Press, 1993.

Sasson, Victor. "An Unrecognized 'Smoke Signal' in Isaiah xxx 27." *Vetus Testamentum* 33 (1983): 90–95.

Sauneron, S., and J. Yoyotte. "Sur la politique palestinienne des rois saïtes." *Vetus Testamentum* 2 (1952): 131–6.

Sawyer, John F. A. "'Blessed Be My People Egypt' (Isaiah 19:25): The Context and Meaning of a Remarkable Passage." Pages 57–71 in *A Word in Season: Essays in Honour of William McKane*. Edited by James D. Martin and Philip R. Davies. Journal for the Study of the Old Testament: Supplement Series 42. Sheffield: JSOT Press, 1986.

Sayed, Ramadan. "Tefnakht ou Horus SI3-(ib)." *Vetus Testamentum* 20 (1970): 116–18.

Schaper, Joachim. "Hebrew and Its Study in the Persian Period." Pages 15–26 in *Hebrew Study from Ezra to Ben-Yehuda*. Edited by William Horbury. Edinburgh: T. & T. Clark, 1999.

Scharbert, Josef. "Fluchen und Segnen im Alten Testament." *Biblica* 39 (1958): 1–26.

Schniedewind, William M. "Aramaic, the Death of Written Hebrew, and Language Shift in the Persian Period." Pages 141–51 in *Margins of Writing, Origins of Cultures*. Edited by Seth L. Sanders. 2d printing. Oriental Institute Seminars 2. Chicago: The Oriental Institute of the University of Chicago, 2007.

Schreiner, Josef. "Segen für die Völker in der Verheißung an die Väter." *Biblische Zeitschrift* 6 (1962): 20–26.

Scott, R. B. Y. "The Book of Isaiah, Chapters 1–39." Pages 175–86 in *The Interpreter's Bible, vol. 5*. Edited by George A. Buttrick. 12 vols. New York: Abingdon-Cokesbury, 1951–1957.

———. "Isaiah XXI 1–10: The Inside of a Prophet's Mind." *Vetus Testamentum* 2 (1952): 278–82.

———. "The Literary Structure of Isaiah's Oracles." Pages 175–86 in *Studies in Old Testament Prophecy Presented to T. H. Robinson*. Edited by H. H. Rowley. Edinburgh: T. & T. Clark, 1950.

——. "The Meaning of massāʾ as an Oracle Title." *Journal of Biblical Literature* 67 (1948): v–vi.

Sedlmeier, Franz. "Israel—'Ein Segen inmitten der Erde': Das JHWH-Volk in der Spannung zwischen radikalem Dialog und Identitätsverlust nach Jes 19,16–25." Pages 89–108 in *Steht nicht geschrieben? Studien zur Bibel und ihrer Wirkungsgeschichte: Festschrift für Georg Schmuttermayr.* Edited by Johannes Frühwald-König, Ferdinand R. Prostmeier, and Reinhold Zwick. Regensburg: Verlag Friedrich Pustet, 2001.

Seeligmann, Isaac Leo. *The Septuagint Version of Isaiah and Cognate Studies.* Edited by Robert Hanhart and Hermann Spieckermann. Tübingen: Mohr Siebeck, 2004.

Seidl, Theodor. "Datierung und Wortereignis: Beobachtungen zum Horizont von Jer 27, 1." *Biblische Zeitschrift* 21 (1977): 23–44, 184–99.

——. "Die Wortereignisformel in Jeremia: Beobachtungen zu den Formen der Redeeröffnung in Jeremia, im Anschluß an Jer 27, 1. 2." *Biblische Zeitschrift* 23 (1979): 20–47.

Seitz, Christopher R. "The Crisis of Interpretation over the Meaning and Purpose of the Exile: A Redactional Study of Jeremiah XXI–XLIII." *Vetus Testamentum* 35 (1985): 78–97.

——. *Isaiah 1–39.* Interpretation: A Bible Commentary for Teaching and Preaching. Louisville: John Knox, 1993.

——. *Theology in Conflict: Reactions to the Exile in the Book of Jeremiah.* Beihefte zur Zeitschrift für die alttestamentliche Wissenschaft 176. Berlin: de Gruyter, 1989.

——. *Zion's Final Destiny: The Development of the Book of Isaiah: A Reassessment of Isaiah 36–39.* Minneapolis: Fortress, 1991.

Sekine, Seizo. *Die tritojesajanische Sammlung (Jes 56–66) redaktionsgeschichtlich untersucht.* Beihefte zur Zeitschrift für die alttestamentliche Wissenschaft 175. Berlin: de Gruyter, 1989.

Smelik, Klaas A. D. "Distortion of Old Testament Prophecy: The Purpose of Isaiah xxxvi and xxxvii." Pages 70–93 in *Crises and Perspectives: Studies in Ancient Near Eastern Polytheism, Biblical Theology, Palestinian Archaeology and Intertestamental Literature.* Oudtestamentische Studiën 24 (1989): 70–93.

Smith, Ralph L. *Micah-Malachi.* Word Biblical Commentary 32. Dallas: Word, 1998.

Soggin, J. Alberto. *Joshua.* Translated by R. A. Wilson. Old Testament Library. London: SCM, 1972.

Sommer, Benjamin D. *A Prophet Reads Scripture: Allusion in Isaiah 40–66.* Stanford: Stanford University Press, 1998.

Spalinger, Anthony. "The Year 712 B.C. and its Implications for Egyptian History." *Journal of the American Research Center in Egypt* 10 (1973): 95–101.

Sparks, Kenton L. *Ethnicity and Identity in Ancient Israel: Prolegomena to the Study of Ethnic Sentiments and their Expression in the Hebrew Bible.* Winona Lake, Ind.: Eisenbrauns, 1998.

Spiegelberg, Wilhelm. *The Credibility of Herodotus' Account of Egypt in the Light of the Egyptian Monuments.* Translated by Aylward M. Blackman. Oxford: Blackwell, 1927.

——. *Die sogenannte demotische Chronik des Pap. 215 der Bibliothèque Nationale zu Paris; nebst den auf der Rückseite des Papyrus stehenden Texten.* Demotische Studien 7. Leipzig: J. C. Hinrichs, 1914.

Stacey, W. David. *Prophetic Drama in the Old Testament.* London: Epworth, 1990.

Stade, B. "Miscellen." *Zeitschrift für die alttestamentliche Wissenschaft* 6 (1886): 122–89.

Steck, Odil Hannes. *Studien zu Tritojesaja.* Beihefte zur Zeitschrift für die alttestamentliche Wissenschaft 203. Berlin: de Gruyter, 1991.

Stenning, J. F. *The Targum of Isaiah.* Oxford: Clarendon, 1949.

Stern, Ephraim. "The Religious Revolution in Persian-Period Judah." Pages 199–205 in *Judah and the Judeans in the Persian Period.* Edited by Oded Lipschits and Manfred Oeming. Winona Lake, Ind.: Eisenbrauns, 2006.

Stern, Ephraim, and Yitzhak Magen. "Archaeological Evidence for the First Stage of the Samaritan Temple on Mount Gerizim." *Israel Exploration Journal* 52 (2002): 49–57.

Stern, Philip. "The 'Blind Servant' Imagery of Deutero-Isaiah and Its Implications." *Biblica* 75 (1994): 224–32.

Stipp, Hermann-Josef. "Probleme des redaktionsgeschichtlichen Modells der Entstehung des Jeremiabuches." Pages 225–62 in *Jeremia und die "Deuteronomistische Bewegung."* Edited by Walter Groß. Bonner biblische Beiträge 98. Weinheim: Beltz Athenäum, 1995.

——. "Zedekiah in the Book of Jeremiah: On the Formation of a Biblical Character." *Catholic Biblical Quarterly* 58 (1996): 627–48.

Stockton, E. "Sacred Pillars in the Bible." *Australian Biblical Review* 20 (1972): 16–32.

Sweeney, Marvin A. *Isaiah 1–4 and the Post-Exilic Understanding of the Isaianic Tradition.* Beihefte zur Zeitschrift für die alttestamentliche Wissenschaft 171. Berlin: de Gruyter, 1988.

——. *Isaiah 1–39.* Forms of the Old Testament Literature 16. Grand Rapids: Eerdmans, 1996.

——. "Jesse's New Shoot in Isaiah 11: A Josianic Reading of the Prophet Isaiah." Pages 103–18 in *A Gift of God in Due Season: Essays on Scripture and Community in Honor of James A. Sanders.* Edited by Richard D. Weis and David M. Carr. Journal for the Study of the Old Testament: Supplement Series 225. Sheffield: Sheffield Academic Press, 1996.

——. *King Josiah of Judah: The Lost Messiah of Israel.* Oxford: Oxford University Press, 2001.

——. "New Gleanings from an Old Vineyard: Isaiah 27 Reconsidered." Pages 51–66 in *Early Jewish and Christian Exegesis: Studies in Memory of William Hugh Brownlee.* Edited by Craig A. Evans and William F. Stinespring. Atlanta: Scholars Press, 1987.

——. "Textual Citations in Isaiah 24–27: Toward an Understanding of the Redactional Function of Chapters 24–27 in the Book of Isaiah." *Journal of Biblical Literature* 107 (1988): 39–52.

Tadmor, Hayim. "The Campaigns of Sargon II of Assur: A Chronological-Historical Study." *Journal of Cuneiform Studies* 12 (1958): 22–40.

——. *The Inscriptions of Tiglath-pileser III, King of Assyria.* Jerusalem: Israel Academy of Sciences and Humanities, 1994.

——. "Philistia under Assyrian Rule." *Biblical Archaeologist* 29 (1966): 86–102.

Talmon, Shemaryahu. "Prophetic Rhetoric and Agricultural Metaphora." Pages 267–79 in *Storia e Tradizioni di Israele: Scritti in onore di J. Alberto Soggin.* Edited by Daniele Garrone and Felice Israel. Brescia: Paideia, 1991.

Täubler, Eugen. "Kharu, Horim, Dedanim." *Hebrew Union College Annual* 1 (1924): 97–123.

Tawil, Hayim. "The Historicity of 2 Kings 19:24 (Isaiah 37:25): The Problem of Yeʾōrê Maṣôr." *Journal of Near Eastern Studies* 41 (1982): 195–206.

Taylor, J. Glen. *Yahweh and the Sun: Biblical and Archaeological Evidence for Sun Worship in Ancient Israel.* Journal for the Study of the Old Testament: Supplement Series 111. Sheffield, JSOT Press, 1993.

Thacker, T. W. "A Note on עָרוֹת (Is. xix 7)." *Journal of Theological Studies* 34 (1933): 163–5.

Thiel, Winfried. *Die deuteronomistische Redaktion von Jeremia 26–45.* Wissenschaftliche Monographien zum Alten und Neuen Testament 52. Neukirchen-Vluyn: Neukirchener Verlag, 1981.

Thomas, D. Winton. "Again 'The Prophet' in the Lachish Ostraca." Pages 244–9 in *Von Ugarit nach Qumran: Beiträge zur alttestamentlichen und altorientalischen Forschung Otto Eissfeldt zum 1. September dargebracht.* Edited by Johannes Hempel and Leonhard Rost. Beihefte zur Zeitschrift für die Alttestamentliche Wissenschaft 77. Berlin: Töpelmann, 1958.

Tomasino, Anthony J. "Isaiah 1.1–2.4 and 63–66, and the Composition of the Isaianic Corpus." *Journal for the Study of the Old Testament* 57 (1993): 81–98.

Toorn, Karel van der. "Anat-Yahu, Some Other Deities, and the Jews of Elephantine." *Numen* 39 (1992): 80–101.

Toorn, Karel van der, Bob Becking, and Pieter W. van der Horst, eds. *Dictionary of Deities and Demons in the Bible*. 2d ed. Leiden: Brill, 1999.

Torczyner, Harry, Lankester Harding, Alkin Lewis, and J. L. Starkey. *The Lachish Letters*. London: Oxford University Press, 1938.

Török, László. *The Kingdom of Kush: Handbook of the Napatan-Meroitic Civilization*. Handbuch der Orientalistik 31. Leiden: Brill, 1997.

Torrey, Charles C. "Some Important Editorial Operations in the Book of Isaiah." *Journal of Biblical Literature* 57 (1938): 109–39.

Tov, Emanuel. "The Text of Isaiah at Qumran." Pages 491–511 in vol. 2 of *Writing and Reading the Scroll of Isaiah*. Edited by Craig C. Broyles and Craig A. Evans. 2 vols. Vetus Testamentum Supplements 70/2. Formation and Interpretation of Old Testament Literature 1/2. Leiden: Brill, 1997.

Tsevat, Matitiahu. "The Neo-Assyrian and Neo-Babylonian Vassal Oaths and the Prophet Ezekiel." *Journal of Biblical Literature* 78 (1959): 199–204.

Tucker, Gene M. "Prophetic Superscriptions and the Growth of the Canon." Pages 56–70 in *Canon and Authority: Essays in Old Testament Religion and Theology*. Edited by George W. Coats and Burke O. Long. Philadelphia: Fortress, 1977.

Uffenheimer, Binyamin. "The Desert of the Sea Pronouncement (Isaiah 21:1–10)." Pages 677–88 in *Pomegranates and Golden Bells: Studies in Biblical, Jewish, and Near Eastern Ritual, Law, and Literature in Honor of Jacob Milgrom*. Edited by David P. Wright, David Noel Freedman, and Avi Hurvitz. Winona Lake, Ind.: Eisenbrauns, 1995.

Unseth, Peter. "Hebrew Kush: Sudan, Ethiopia, or Where?" *Africa Journal of Evangelical Theology* 18 (1999): 143–59.

Vermeylen, Jacques. *Du prophète Isaïe à l'apocalyptique: Isaïe, I–XXXV*. 2 vols. Etudes bibliques. Paris: Gabalda, 1977–78.

——. "L'Unité du livre d'Isaïe." Pages 11–53 in *The Book of Isaiah—Le Livre de Isaïe: Les oracles et leurs relecture. Unité et complexité de l'ouvrage*. Edited by Jacques Vermeylen. Bibliotheca ephemeridum theologicarum lovaniensium 81. Leuven: Peeters, 1989.

——. "Hypothèses sur l'origine d'Isaïe 36–39." Pages 95–118 in *Studies in the Book of Isaiah: Festschrift Willem A. M. Beuken*. Edited by Jacques van Ruiten and Marc Vervenne. Bibliotheca ephemeridum theologicarum lovaniensium 132. Leuven: Leuven University Press, 1997.

Vink, J. G. "The Date and Origin of the Priestly Code in the Old Testament." Pages 1–144 in *The Priestly Code and Seven Other Studies*. Edited by P. A. H. de Boer. *Oudtestamentische Studiën* 15. Leiden: Brill, 1969.

Vittmann, Günther. *Der demotische Papyrus Rylands 9*. 2 vols. Ägypten und Altes Testament 38. Wiesbaden: Harrassowitz, 1998.

Vogels, Walter. "Egypte mon peuple: L'Universalisme d'Is 19,16–25." *Biblica* 57 (1976): 494–514.

Walsh, Carey Ellen. *The Fruit of the Vine: Viticulture in Ancient Israel*. Harvard Semitic Monographs 60. Winona Lake, Ind.: Eisenbrauns, 2000.

Wanke, Gunther. "אוֹי und הוֹי." *Zeitschrift für die alttestamentliche Wissenschaft* 78 (1925): 215–18.

Ward, William A. "The Semitic Biconsonantal Root *sp* and the Common Origin of Egyptian *ćwf* and Hebrew *sûp*: 'Marsh(-Plant).'" *Vetus Testamentum* 24 (1974): 339–49.

Watts, John D. W. *Isaiah 1–33*. Word Biblical Commentary 24. Dallas: Word, 1985.

——. *Isaiah 1–33*. Rev. ed. Word Biblical Commentary 24. Nashville: Thomas Nelson, 2005.

Weidner, Ernst F. "Šilkan(ḫe)ni, König von Muṣri, ein Zeitgenosse Sargons II. nach einem neuen Bruchstück der Prisma-Inschrift des assyrischen Königs." *Archiv für Orientforschung* 14 (1941–44): 40–53.

Weinberg, Joel. "Gedaliah, the Son of Ahikam in Mizpah: His Status and Role, Supporters and Opponents." *Zeitschrift für die alttestamentliche Wissenschaft* 119 (2007): 356–68.

Weinfeld, Moshe. "The Worship of Molech and of the Queen of Heaven and its Background." *Ugarit-Forschungen* 4 (1972): 133–54.

Weis, Richard D. "A Definition of the Genre Maśśāʾ in the Hebrew Bible." Ph.D. diss., Claremont Graduate School, 1986.

——. "Oracle, Old Testament." Pages 28–9 in vol. 5 of *Anchor Bible Dictionary*. Edited by David Noel Freedman. 6 vols. New York: Doubleday, 1992.

Wellhausen, Julius Wellhausen. *Die Composition des Hexateuchs und der historischen Bücher des Alten Testaments*. 3d ed. Berlin: Georg Reimer, 1899.

Welsby, Derek A. *The Kingdom of Kush: The Napatan and Meroitic Empires*. London: British Museum Press, 1996.

Wendel, Ute. *Jesaja und Jeremia: Worte, Motive und Einsichten Jesajas in der Verkündigung Jeremias*. Biblisch-Theologische Studien 25. Neukirchen-Vluyn: Neukirchener-Verlag, 1995.

Werner, Wolfgang. *Studien zur alttestamentlichen Vorstellung vom Plan Jahwes*. Beihefte zur Zeitschrift für die alttestamentliche Wissenschaft 173. Berlin: de Gruyter, 1988.

Westermann, Claus. *Basic Forms of Prophetic Speech*. Translated by H. C. White. Philadelphia: Westminster, 1967. Repr. Cambridge: Lutterworth; Louisville: Westminster/John Knox, 1991.

——. *Isaiah 40–66*. Translated by David M. G. Stalker. Old Testament Library. London: SCM, 1969.

Whedbee, J. William. *Isaiah & Wisdom*. Nashville: Abingdon Press, 1971.

Wildberger, Hans. *Isaiah 1–12*. Translated by Thomas H. Trapp. Minneapolis: Fortress, 1991.

——. *Isaiah 13–27*. Translated by Thomas H. Trapp. Minneapolis: Fortress, 1997.

——. *Isaiah 28–39*. Translated by Thomas H. Trapp. Minneapolis: Fortress, 2002.

——. "Jesajas Verständnis der Geschichte." Pages 83–117 in *Congress Volume: Bonn, 1962*. Vetus Testamentum Supplements 9. Leiden: Brill, 1962.

Williams, James G. "The Alas-Oracles of the Eighth-Century Prophets." *Hebrew Union College Annual* 38 (1967): 75–91.

Williamson, H. G. M. *The Book Called Isaiah: Deutero-Isaiah's Role in Composition and Redaction*. Oxford: Oxford University Press, 1994.

——. *Isaiah 1–27*. 3 vols. International Critical Commentary. London: T. & T. Clark, 2006–.

——. "Isaiah xi 11–16 and the Redaction of Isaiah i–xii." Pages 343–57 in *Congress Volume: Paris, 1992*. Edited by J. A. Emerton. Vetus Testamentum Supplements 61. Leiden: Brill, 1995.

——. "On Getting Carried Away with the Infinitive Construct of נשא." Pages 357*–367* in *Shai le-Sara Japhet: Studies in the Bible, its Exegesis and its Language*. Edited by M. Bar-Asher, E. Tov, D. Rom-Shilony, and N. Wazana. Jerusalem: Bialik Institute, 2007.

——. "Sound, Sense and Language in Isaiah 24–27." *Journal of Jewish Studies* 46 (1995): 1–9.

——. "Synchronic and Diachronic in Isaian Perspectives." Pages 211–26 in *Synchronic or Diachronic?: A Debate on Method in Old Testament Exegesis*. Edited by Johannes C. de Moor. Oudtestamentische Studiën 34. Leiden: Brill, 1995.

——. *Variations on a Theme: King, Messiah and Servant in the Book of Isaiah*. Carlisle: Paternoster, 1998.

Willis, John T. "Isaiah 2:2–5 and the Psalms of Zion." Pages 295–316 in vol. 1 of *Writing and Reading the Scroll of Isaiah*. Edited by Craig C. Broyles and Craig A. Evans. 2 vols. Vetus Testamentum Supplements 70. Leiden: Brill, 1997.

Wilson, J. V. Kinnier. "A Return to the Problems of Behemoth and Leviathan." *Vetus Testamentum* 25 (1975): 1–14.

Wilson, Robert R. *Prophecy and Society in Ancient Israel*. Philadelphia: Fortress, 1980.

Wiseman, Donald J. *Nebuchadrezzar and Babylon*. Schweich Lectures. Oxford: Oxford University Press, 1985.

Wolff, Hans Walter. "The Kerygma of the Yahwist." *Interpretation* 20 (1966): 131–58.

Yahuda, A. S. "Hebrew Words of Egyptian Origin, 6." *Journal of Biblical Literature* 66 (1947): 85–6.

Yamauchi, Edwin. "Cambyses in Egypt." Pages 371–92 in *Go to the Land I Will Show You: Studies in Honor of Dwight W. Young*. Edited by Joseph E. Coleson and Victor H. Matthews. Winona Lake, Ind.: Eisenbrauns, 1996.

Younger, K. Lawson Jr. "Assyrian Involvement in the Southern Levant at the End of the Eighth Century B.C.E." Pages 235–63 in Jerusalem in Bible and Archaeology: The First Temple Period. Edited by Andrew G. Vaughn and Ann E. Killebrew. Society of Biblical Literature Symposium Series 18. Atlanta: Society of Biblical Literature, 2003.

——. "The Fall of Samaria in Light of Recent Research." *Catholic Biblical Quarterly* 61 (1999): 461–82.

Yurco, Frank J. "Sennacherib's Third Campaign and the Coregency of Shabaka and Shebitku." *Serapis* 6 (1980): 221–40.

——. "The Shabaka-Shebitku Coregency and the Supposed Second Campaign of Sennacherib against Judah: A Critical Assessment." *Journal of Biblical Literature* 110 (1991): 35–45.

Zimmerli, Walther. *Ezekiel 2*. Translated by James D. Martin. Hermeneia. Philadelphia: Fortress, 1983.

Zorn, Jeffrey R. "Mizpah: Newly Discovered Stratum Reveals Judah's Other Capital." *Biblical Archaeology Review* 23/5 (1997): 28–38.

——. "Tell en-Naṣbeh and the Problem of the Material Culture of the Sixth Century." Pages 413–47 in *Judah and the Judeans in the Neo-Babylonian Period*. Edited by Oded Lipschits and Joseph Blenkinsopp. Winona Lake, Ind.: Eisenbrauns, 2003.

Zsengellér, József. *Gerizim as Israel: Northern Tradition of the Old Testament and the Early History of the Samaritans*. Utrechtse Theologische Reeks 38. Utrecht: Faculteit der Godgeleerdheid, Universiteit Utrecht, 1998.

INDEX OF AUTHORS

INDEX OF TEXTS

INDEX OF SUBJECTS